THE PERSUADABLE VOTER

THE PERSUADABLE VOTER

WEDGE ISSUES IN PRESIDENTIAL CAMPAIGNS

D. Sunshine Hillygus and Todd G. Shields

PRINCETON UNIVERSITY PRESS   PRINCETON AND OXFORD

Copyright © 2008 by Princeton University Press
Published by Princeton University Press, 41 William Street,
Princeton, New Jersey 08540
In the United Kingdom: Princeton University Press, 6 Oxford Street,
Woodstock, Oxfordshire OX20 1TW

Hillygus, D. Sunshine.
The persuadable voter : wedge issues in presidential campaigns /
D. Sunshine Hillygus and Todd G. Shields.
Includes bibliographical references and index.
ISBN: 978-0-691-13341-6 (hardcover : alk. paper)
1. Presidents—United States—Election. 2. Voting—United States.
3. United States—Politics and government. I. Shields, Todd G., 1968–
II. Title.
JK528.H55 2008
324.70973—dc22   2007037758

British Library Cataloging-in-Publication Data is available

This book has been composed in Palatino

Printed on acid-free paper. ∞

press.princeton.edu

Printed in the United States of America

10 9 8 7 6 5 4 3 2 1

In memory of Diane D. Blair, 1938–2000

Contents

List of Illustrations ⸻

List of Tables

Acknowledgments ————————————————————————————

THIS STARTED OUT as a completely different book. We had planned on writing a book about voting behavior in the South as a tribute to our friend and mentor, Diane Blair. But intellectual ideas from a variety of projects bled together so that, ultimately, we have written a book about presidential campaigns, with just a single chapter focused on the South (although that chapter is one of our favorites). This topic is perhaps just as fitting for a book dedicated to Diane Blair—she was the rare academic who contributed both to political science and to the real world of campaign politics. Diane seamlessly blended her passion for research and teaching with her passion for politics—and that passion was infectious. As a freshman at the University of Arkansas in 1992, Sunshine got caught up in the excitement of the presidential campaign, and with Diane as a role model, changed her major to political science. To Todd, Diane served as a mentor when he was a young assistant professor at the University of Arkansas, demonstrating to him the direct link between scholarly research and real politics with her work during the 1996 presidential campaign.

The Diane D. Blair Center for Southern Politics and Society was created to honor Diane's legacy, and this book would not have been possible without the center's generous funding of two unique surveys. Funding from the Institute for Quantitative Social Science and a fellowship at the Shorenstein Center for the Press, Politics, and Public Policy gave Sunshine a full year of research leave to devote to writing. And because of the generous support of the Center for American Political Studies at Harvard University, we were able to hold a book conference around the first draft of the manuscript, providing critical feedback *before* it was too late to make changes.

We were able to include a great variety of data sources and analyses in this work only because of the willingness of so many scholars to share their data. Daron Shaw provided us with data on state-by-state candidate advertising and visit numbers from the 2000 and 2004 campaigns. Lee Sigelman and Emmet Buell shared their content analysis of *New York Times* coverage of the 1952–2004 presidential campaigns. Joel Rivlin with the Wisconsin Advertising Project gave us the issue content of the television advertising in the 2004 presidential campaign. We are especially grateful to Doug Rivers, Simon Jackman, and Norman Nie for their willingness to share the massive 2000 Knowledge Networks Election Study, which first gave Sunshine a chance to study campaigns as a graduate student at Stanford University. We also owe a special thanks to David Magleby, Kelly Patterson, and Quin Monson of the Center for the Study of Education and Democracy at Brigham Young University for providing access to the 2004 Campaign Communications Study. Quin Monson, in particular, provided critical help and advice for our analysis of the 2004 presidential direct mail.

As the topic of this book evolved, we greatly benefited from the valuable feedback and intellectual support of some of the smartest people in the discipline. We are especially grateful to those who were willing to read the entire manuscript draft: Adam Berinsky, Daron Shaw, Richard Johnston, Bob Shapiro, Paul Sniderman, Matt Baum, Mike Alvarez, Markus Prior, Eric Schickler, Sidney Verba, Mo Fiorina, Paul Peterson, Dennis Thompson, Sam Popkin, Norman Nie, Dave Peterson, Steven Kelts and Justin Grimmer. A very special thanks (its own sentence worth!) to Jennifer Lawless for going through the manuscript draft line by line just days before it was due. A number of other colleagues provided critical advice and suggestions at various stages in the project: Pippa Norris, Jane Junn, Gary King, Don Kelley, Shannon Davis, Jon Krosnick, and Tasha Philpot.

Along the way, we have received helpful suggestions and stimulating questions in presenting the project to different audiences—political science conferences as well as seminars at Vanderbilt University, Columbia University, University of Chicago, Harvard University, University of Minnesota, Stanford University, Brigham Young University, the Massachusetts Institute of Technology, and the Boston chapter of the Institute of Electrical and Electronics Engineers. For especially thought-provoking and helpful comments, we would like to thank Gabe Lenz, Joanne Miller, Jeremy Pope, John Sides, Dan Carpenter, Andrea Campbell, Chap Lawson, Noah Kaplan, Phil Klinker, Bob Erikson, and Kirby Goidel. For their hard work, we would like to thank the terrific group of Harvard research assistants: Raul Campillo, Tiffany Washburn, Karen Harmel, David Daniels, Kevin Papay, and Matt Smith.

And, for helpful conversations—occasionally about the book, but more often about more interesting topics—Sunshine is grateful to Barry Burden, William Howell, Steven Kelts, Shawn Treier, Jennifer Jerit, Maggie Penn, John Patty, Jason Barabas, Cara Wong, and Jake Bowers. Todd also expresses his sincere appreciation to Jim Blair for his invaluable support and advice and for the positive and significant contributions he has made to Todd's life and career.

We would also like to thank Chuck Myers, senior editor at Princeton University Press, for his enthusiastic endorsement of this project.

He has helped to make the publication process the very easiest part of this project.

Last, but not least, we would like to express our gratitude to our families. If not for the unwavering encouragement, infinite patience, and numerous sacrifices of Joel Hillygus, this book—and Sunshine's academic career—would not have been possible. Karen Shields—Todd's wife for the past sixteen years and best friend for the past eighteen years—as well as his children, Savannah and Dane, have also been exceptionally supportive throughout this project.

THE PERSUADABLE VOTER

One

Wedge Issues in Presidential Campaigns

AT THE 2004 Democratic National Convention in Boston, Massachusetts, the topic of stem cell research received top billing in a prime-time speech by the son of former president Ronald Reagan.

> A few of you may be surprised to see someone with my last name showing up to speak at a Democratic convention. Let me assure you, I am not here to make a political speech. . . . I am here tonight to talk about the issue of research into what may be the greatest medical breakthrough in our or in any lifetime: the use of embryonic stem cells.[1]

Network news coverage of the nominating conventions reached an all-time low in 2004, dropping from twenty-six hours of coverage in 1976 to a measly three hours in 2004, so Ronald Prescott Reagan's speech appeared during an especially coveted and carefully scripted time slot. With the United States embroiled in a controversial war in the Middle East and the economy faltering, why would the Democrats prioritize a "nonpolitical" speech about stem cell research?

The answer points to the heart of contemporary electoral contests. Democrats emphasized their support of stem cell research during the convention and later in stump speeches and campaign mail because they believed the issue offered them an advantage among Independents and Republicans who disagreed with President Bush's policy limiting it. Democratic pollster Peter Hart explained that the issue of stem cell research had the potential to "attract support from disease sufferers and families who otherwise agree with Bush on public policy but feel 'alienated' by his decision to restrict federal funding for embryonic stem cell research."[2] Republican pollster Robert Moran offered a similar assessment, "This is not an issue you can run and hide from. . . . If this is going to negatively impact President Bush, it will likely be in places like the Philadelphia suburbs, where you have moderate swing-voting economic conservatives."[3] Ron Reagan's highly touted

---

[1] Full transcript of the speech was published by the *New York Times*, 27 July 2004, A1.

[2] Ceci Connolly, "Kerry Takes on Issue of Embryo Research; Campaign Broadens Challenge to Include President's Commitment to Science," *Washington Post*, 8 August 2004, A5.

[3] Ibid., "Stem Cell Proponents Enter Campaign Fray," *Washington Post*, 26 July 2004, A11.

speech was an appeal not to core Democratic supporters, but to otherwise Republican voters. In other words, the Democrats were using stem cell research as a wedge issue to divide the traditional coalition of Republican supporters.

Turning the clock back four years, we find then-candidate George W. Bush using stem cell research as part of a parallel strategy in the 2000 presidential campaign. Most people do not remember that this was even an issue in that campaign, as it was not mentioned in the nominating speeches of either candidate, was not covered in their television advertising or raised in the presidential debates, and the candidates' positions were not available on their campaign Web sites. In fact, a CNN/*USA Today* poll at the time found that 56 percent of respondents "didn't know enough to say" when asked their opinion on the issue. Yet in the midst of the 2000 presidential campaign, Bush sent a letter to the U.S. Conference of Catholic Bishops in which he underscored his position that "taxpayer funds should not underwrite research that involves the destruction of live human embryos."

The Bush campaign was trying to make inroads into the Catholic vote, a traditionally Democratic constituency that often disagreed with the national party on moral issues. Opposition to abortion and stem cell research offered Bush common ground with religious voters of different denominations and across party affiliations. So, again, the issue of stem cell research was raised not to throw "red meat" to the partisan faithful, but as a wedge issue aimed at pulling away voters from the opposition camp. Because stem cell research was a relatively obscure scientific question in 2000, Bush was able to narrowly target a campaign promise on the issue without much concern that the position would carry electoral risk with the broader electorate. But in staking a position on the issue, Bush created a strategic opportunity for Democrats to use stem cell research as a wedge issue in the 2004 campaign.

Stem cell research is just one of a long list of divisive issues—abortion, gay marriage, minimum wage, school vouchers, immigration, and so on—that have become standard playbook fare in contemporary presidential campaigns. The prominence of these controversial issues challenges the conventional wisdom in political science that rational candidates should run to the center on public policy matters and avoid controversial issues at all costs in their efforts to be elected to office. What explains candidates' willingness to campaign on these divisive issues?

In this book, we offer three key arguments that help to answer this question: First, some of the most persuadable voters in the electorate—those voters most likely to be responsive to campaign information—are partisans who disagree with their party on a policy issue they care about, like the aforementioned pro-life Democrats or pro–stem cell re-search Republicans. Second, candidates have a chance to attract (or at least disaffect) these persuadable voters by emphasizing the issues that are the source of internal conflict. Third, advances in information and communication technologies have encouraged the use of wedge issues by making it easier to identify who should be targeted and with what campaign messages. In the 2004 campaign, both candidates used direct mail, telephone calls, email, and personal canvassing to target different policy messages to persuadable voters on the particular wedge issues for which they were expected to be receptive.

Our theory of the persuadable voter challenges three widespread myths about contemporary American politics. First, there is a popular perception that recent presidential candidates have campaigned on di-visive issues as a way to fire up their core partisan base. Political pun-dits and journalists commonly argued that Bush's attention to abor-tion, gay marriage, and stem cell research in the 2004 campaign was an appeal to his extremist core supporters: "Instead of edging toward the middle, Bush ran hard to the right. Instead of trying to reassure uncertain moderates, he worked hard to stoke the passions of those who needed no convincing."[4] Academic works have similarly con-cluded that candidates will be willing to take extreme positions on con-troversial issues to pander to their partisan base—either because they need to win party primaries or to obtain the campaign contributions and other resources necessary to run for office.[5] In contrast, we argue that divisive issues are often used to appeal to persuadable voters, often from the opposing partisan camp.

Looking back in history, there are clear examples of such wedge campaign strategies—most notably, the efforts of Republican candi-dates Richard Nixon and Ronald Reagan to appeal to southern conser-vative Democrats. Indeed, political scientist E. E. Schattchneider long ago argued that the effort of *all* political struggles "is to exploit cracks in the opposition while attempting to consolidate one's own side."[6] Yet such wedge strategies might seem obsolete if the electorate has polar-ized along partisan and ideological lines, as is generally thought to be the case today. The second myth we take on in this book is the wide-spread view that the polarization we observe in Washington has led to or has followed similar polarization in the electorate. The reality is that in a complex and pluralistic society, political parties are inherently co-

---

[4] Hamburger and Wallsten, *One Party Country,* 138.
[5] For a review of the literature see Fiorina, "Whatever Happened to the Median Voter."
[6] Schattschneider, *The Semisovereign People,* 67.

alitions of diverse individuals. The choice of only two major parties ensures that some partisans will be incongruent on some issues, thereby creating policy cleavages within the party coalitions. We argue that these cross-pressures between partisan loyalties and policy preferences have clear implications for the behavior of both voters and candidates in the campaign.

Cross-pressured partisans are willing to reassess their expected support for their party's nominee if they come to believe that an issue about which they disagree with their party is at stake in the election. These voters might find the salience of a conflicting issue increased by real-world events or personal experiences, but a political campaign can also activate a policy disagreement by highlighting the candidates' differences on the issue and calling attention to one's own party's failings and the opposition's virtues on the issue.

Finally, the third myth that we challenge in our analysis is the enduring conventional wisdom that persuadable voters are the least admirable segment of the electorate—poorly informed and lacking in policy attitudes. The prevailing perception about the persuadable segment of the electorate is that "its level of information is low, its sense of political involvement is slight, its level of political participation is not high."[7] It is thought that these muddled voters make up their minds on the basis of nonpolicy considerations, like candidate personality, charisma, and the "guy you'd wanna drink a beer with" criteria. In contrast, our theory suggests that policy issues are often central to how persuadable voters make up their minds. To be clear, this book is not a polemical account of an American populace composed of ideal citizens highly engaged and fully informed across all policy domains. Rather, we argue simply that for those voters who find themselves at odds with their party nominee it is the campaign that often helps to determine whether partisan loyalties or issue preferences are given greater weight in their vote decision.

A Broad View: The Reciprocal Campaign

In this book, we explore the interactions between voters and candidates during contemporary presidential campaigns. We argue that there is a reciprocal relationship between candidates' campaign strategies and voter decision making. Voter behavior cannot be fully understood without taking into account campaign information, and the behavior of candidates rests fundamentally on perceptions about what

---

[7] Key, *The Responsible Electorate*, 92.

the voters care about and how they make up their minds in a campaign. Thus, our analysis is broadly motivated by two interrelated research questions: Who in the electorate can be persuaded by campaign information? What strategies do candidates use to appeal to these persuadable voters?

In answering the former question, we argue that campaign information can influence voter decision making when the factors underlying an individual's vote decision are in conflict. The most persuadable voters in the electorate are those individuals with a foot in each candidate's camp. A Pew Survey conducted late in the 2004 campaign, for instance, found that 76 percent of likely voters who had not yet made up their minds said they agreed with Republican George Bush on some important issues and with Democrat John Kerry on other issues.[8] This group of persuadable voters includes some political Independents who are closer to the Republican candidate on some issues and the Democratic candidate on other issues, but it is primarily composed of partisans who disagree with their party on a personally important policy issue. These are the "but otherwise" Democrats and Republicans, as in the voter who is "pro-life, but otherwise Democratic" or "opposed to the Iraq War, but otherwise Republican." These cross-pressured voters have a more difficult time deciding between the candidates, so they turn to campaign information to help decide between the competing considerations.

As highlighted by our stem cell research example, our expectations about individual-level voter behavior provide a framework for understanding candidates' campaign strategies. As V. O. Key long ago recognized, "perceptions of the behavior of the electorate . . . condition, if they do not fix, the types of appeals politicians employ as they seek popular support."[9] Identifying who is persuadable and who is not helps to explain why candidates behave the way they do. The key implication of our arguments for campaign strategy is that candidates have an incentive to emphasize wedge issues to appeal to the persuadable voters in the electorate if they cannot win the election with their partisan base alone. Strategic candidates will exploit the tensions that make campaigns matter. By emphasizing the issues that are the source of internal conflict, candidates can potentially shape the vote decision of these persuadable voters.

Although candidates have always had reason to look for wedge issues to highlight during their campaigns, the contemporary informa-

---

[8] "Swing Voters Slow to Decide, Still Cross-pressured," *Pew Research Center Survey Report*, 27 October 2004.

[9] Key, *The Responsible Electorate*, 7.

tion environment has made it easier to identify potential wedge issues and to target issue messages to narrow segments of the population. With a wealth of information about individual voters, candidates are increasingly able to microtarget personalized appeals on the specific issues for which each voter disagrees with the other candidate. This fragmentation of the candidates' campaign communications leads to *dog-whistle politics*—targeting a message so that it can be heard only by those it is intended to reach, like the high-pitched dog whistle that can be heard by dogs but is not audible to the human ear.[10] By narrowly communicating issue messages, candidates reduce the risk of alienating other voters, thereby broadening the range of issues on the campaign agenda. For instance, our analysis finds that the candidates in the 2004 presidential election staked positions on more than seventy-five different policy issues in their direct-mail communications. Thus, new information and communication technologies have changed not only how candidates communicate with voters, but also who they communicate with and what they are willing to say.

In building a theory of campaigns that attempts to explain both voter and candidate behavior, we will inevitably oversimplify the political world, make sweeping and controvertible assumptions, and gloss over the many important nuances of both candidate and voter behavior. On the candidate side, for instance, we focus on the incentives in place for candidates to microtarget wedge campaign messages, but we must recognize that candidates still devote most of their campaign efforts to "macrotargeting" on the broad issues of the day. Moreover, a candidate's campaign strategy plans are rarely perfectly implemented. Even the best-laid plans can be derailed by a scandal or a powerful opposition attack once the campaign hits full swing.

On the voter side, we do not challenge the enduring view that the mass public generally has limited political information and incoherent ideological worldviews. But just because voters do not have constrained ideologies does not necessarily mean that they do not hold policy preferences. As Phil Converse himself wrote in his classic piece assailing the ideological capabilities of the public, "A realistic picture of political belief systems in the mass public . . . is not one that omits issues and policy demands completely nor one that presumes widespread ideological coherence; it is rather one that captures with some fidelity the fragmentation, narrowness, and diversity of these demands."[11] Although there are undoubtedly some ill-informed voters who "respond in random fashion to the winds of the campaign," the

---

[10] The classic example comes from the 2001 Australian federal election campaign in which Prime Minister John Howard infamously said, "We don't want those sorts of people here," referring to asylum seekers coming to the country on unauthorized boats.

[11] Converse, "The Nature of Belief Systems in Mass Publics," 247.

heart of our argument is that some voters are persuadable not because of the *absence* of political preferences, but rather because of the *complexity* of those preferences.[12] The voters' individual patterns of political preferences (reinforcing or conflicting) shape how voters respond to political information, as well as how candidates attempt to win them over.

In exploring campaign effects and candidate strategy, we build on a diverse body of research in political psychology, political communication, voting behavior, and candidate position taking. And we evaluate our expectations about the dynamics of presidential campaigns using a wide variety of different data sources and methodological approaches—cross-sectional, longitudinal, and panel surveys, a survey experiment, a data collection of direct mail from the 2004 presidential election, historical and archival research about campaign strategy, content analysis of party platforms and campaign speeches, and personal interviews with campaign practitioners. Each method has its own strengths and weaknesses; we hope our pluralistic approach offers a more comprehensive and compelling examination of campaign effects and candidate strategy. Sections of our story will span American political history, but the bulk of our empirical analysis is focused on the 2000 and 2004 presidential elections. In today's political environment, in which election outcomes are determined by razor-thin margins and the balance of power in Washington is evenly divided, it is increasingly important to understand the nature and influence of presidential campaigns. Our perspective is that campaigns play an intermediary role between the governed and the governors, a role that fundamentally hinges on information about both the candidates and the voters. Candidates develop their issue agendas and campaign strategies on the basis of information about the voting public. The voters, in turn, select a preferred presidential candidate using information learned during the campaign. Although the translation of information between candidates and voters is neither flawless nor complete, it is the key mechanism by which elections are thought to serve a democratic function.

Contributions to Campaign Effects Research

There is perhaps no wider gulf in thinking than that between academics and political practitioners on the question of "do campaigns matter?" Campaign professionals tend to view election outcomes as singularly determined by the campaign itself, while political scholars often treat election outcomes as a foregone conclusion. Since the earliest voting behavior research, the prevailing academic perspective has been

---

[12] Key, *The Responsible Electorate*, 8.

that presidential campaigns are "sound and fury signifying nothing";
it is possible to predict how people will vote and who will win the
election long before the campaign even begins.[13] A virtual renaissance
of recent research has since offered compelling evidence that campaigns can and do shape voter behavior and election outcomes, and to
that growing literature we offer a number of unique contributions.[14]

First, we examine not whether campaigns matter, but rather, for
whom and under what conditions campaigns influence voter decision
making. We identify the persuadable voters on the basis of durable
attitudes and beliefs, and we show how previous definitions of swing
voters that use group characteristics (e.g., Catholics or suburban
women) or past or intended behavior (e.g., the "undecideds" in response to a poll) provide an incomplete picture of who is responsive
to the campaign and why. Our perspective recognizes that a campaign
will have little influence on some in the electorate, but for others the
campaign provides critical information for selecting between two candidates, neither of whom is a perfect match to their preferences. Traditional analyses of aggregate state or national vote totals mask this variation in individual-level campaign effects.[15]

At the same time, in a competitive electoral environment, even this
small set of persuadable voters can be decisive. The number of partisan
defectors in the electorate was large enough to make the difference between the winner and loser in ten of the last fourteen presidential elections.[16] In the 2004 presidential election, our analysis estimates that
roughly 25 percent of the voting public were persuadable partisans
(another 9 percent were persuadable Independents), clearly sufficient
numbers of voters to swing victory to either candidate. Of course, not
all of these voters were persuaded to vote against their party's nominee. But our analysis estimates a campaign effect of some 2.8 million
partisans switching their expected vote choice in the sixteen key battleground states of the 2004 presidential campaign. Bush's margin of victory over Kerry in those states was just 200,000 votes.

---

[13] Campbell et al., *The American Voter*; Fair, *Predicting Presidential Elections and Other Things*.

[14] Most prominently, Johnston et al., *The 2000 Presidential Election and the Foundations of Party Politics*; Holbrook, *Do Campaigns Matter?*; Shaw, *The Race to 270*.

[15] For instance, Shaw, "The Effect of TV Ads and Candidate Appearances on State-wide Presidential Votes."

[16] This estimate does not include Independents who "lean" toward one party or an-other. The number of 'leaning' and 'pure' Independents alone has exceeded the winners' margin of victory in every election between 1952 and 2004, except 1964. Data source is the American National Election Study cumulative file.

Second, our analysis suggests that the particular issues emphasized during a presidential campaign shape who votes how and why. Much of the recent research on campaign effects has evaluated the influence of campaign volume—the number of television ads or candidate visits, the amount of media coverage, or the intensity of campaign efforts.[17] Much less is known about the nature and influence of campaign *content*. Is it consequential, for instance, not only that Bush ran more ads than Kerry in Ohio in 2004, but also that those ads focused primarily on issues of national security? Scholars have often concluded that campaign dynamics are predictable from one campaign to the next, implying that the specific content of the campaign is largely inconsequential.[18] Most prominently, it is thought that campaigns largely serve to activate and reinforce partisan attachments, bringing home any wayward partisans by Election Day. Political scientist James Campbell sums up this perspective: "Campaigns remind Democrats why they are Democrats rather than Republicans and remind Republicans why they are Republicans rather than Democrats."[19] In contrast, our analysis demonstrates that campaigns often serve to pull persuadable partisans away from their party's nominee. And depending on the nature of campaign dialogue, conflicting predispositions might rest peacefully unnoticed in one election but be the basis for defecting in the next.

Finally, our analysis examines the impact of the campaign not only on final vote choice, but also on the process by which voters make up their mind. Classic political science research offers extensive theories about the correlates of the final vote decision, but we know much less about any dynamics in the process by which voters come to that decision. As Thomas Holbrook observes, "A political campaign must be understood to be a process that generates a product, the election outcome, and like any other process, one cannot expect to understand the process by analyzing only the product."[20] Even if we are able to accurately predict an individual's final vote choice with long-term demographic and political characteristics, knowing if it was a bumpy ride to reach that decision helps us to evaluate the persuasiveness of campaign communication. There is a noteworthy difference between the partisan who remains a committed loyalist through the entire campaign and the one who switches back and forth between candidates or remains undecided until "coming home" on Election Day. Focusing on

[17] For instance, Shaw, *The Race to 270*.

[18] Gelman and King, "Why Are American Presidential Election Campaign Polls So Variable When Votes Are So Predictable?"

[19] Campbell, "Presidential Election Campaigns and Partisanship," 13.

[20] Holbrook, *Do Campaigns Matter?*, 153.

the dynamics of the presidential campaign, we find that persuadable partisans exposed to campaign dialogue are not only more likely to defect on Election Day, they are also more likely to change their mind over the course of the campaign and in response to campaign events. With the amount and type of movement we identify, it is clear why candidates and campaign strategists go to such lengths to reach persuadable voters.

Contributions to Campaign Strategy Research

Knowing who is responsive to campaign messages helps us understand the actions of candidates in presidential campaigns. Our view of campaign responsiveness suggests that presidential candidates should emphasize wedge issues in order to appeal to persuadable voters in the electorate. It is risky for a candidate to make a policy promise in a campaign—it might alienate voters who disagree and it can constrain position taking and policy making down the line—so candidates will avoid taking positions on issues when possible. Research has documented, for instance, that congressional candidates are less likely to talk about issues if they are in a less intense or uncompetitive campaign.[21] Yet, presidential contests are always competitive. Candidates must win over persuadable voters—a candidate's partisan base is simply not sufficient to win the White House. In 2004, for instance, self-identified Republicans composed just 35 percent of the voting public, and self-identified Democrats made up 32 percent.[22] In an electoral context in which the parties are evenly divided, it is Politics 101—to beat the other candidate, you must get not only the votes of your own supporters but also a few from the other side (in the concluding chapter, we consider contexts outside U.S. presidential elections). In contrast to previous expectations that candidates will appeal to the moderate median voter with centrist policy promises, we argue that candidates try to build a winning coalition between their base supporters and subsets of the persuadable voters by activating persuadable voters on the issues on which they disagree with the other candidate. As Sam Popkin observes, "Politicians and parties do not introduce [government policy] programs to . . . build a consensus on what is good for America, despite pious claims to the contrary. They defend or promote obligations to renew and build constituencies, or to split the opposition."[23]

---

[21] Kahn and Kenney, *The Spectacle of U.S. Senate Campaigns.*

[22] Including leaners increases the percentages to 46 percent Republicans and 48 percent Democrats. Data source is the 2004 National Election Study.

[23] Popkin, "Public Opinion and Collective Obligations," 2.

It should perhaps not be surprising that presidential candidates develop their issue agendas with an eye on persuadable voters. After all, strategic candidates target all their resources—political and financial—for the greatest electoral impact. Candidates target their policy promises to the pivotal voters, just as they target their campaign spending to the pivotal states. In the 2004 presidential contest, thirty-three states received no television advertising dollars from the presidential campaigns or the national parties, while battleground states received more than $8 million, and Florida alone received $36 million.[24] Candidates similarly design their policy agendas to get the biggest bang for the buck. As one consultant explained, "once we have identified how to win ... [and] our voters have been defined, the campaign's resources—money, time, effort, and most of all, message—are directed only to those voters. *No effort is directed anywhere or at anyone else*" (italics in original).[25] More narrowly still, the campaign agendas of presidential candidates are focused on the policy preferences of persuadable voters in the most competitive states. As a 1976 campaign strategy memo for President Ford bluntly explained, "Because of our electoral college system, 'swing voters' in target states which we believe can be won, are the only 'swing voters' we should focus on. It does no good to capture 100% of the 'swing vote' in a state which goes to our opponent because of his overwhelming initial advantage."[26]

Because taking a stand on a wedge issue runs the risk of losing voters, a candidate's use of a wedge strategy fundamentally depends on having information about the wants and desires of the persuadable voters in the electorate. The more uncertain the candidate is about the preferences of the voters, the more ambiguous campaign appeals are likely to be. Likewise, the broader the audience to whom candidates are communicating, the more moderate the issue message. Since the turn of the twenty-first century, candidates have had more information about the electorate than ever before. By combining computerized voter registration lists—which contain a voter's name, address, and in most states, party registration and vote history—with information from census data, consumer databases, and political polls, candidates are better able to predict whether an individual citizen will turn out and who he or she might support. Candidates can then narrowly target the issue mes-

---

[24] Estimates computed from data generously provided by Daron Shaw.

[25] Political consultant Joel Bradshaw, "Who Will Vote for You and Why: Designing Campaign Strategy and Message," 39.

[26] Campaign Strategy Plan (drafted by White House aide Michael Raoul-Duval), August 1976; folder "Presidential Campaign—Campaign Strategy Program (1)-(3)," box 1, Dorothy E. Downton Files, Gerald R. Ford Library.

sages most likely to resonate with the individual. In talking about the importance of information for campaign strategy, one campaign consultant explained, "I think politics has always been driven by data; it's just that the data on the electorate was never very accurate. The reason traditional politics has been about class or race politics is because individual policy preferences could only be meaningfully categorized by class or race. Now I can differentiate between nine gradations of nose-pickers."[27] Candidates use information about the voters to target policy appeals in email, direct mail, phone calls, and so on in an effort to prime different individuals to vote on the basis of different issues. Recent research has recognized that candidates will emphasize those issues that offer them a strategic advantage, but our theoretical expectations account for variations in candidates' policy agendas by identifying who in the electorate confers the strategic advantage and why.

In 2004, for instance, the Republican Party identified thirty different target groups—like "traditional-marriage Democrats," "education Independents," and "tax-cut conservative Republicans"—each of which was told that their particular issue priorities were at stake in the election.[28] In their book, *One Party Country*, political journalists Tom Hamburger and Peter Wallsten outline the efforts of the Bush campaign to "slice away pieces" of the traditional Democratic coalition with custom-tailored messages sent to business-oriented Asians, church-going black suburbanites, second-generation Indian Americans, Orthodox Jews, and other "once-Democratic swingers."[29] One pro-Bush direct-mail piece in our analysis features a Jewish Democratic woman saying, "I remember 9/11 as if it happened yesterday. . . . Like most Democrats, I disagree with President Bush on a lot of issues, but he was right to act quickly and decisively after we were attacked. . . . I've always been a pro-choice Democrat, but party loyalties have no meaning when it comes to my family's safety."

George Bush is by no means the only presidential candidate to use wedge issues to target persuadable voters. In 1996 President Bill Clinton's campaign "went through the average woman's day and said, we're going to appeal to her at every step of that day," using policies like education to "drive a wedge between the GOP and suburban families."[30] Pollster Mark Penn explained the process by which the cam-

---

[27] As quoted in Howard, *New Media Campaigns and the Managed Citizen*, 229.

[28] Interview of Sara Taylor conducted by Sunshine Hillygus on 21 November 2005. The segments were calculated by state, and varied somewhat in number and content across states, depending on the type and quality of data available.

[29] Hamburger and Wallsten, *One Party Country*, 140.

[30] Rich Lowry, "Wedge Shots," *The National Review*, 1 September 1997. 49 (16): 22–23.

paign developed Clinton's issue agenda. Using extensive polling data, "we figured out who those [swing] voters were, everything from their sports, vacations, and lifestyles," and then divided them into nine different groups—like "balanced-budget swing voters" or "young social conservatives."[31] Finally, they were polled about a variety of different policy proposals to see how much more likely they would be to support Clinton if he offered each proposal, allowing Clinton to then emphasize the policies with the greatest appeal among these critical swing voters.

Democratic Implications of Changing Candidate Strategies

Changes in presidential campaign strategies and tactics made possible by a hyperinformation environment have broader implications for American democracy. In the campaign, the efficiency of candidate targeting strategies has heightened political inequality by improving the ability of candidates to ignore large portions of the public—nonvoters, those committed to the opposition, and those living in uncompetitive states. Critically, the preferences of these individuals are not unknown; they are deliberately ignored. Candidates consider it a waste of effort to reach out to individuals with a low expected probability of voting for them.

We can easily see this change in campaign strategy over time by looking at trends in self-reported campaign contact in the 1952–2004 American National Election Study (NES) cumulative file. Displayed in figure 1.1 are the percentages of respondents, by voter-registration status, reporting they were contacted by one of the political parties. By the late 1990s, corresponding with the computerization of voter registration files, the gap in party contact between those registered to vote and those not registered dramatically increased. In 2004 just 14 percent of those not registered to vote were contacted by either of the political parties, compared to 47 percent of those registered to vote, and 58 percent of registered voters in battleground states.[32]

The fragmentation of campaign dialogue also has potential implications beyond the electoral contest itself. Elections have always been a blunt instrument for expressing the policy preferences of the public, but the multiplicity of campaign messages makes it even more difficult to evaluate whether elected representatives are following the will of

[31] Sosnik et al., *Applebee's America*, 22.

[32] Competitive states defined by a winning margin of 5 percentage points or less in the previous election.

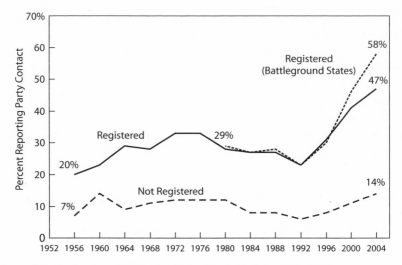

Figure 1.1: Campaign Contact by Voter Registration, 1952–2004
Note: Figure illustrates increasing gap in party contact since the early 1990s.
Data source is the American National Election Study cumulative file.

the people. Microtargeting enables candidates to focus attention on the issues that will help them win, irrespective of whether they are of concern to the broader electorate. In the months leading up to the 2004 Democratic National Convention, for instance, the monthly Gallup Poll open-ended question asking about the most important problem facing the nation never once registered stem cell research in its top twenty issues.[33] It is also hard to imagine that snowmobiling policy topped the public's list of political concerns in 2006, but in the Michigan governor's race, Republicans microtargeted working-class snowmobilers with the message that the Democratic candidate's environmental views stood in the way of better snowmobiling opportunities.[34] Will political dialogue be consumed by "superficial politics" instead of addressing the critical issues of concern to the general public? How does a winning candidate interpret the policy directive of the electorate if different individuals intended their vote to send different policy messages? Can politicians claim a policy mandate if citizens are voting on the basis of different policy promises?

[33] Survey by Gallup Organization, January–October, 2004. Retrieved 22 November 2006 from the iPOLL Databank, Roper Center for Public Opinion Research, University of Connecticut.
[34] Tom Hamburger and Peter Wallsten, "GOP Mines Data for Every Tiny Bloc," *Los Angeles Times*, 24 September 2006, A1.

We return to these questions in the conclusion of this book, but raise them here to point out the potential ramifications of a microtargeting strategy taken to the extreme. To be sure, in many cases we are making predictions for the future rather than identifying today's empirical reality. Microtargeting strategies continue to evolve in fits and starts as political operatives figure out issues of file management, data relevance, and analytic methods. But it is also clear that, in today's hyper-information environment, microtargeting is not going away. Democratic consultant Hal Malchow explains "Microtargeting is still in the early phases in politics. . . . It will become bigger as the campaigns start to understand it better and the data become more relevant. Then it will really reshape politics."[35] While campaign strategists and political consultants focus attention on trying to evaluate whether microtargeted appeals have some influence on the voters, in this book we consider how this campaign tactic has changed the incentives and behaviors of the candidates.

At least in the case of government policy on stem cell research, the electoral process has not yet brought stem cell policy more closely in step with current public opinion on the issue. In July 2006 Bush issued the first veto of his administration to reject the Republican Congress's effort to expand federal funding of embryonic stem cell research, even as polls found that 68 percent of Americans support such a policy and 58 percent disapproved of his veto.[36]

Overview of Chapters

We cover a lot of ground in this book: voter decision making, candidate strategy, and the campaign spectacle that connects the two. We lean on a number of different theoretical perspectives, including work on information processing, attitudinal ambivalence, political persuasion, campaign strategy, and campaign effects. And we evaluate our expectations about the dynamics of presidential campaigns using a wide variety of different data sources—sample surveys, a survey experiment, a data collection of presidential direct mail, historical and archival data, and personal interviews. With this multimethod approach and

---

[35] Telephone interview with Hal Malchow conducted by Sunshine Hillygus on 16 April 2007.

[36] *Survey by USA Today and Gallup Organization, 21–23 July 2006. Survey by NBC News, Wall Street Journal and Hart and McInturff Research Companies, 21–24 July 2006.* Both retrieved 19 December 2006 from the iPOLL Databank, Roper Center for Public Opinion Research, University of Connecticut.

broad theoretical perspective, we hope to provide a better understanding of who is responsive in presidential campaigns, why they are responsive, and how candidates attempt to sway them.

In the next chapter, we develop our theoretical arguments about how campaigns influence persuadable voters as well as how the information environment shapes the incentives that candidates face when they develop campaign strategy. We compare our expectations about campaign effects and candidate behavior with the conventional academic and popular wisdom. We argue there is an interactive flow of information and influence between candidates and voters in presidential campaigns, and cross-pressured partisans are often in the center of this reciprocal relationship.

Before turning to our analysis of campaign persuasion and candidate strategy in later chapters, we focus in chapter 3 on the fundamental issues of data, definition, and measurement. We begin the chapter with a thorough discussion of the challenges of measuring cross-pressures and an overview of the data sources used in the analysis throughout the book. We then evaluate the key assumption underlying our theoretical expectations—that there are indeed persuadable partisans in the contemporary American electorate. This chapter provides a careful examination of the contemporary policy fractures between and within the American political parties, offering a new perspective on the so-called culture wars and the surrounding debate over the degree of partisan and ideological polarization in the mass public.

Chapter 4 presents our key empirical tests of campaign persuasion by examining the way in which cross-pressures interact with the campaign environment to shape voter decision making. More broadly, this chapter addresses the question: when and how campaigns shape voter behavior. We evaluate the responsiveness of persuadable voters to campaign information in both the 2000 and 2004 presidential elections using multiple tests across multiple data sources, including a cross-sectional survey, a panel survey, and a survey experiment. This comprehensive analysis provides compelling evidence that campaigns can have measurable effects on voter decision making and these effects often serve to activate issues at the expense of partisan loyalties.

In the next two chapters, we shift our focus to more carefully consider the implications of our story for candidate strategy. In chapter 5, we offer a more detailed evaluation of our expectations about the link between voter preferences, candidate position taking, and campaign effects with an in-depth analysis of the Republican "southern strategy." We examine the origins of this wedge-issue campaign strategy and trace its evolution and influence as it changed from an emphasis on racial wedge issues, like civil rights and busing in the late 1960s and early 1970s, to a focus on moral wedge issues, such as gay marriage and stem cell research by the turn of the century. This chapter offers an in-depth qualitative and archival analysis of candidate strategy that highlights the long-standing incentive for candidates to use wedge issues and then turns to a quantitative analysis of voter behavior to evaluate the impact of candidate strategy on voter decision making.

In chapter 6, we examine candidates' strategies in the 2004 presidential election, focusing on the link between the information environment and candidates' incentive to microtarget a wide range of wedge issues. Looking at the volume, content, and targeting of direct-mail and television advertising in the 2004 presidential election, we test whether candidates were primarily using controversial wedge issues in an effort to mobilize their base partisan supporters or as a tactic for influencing persuadable voters. Finally, we consider the implications of these campaign strategies for political representation and inequality.

In the final chapter, we discuss the limits of our investigations and the extent to which our theory might generalize beyond American presidential elections. We conclude with a discussion of the potentially troublesome implications of our findings for electoral accountability and democratic governance.

Two

The Reciprocal Campaign

IN EVERY PRESIDENTIAL ELECTION, the media focus attention on swing voters in the electorate. Everyone wants to know who they are, what they want, and how they will make up their minds. Swing voters dictate the candidates' efforts, they provide fodder for media discussion, and they ultimately decide the election. "Mushy Swings are Wavering Election Kings," summed up one newspaper headline.[1] Political journalists and pundits variously define this group as undecided voters, political Independents, ticket splitters, ideological moderates, or more creatively, soccer moms, NASCAR dads, or some other demographic group du jour. It is commonly recognized that these swing voters are individuals who might be available to either candidate, but there are few guiding principles—and certainly no well-grounded theory—about who these voters are or what makes them persuadable. Political scientist Daron Shaw recently observed, "The concept of swing voting is something that has miraculously escaped the empirical scrutiny of scholars. . . . We are clearly enamored with the idea that certain voters are more persuadable and therefore disproportionately important for our understanding of close elections. . . . But we are not quite sure what we want to say on the matter."[2]

As the title of our book implies, we offer a theoretical perspective that identifies the persuadable voters in the electorate. More broadly, though, we argue that to understand campaign dynamics it is necessary to understand the interaction between the persuadable voters and the political candidates who attempt to sway them. In this chapter, we consider the incentives, motives, and interests of both voters and candidates in a presidential campaign, outlining our theoretical expectations about the behaviors of both of these actors. We begin by explaining why cross-pressured partisans—those who disagree with their affiliated party on a policy issue—are among the persuadable voters, and then we consider the implications for candidate strategy.

[1] Peter Callaghan, "Mushy Swings Are Wavering Election Kings," *The News Tribune*, 12 October 2004, B1.

[2] Shaw, *The Race to 270*, 169–70.

A THEORY OF PERSUADABLE VOTERS

Voter decision making is a dynamic process. Voters have a set of pre-dispositions—existing beliefs and attitudes—and they are charged with the task of matching those predispositions with a candidate selection. As voters learn new information over the course of the campaign, they are better able to match their predispositions with their candidate choice. Some voters find this an easier task than others, so there is variability in the likelihood that voters will use campaign information in making up their minds. Existing research on vote choice dynamics emphasizes that political sophistication and the strength of predispositions determine whether an individual will change her candidate choice during a campaign. We argue that responsiveness to new information is determined not only by the strength of existing predispositions, but also by the relationship between those predispositions.

In proposing that persuadable voters are those with conflicting predispositions underlying their vote decision, we use the term *predisposition* to refer to a durable political inclination relevant to selecting a preferred political candidate. These predispositions might include partisan loyalties, group attachments, political values, policy attitudes, incumbent evaluations, or other political considerations.[3] Voting requires making a choice between these sometimes competing considerations, and we argue that the campaign context helps determine how voters resolve any internal conflict between them. We expect our basic theoretical predictions might hold for any set of conflicting considerations, but we focus specifically on the tension between party affiliation and policy preferences as perhaps the most overlooked and most consequential for the dynamics we observe in presidential campaigns.[4]

Electoral campaigns, especially presidential contests, are structured around partisan competition for office and the policy alternatives offered by the opposing candidates. A party attachment provides an anchor, a latent expectation about which candidate a voter will support in a generic election. Voters are not asked to select their preferred candidate from among all eligible citizens in the country, but rather they must choose between a Democratic and Republican (and occasionally a minor party) nominee. A party affiliation predisposes a voter to sup-

---

[3] Although some scholars distinguish between a predisposition and a consideration, we use the terms interchangeably as primitives to the vote decision. To be sure, the particular criteria that people use in making up their mind might differ across individuals. Rivers, "Heterogeneity in Models of Electoral Choice."

[4] For instance, we expect political Independents to be persuadable if they are cross-pressured between competing issues pulling them in different directions.

port one candidate or the other—an initial expectation of support for the party's nominee. A more general model examining conflicts between different issue positions or competing political values, then, would miss the unique and important role that party identification has on the vote decision beyond serving as an issue placeholder. In addition to party identification, policy preferences are the other key factor to voter decision making. Political issues are the very things that campaigns are made of—the "basic unit of political analysis for campaigns, candidates, journalists, and other members of the chattering classes. It's what makes up the subheadings on a candidate's website, it's what sober, serious people wish election outcomes hinged on, it's what every candidate pledges to run his campaign on, and it's what we always complain we don't see enough coverage of."[5]

Cross-pressured partisans, then, have competing considerations pulling them in opposing directions. As a result, they are more likely to hold a candidate preference that is weakly anchored and thus more pliable. In contrast, partisans with reinforcing policy preferences can easily converge on a vote decision and are unlikely to change it over the course of the campaign.[6] These congruent partisan voters are a candidate's base supporters, likely to support the candidate through thick and thin, in the face of missteps or scandal.

At some level, it is perhaps obvious that it should be easier to change the minds of voters who are closer to indifferent between the candidate choices, simply by virtue of the fact that it takes less to move them from one side to the other. If we conceive of everyone in the electorate holding a latent probability of voting for a particular party in a generic election—ranging from 0 percent to 100 percent chance of voting for the Republican over the Democratic candidate—then it seems intuitive that the individuals near 50 percent will be the most persuadable. It should take less to change the expected vote of the individuals with a 45 percent probability of voting Republican than those with just a 15 percent probability of doing so. Suppose, for instance, that the Republican candidate makes a new policy promise (say, an across-the-board tax rebate) that increases every voter's probability of voting Republican by 10 percentage points, then the candidate has now won over the first voter but not the second.

---

[5] Christopher Hays, "Decision Makers," *The New Republic Online*, posted on 17 November 2004.

[6] This assumes the candidate takes positions consistent with the party platform, a reasonable assumption in presidential races but perhaps not always the case in lower-level races, a distinction discussed in the concluding chapter.

But cross-pressured partisans are also more responsive to campaign appeals because the conflicting issue creates an opportunity for messages from the opposition-party candidate to be influential. In contrast to our hypothetical example, political psychology research suggests that the campaign message from a Republican candidate will not in fact increase every voter's level of support equally. Rather, some voters will resist the message; how individuals respond to new information depends on their existing predispositions. When individuals encounter new information, it is gauged against existing beliefs and attitudes, with congruent evidence being uncritically assimilated and inconsistent evidence being vigorously counterargued, rationalized, or ignored.[7] Previous research has concluded that partisan predispositions, in particular, filter out countervailing political information. John Zaller most explicitly argues this perspective: "Given reception of a range of campaign messages, people tend to accept what is congenial to their partisan values and to reject what is not."[8] Whereas he suggests that party identification serves as a perceptual screen leading partisans to resist information from the opposing party, we explicitly identify the conditions under which partisans may be receptive to messages from the opposition.

When partisans with reinforcing policy preferences encounter campaign information from the opposing party candidate, we expect that they will counterargue it as previous studies have predicted. But for those partisans who disagree with their party on an issue, we expect them to be more receptive to information from the opposition party on that conflicting issue. And a message on a conflicting issue from their own party's nominee actually serves to exacerbate tensions. For example, following President Bush's announcement that he would support a constitutional amendment banning gay marriage, the Log Cabin Republicans (a national group of gay Republicans) issued an immediate press release rebuking the position, and they ultimately decided to withhold endorsing Bush, the first time in history the group refused to endorse the Republican nominee.

We argue that campaigns help cross-pressured voters choose between competing considerations. Depending on the issues emphasized in the campaign, cross-pressures may lie dormant in one election but be the basis for defecting in the next. In other words, priming is the mechanism by which campaigns can persuade a cross-pressured partisan to support one candidate or the other. While previous research on

---

[7] Taber and Lodge, "Motivated Skepticism in the Evaluation of Political Beliefs"; Bartels, "Beyond the Running Tally: Partisan Bias in Political Perceptions."

[8] Zaller, *The Nature and Origins of Mass Opinion*, 241.

priming has recognized that the campaign can heighten the salience of an issue, we evaluate how campaign priming interacts with policy incongruence to influence voter decision making. An environmentalist Republican might not fret over the candidates' positions on global warming if she does not think the policy is at stake in the election. If, however, she is bombarded with messages about the Republican candidate's heinous record on the environment and the Democratic candidate's stellar accomplishments, the cross-pressure will be activated and she will be more likely to switch support to the Democratic candidate.

Our conception of persuadable voters builds on V. O. Key's "party switchers" in *The Responsible Electorate*. Key argued that a voter who supported candidates of different parties in adjacent elections was not the "erratic and irrational fellow" so commonly conceived, but was someone "moved by concern about central and relevant questions of public policy, or governmental performance, and of executive personality."[9] But while Key looked at changes in vote choice *across* elections, our focus is *within* elections. Key also explicitly discounted the role of campaigns in shaping vote dynamics—equating campaign effects to "manipulation by skilled humbugs." In contrast, we argue that campaign information helps to determine whether a cross-pressured partisan remains loyal or defects to the opposition.

To be clear, when we talk about "persuadable" voters, our notion of campaign persuasion refers to campaign-induced changes in *vote choice*. Candidates are not changing a voter's underlying predispositions; rather they are changing how she translates those predispositions into a candidate selection. At times in our analysis, we observe individual-level changes in vote choice directly. With repeated interviews of the same individuals over the course of the 2000 campaign, our analysis directly traces movement in support for one candidate to another. At other times, we look for evidence of the persuasive influence of campaigns by examining voters' deviation from their expected (but unmeasured) support for a candidate. More precisely, we examine whether partisan defection—in which a partisan identifier casts a ballot for the opposing party candidate—is related to the campaign.

Our notion of persuasion differs from how the term has been used in some previous research, which has defined it only as campaign-induced changes in the attitudes or considerations that underlie the vote decision. For instance, Adam Simon looks for evidence that a television advertisement about a candidate's view on the death penalty changes the voters' position on the issue.[10] Although revising an individual's policy attitudes is certainly one type of persuasion, campaign commu-

[9] Key, *The Responsible Electorate*, 4, 7–8. A similar argument is made in Daudt, *Floating Voters and the Floating Vote*.

[10] Simon, *The Winning Message*.

nications are fundamentally directed toward influencing the vote decision rather than underlying predispositions. Campaigns do not typically manipulate individuals to vote against their predispositions; rather, campaigns have an influence because of the diversity of voter predispositions. Campaigns help voters sort through a variety of preferences, shaping which ones voters bring to bear in selecting a preferred candidate.

Despite the differences between our definition of persuasion and existing research, our conception of campaign persuasion closely correlates with popular use of the term. When using the term *persuadable voter*, for instance, political commentators reference those individuals who might be convinced to support either political candidate.[11] Candidates similarly recognize the difficulty of changing voters' policy attitudes, especially on the divisive positional issues that are the focus of our analysis. Campaign efforts are instead directed toward influencing the public by changing how voters make up their minds, a process some call deliberate priming or heresthetics.[12] A rich literature has shown that campaigns can affect the electorate by priming the criteria on which voters base their vote decisions, either by increasing the accessibility or importance of particular criteria (or simply informing the public where the candidates line up on different criteria).[13] We identify the conditions under which these priming effects will produce changes in candidate support.

Conventional Wisdom about Persuadable Voters

When political pollsters and journalists talk about persuadable voters, they commonly define them as individuals who are "undecided" in response to a poll or survey asking about their candidate preferences.[14]

---

[11] For example, Joe Hadfield, "Guns Versus Jobs: Some Voters Pulled in Different Directions at the Polls," *Campaigns & Elections*, Oct/Nov 2004, 28–30. A number of scholars also define campaign persuasion effects as those that influence voter preference. See, for instance, Iyengar and Simon, "New Perspectives and Evidence on Political Communication and Campaign Effects;" Holbrook, *Do Campaigns Matter?*

[12] Johnston et al., *Letting the People Decide: Dynamics of a Canadian Election*; Carsey, *Campaign Dynamics: the Race for Governor*; Riker, *The Strategy of Rhetoric*; Medvic, *Political Consultants in U.S. Congressional Elections*; Druckman et al., "Candidate Strategies to Prime Issues and Image."

[13] Druckman, "Priming the Vote: Campaign Effects in a U.S. Senate Election." Much of the early research was focused on priming effects and evaluations of a candidate or other object. For instance, Miller and Krosnick, "News Media Impact on the Ingredients of Presidential Evaluations."

[14] Similar to the undecided measure is William Mayer's definition of swing voters as those rating both candidates within fifteen degrees of each other on a thermometer rating in a political survey. Mayer, "The Swing Voter in American Presidential Elections."

In an article about swing voting, one journalist lamented, "for those who follow politics, there are few things more mysterious, more inscrutable, more maddening than the mind of the undecided voter."[15] As interesting as these elusive, uncommitted voters are, being undecided in response to a poll is not a theoretically compelling measure of persuadability. Although some undecided voters are truly persuadable, others are nonvoters or reliable partisans who have just not yet come home.

The size of the undecided contingent also very much depends on the timing of the poll in the campaign, the wording of the question, and the coding decisions of the particular polling house. Pollsters vary widely in how they ask about candidate preference, with many asking how respondents "lean" in an effort to classify as many individuals as possible into one camp or the other. Not surprisingly, polls from early in the campaign will have more undecided voters than polls later in the campaign. The undecided measure also misses those individuals who change their candidate choice over the course of the campaign, offering the clearest evidence of persuasive effects.

More importantly, being undecided about candidate preference is a behavioral consequence, rather than a determinant, of persuadability. The undecided measure offers no theoretical guidance as to who in the electorate will be persuadable outside the context of the current poll (and the specific election). To understand campaign dynamics, we need to be able to identify the persuadable voters *before the campaign begins*. We offer a theoretically grounded explanation of who is persuadable in the electorate based on voter attitudes rather than on intended behavior. Measures that rely on an individual's past voting history face the same conceptual limitation in that they do not offer a theoretical reason about why an individual is persuadable or not.[16] By forcing a choice between only two alternatives, an individual's behavior of casting (or intending to cast) a ballot for one candidate or the other masks the complexity of attitudes that might motivate that behavior. As such, behavioral measures fail to recognize the potential role of the campaign in determining whether the persuadable voters will be undecided or able to settle on a preferred candidate.

[15] Christopher Hayes, "Decision Makers: Lessons Learned about Undecided Voters," *New Republic Online*, posted on 17 November 2004.

[16] Such measures are also problematic in that they miss individuals with no voting history (the young or newly mobilized) and are dependent on the previous electoral context. Given Ronald Reagan's high level of support among Republicans, for instance, this measure would lead us to predict that few Republicans were persuadable in 1988, when in fact George H.W. Bush won a smaller percentage of Republican votes than Reagan did in either 1980 or 1984.

Swing voters are alternatively defined as political Independents. For example, a recent PBS report observed, "In a country where many voters identify with a particular political party, 'swing voters'—those who do not have a strong party affiliation—often take center stage in an election year."[17] It seems intuitive that individuals who call themselves political Independents will be more persuadable than partisan identifiers. Without a party attachment to anchor their choice, Independents should be more likely to start the campaign with an open mind about the two candidates. But the numbers of true Independents in the voting public is smaller than often assumed, and they often do not know about or care about politics.

To be sure, we expect that Independents will be persuadable if they agree with each of the candidates on a different policy issue, if they care about both issues, and if they actually plan to vote. Unfortunately, it is difficult, conceptually and empirically, to identify these persuadable Independents. For one, scholars have long argued that many independents are closet partisans in their attitudes and behaviors. These so-called Independent-leaners—self-identified Independents who say they are closer to one party or the other—are often just as partisan (or more so) in their attitudes and behavior as weak identifiers.[18] Like partisan identifiers, such Independents will start the campaign with an expected level of support for one candidate or the other. Thus, in terms of candidate strategy, these Independents should be targeted on the issues about which they disagree with the opposing party candidate.

It is also problematic to distinguish between persuadable Independents and those who are indifferent about politics altogether, making it difficult to determine if volatility in vote choice reflects deliberative decision making or random response instability. Ultimately, candidates care only about persuadable *voters*—those who actually show up on Election Day. Compared to partisan identifiers, Independents are generally less politically engaged than partisans. In the 2004 National Election Study, just 46 percent of pure Independents (59 percent including Independents who leaned toward one of the political parties) reported voting in the 2004 presidential election, compared to 70 percent of self-identified Democrats and 83 percent of self-identified Republicans. In the 2004 election, we estimate that pure Independents composed 16 percent of the populace, but as a percentage of the voting public, those Independents who hold both liberal and conservative is-

[17] Sheryl Silverman, "Politics 101: Swing Voters." PBS, Online News Hour: 2004 Vote General   Election.   http://www.pbs.org/newshour/vote2004/politics101/politics101 _swingvoters.html.

[18] For similar arguments see Keith et al., *The Myth of the Independent Voter.*

sues on which they are politically knowledgeable made up just 4 percent of the electorate.

Even if we are better able to identify Independents, using political independence alone as a gauge of persuadability misses the many more persuadable partisans in the electorate. As discussed in the next chapter, we find that the number of persuadable partisans in the electorate is nearly three times the size of persuadable Independents. Where possible, we include analyses of Independents throughout the book. But we focus on persuadable partisans because they have been so often overlooked in previous research, they make up a larger share of the electorate, and they offer the most conservative and clearest evidence of the tradeoff voters must make when the considerations underlying their vote decision are in conflict.

Perspectives on Cross-pressured Partisans

Our argument that cross-pressured partisans will be responsive to campaign information is at first glance difficult to reconcile with some of the prominent theories of voting behavior. Scholars typically assume that there will be (or should be) congruence between party identification and issue preferences. On one side, the Michigan school perspective expects party identification and issues to be consistent because issue positions are thought to reflect the partisan paradigm that so dominates an individual's political thinking. According to this view, partisans are expected to fall lockstep in line with partisan elites on most, if not all, policy positions. On the other side, the rational choice perspective also assumes that issue positions and party identification will be congruent but because individuals align themselves with the party that most closely approximates their ideological viewpoints. Morris Fiorina argues that "controversies about issue voting versus party identification miss the point: the 'issues' are *in* party identification" (italics in original).[19] But both traditions tend to overlook the extent to which partisans might disagree with their political party on an issue without it leading to a change in either their partisanship or policy attitude.

Our perspective recognizes that while party identification is closely connected to attitudes on most policy issues, it remains a conceptually distinct consideration in the minds of voters. As Donald Green, Brad Palmquist, and Eric Schickler recently observed, "Ideological proclivities and partisanship overlap somewhat but less than is often supposed,

---

[19] Fiorina, *Retrospective Voting In American National Elections*, 200.

and each contributes to the predictive accuracy of the [vote choice] model."[20] Even if individuals are affiliated with the party that best matches most of their policy preferences, there remains room for consequential policy disagreements. After all, the source of policy attitudes are diverse and far-reaching, including an ideological worldview, core political values, material self-interest, group identity and attachment, or political events and experiences.[21] Voters can and do identify with a political party while actively disagreeing with some of the policy tenets of that party. There are Democrats who support school vouchers, oppose abortion, or oppose environmental regulation, just as there are Republicans who support gun control, oppose tort reform, or support universal health care. In accepting the Republican nomination in 1996, presidential candidate Robert Dole recognized this point, proclaiming the Republican Party to be "broad and inclusive. It represents many streams of opinion and many points of view." More colorfully, former House Speaker Jim Wright made a similar point about the Democratic Party, calling it "a mixture, an amalgam, a mosaic. Call it a fruitcake."[22]

The prevailing assumption of congruence between party identification and issue preference was reinforced by early psychological research on cognitive dissonance, which concluded that when related cognitions conflict, one will be changed to restore consistency.[23] But given the variety of cognitions that can influence any life decision, it is unrealistic to assume that individuals will necessarily be able to make all cognitions congruent. Peter Sperlich forcefully makes this point: "Human existence . . . is unthinkable apart from tension and conflict. Without contrast there can be no perception, without categorization no thought, without friction no movement, without differentiation no identity, without obstacles no accomplishment. . . . It is plainly false to assume that all action has the purpose to reduce drives and disturbances."[24] Jennifer Hochschild similarly argues that politics is fundamentally about conflict among various beliefs and values within the individual voter, and such conflict is critical to the functioning of democracy:

> A democracy composed of consistent, tranquil, attitudinally constrained citizens is a democracy full of smug people with no incentive and perhaps no ability to think about their own circumstances. They know who they are, how things fit together—and woe betide anyone who questions or violates

[20] Green et al., *Partisan Hearts and Minds*, 214.
[21] Kinder, "Diversity and Complexity in American Public Opinion."
[22] Quoted in Mayer, *Divided Democrats*, 1.
[23] Festinger and Carlsmith, "Cognitive Consequences of Forced Compliance."
[24] Sperlich, *Conflict and Harmony in Human Affairs*, 1, 57.

the standard pattern. Conversely, a democracy composed of citizens coping with disjunction and ambivalence is full of people who question their own righteousness, who may entertain alternative viewpoints, and who, given the right questions, are more driven to resolve problems than to ignore them.[25]

More recent research in political psychology now recognizes that when two conflicting cognitions are central to a decision, individuals may simply temporarily change the importance of one consideration or develop a rhetorical strategy to explain the inconsistency.[26]

Original Cross-pressures Theory

Although scholars have generally overlooked cross-pressures between policy preferences and party identification, we are by no means the first to recognize the role and influence of internal conflict in political decision making. The earliest voting behavior research, the pioneering Columbia studies of the 1940 and 1948 presidential campaigns, were the first to offer a theory of cross-pressures. Their focus, however, was on conflicting "social pressures" that might result from conflict between group attachments—being a wealthy business owner and a Catholic was the classic example. They found that individuals who faced cross-cutting social pressures took a longer time to reach a vote decision, were more likely to shift their support between candidates during the course of the campaign, and were less likely to vote on Election Day. Yet, the original cross-pressures theory eventually fell out of favor; as one scholar wrote, the arguments moved into the "category of plausible theories whose empirical support has been cut out from under them."[27] Our theoretical perspective differs from this early work in at least three important ways.

First, the conclusions of this early research rested on the assumption that vote choice is determined by social and group identity, so that vote decision becomes more difficult "when the political complexion of friends and co-workers is divided."[28] This sociological perspective—who you are determines how you vote—has given way in political science to a recognition that other factors play a more prominent and proximate role in voter decision making. In particular, party identification and policy preferences are thought to be the critical determi-

---

[25] Hochschild, "Disjunction and Ambivalence in Citizens' Political Outlooks," 206.
[26] Billig, *Arguing and Thinking*.
[27] Horan, "Social Positions and Political Cross-pressures," 659.
[28] Berelson et al., *Voting*, 98.

nants of the vote.[29] Whereas the person in conflicting social networks may be able to simply avoid discussing politics, voters have a much more difficult time avoiding the tensions between party affiliation and issue preferences if the ubiquitous swirl of presidential campaign dialogue is focused on a conflicting issue.

A second distinction is that we focus on a voter's decision to support one candidate over the other, rather than her decision about whether to vote at all. Lazarsfeld and his colleagues argued that cross-pressures lead to a decline in interest and attention, with conflicted individuals eventually withdrawing from politics altogether. The original cross-pressures theory largely faded from the discipline because subsequent attempts to empirically link social group cross-pressures to turnout were largely unsuccessful.[30] Using more compelling measures and methods, Diana Mutz has recently revived the theory that individuals in cross-cutting social networks might be less inclined to participate in politics.[31] Without questioning the potential for such tensions to influence political engagement, we argue that cross-pressures between party and policy positions should have significant consequences for the vote decision. There are a great many individuals who vote even in the face of tensions between their partisan loyalties and the policies they care about, especially in a high-profile presidential race. Comparing nonvoters and voters in the 2004 presidential election, we found that nonvoters were just 4 percentage points more likely to hold a policy disagreement with their affiliated party than were voters. Panel data also finds greater variability in candidate preference than turnout intention over the course of a presidential campaign.[32]

Our final, and most significant, point of departure from the early cross-pressure theory is the assumed mechanism by which cross-pressures increase susceptibility to persuasion. Lazarsfeld and his colleagues argued that cross-pressures influenced voting behavior by depressing political interest and engagement. In their view, any changes in vote choice came not from reasoned deliberation, but from cross-pressured voters "simply not caring much one way or the other about the election."[33] In *The People's Choice*, they conclude: "The notion that the people who switch parties during the campaign are mainly the rea-

[29] Classically, Campbell et al., *The American Voter.*

[30] For instance, Abelson et al., *Candidates, Issues and Strategies*, 74–76.

[31] Mutz, *Hearing the Other Side.*

[32] In the 2000 Knowledge Networks Election Study data, 20 percent of respondents switched their turnout intentions, while more than 40 percent changed their candidate choice (including moving from undecided to a decision).

[33] Lazarsfeld et al., *The Peoples' Choice*, 19.

soned, thoughtful, conscientious people who were convinced by the issues of the election is just plain wrong. Actually, they were mainly just the opposite."[34]

Their conclusion that the persuadable voters were also the least informed and least interested segment of the electorate continued as a common thread through political science, even as the discipline replaced sociological explanations of voter behavior with psychological ones. Whether looking at the "floating voters" who shift support from one party candidate to another across elections or "waverers" who change their vote within a given election, it has been thought that the persuadable voters are the segment of the electorate that is "least involved in politics, psychologically speaking, and whose information about details of policy is most impoverished."[35] By extension, it was thought that any observed volatility during the campaign reflected irrational behavior among the unsophisticated members of the electorate. In his classic article, "Information Flow and the Stability of Partisan Attitudes," Phil Converse most pointedly argued that "not only is the electorate as a whole quite uninformed, but it is the least informed members within the electorate who seem to hold the critical 'balance of power.'" Ben Harper perhaps best sums up this perspective, "You change your mind so many times, I wonder if you have a mind at all."[36] Although politically unsophisticated respondents might very well be volatile in their survey responses, we argue that there are a great many voters who incorporate campaign information as part of a deliberative process of reasoned decision making. Nevertheless, throughout our investigations we will try to account for this alternative source of vote instability to attempt to better distinguish policy-based campaign effects from those reflecting political ineptitude.

To be clear, we are not suggesting that voters have complete information or are always fully rational. But citizens do typically receive the information necessary to connect their predispositions to a candidate selection by the end of a political campaign, often in the course of going about their daily lives.[37] Morris Fiorina explains, "There is no question of information costs, no question of deciding to gather information as opposed to doing something else. Just as exposed portions of the skin get tanned by the sun when people walk around out of doors, so people become informed as they go about their daily busi-

---

[34] Ibid., 69.

[35] Campbell et al., *The American Voter*, 547.

[36] Ben Harper, "Show Me a Little Shame," *Burn to Shine*, Virgin Records.

[37] Popkin, *The Reasoning Voter*.

ness."[38] The general public might not conform to the civics-book ideal of a fully informed citizenry, but by the end of the campaign most voters are generally capable of recognizing the broad policy differences between the opposing presidential candidates and cast their ballots accordingly.[39] The task is made easier when voters consider the issues important and candidates present clear policy alternatives.[40] In our view, then, the persuadable voter is also a reasoning voter.

In many respects, our perspective offers a bridge between the sociological and psychological schools of thought about voting behavior. We argue that campaign responsiveness is a function of psychological tension between the competing considerations underlying the vote decision, though sociological characteristics, like race, class, religion, may well give rise to the policy attitudes that are the source of conflict. But in contrast to the conclusion of Lazarsfeld and his colleagues that "a person thinks, politically, as he is, socially"[41] we recognize that sociological group identity is not necessarily a marker for a particular set of policy preferences. So, when swing voters are defined by a particular demographic—Catholics, Latinos, white southerners, soccer moms (suburban women with children), or NASCAR dads (working-class white men)—missing is the psychological basis of persuadability. Not all Catholics will be receptive to a pro-life campaign message from a Republican candidate because not all Catholics are opposed to abortion. But, in contrast to those scholars who view persuasion purely as a function of sophistication and party identification, we do recognize that pro-life Democrats might well be receptive to a conservative abortion message from a Republican candidate.

Attitudinal Ambivalence

Reminiscent of the early cross-pressure research, the growing literature about attitudinal ambivalence also recognizes that individuals often hold conflicting considerations about an issue, policy, individual, or group.[42] *Ambivalence* is typically defined as the coexistence of both positive and negative tendencies directed toward the same attitude object.

---

[38] Fiorina, "Information and Rationality in Elections," 338.

[39] Mayer, *Divided Democrats,* 7. In the 2004 NES, for instance, the vast majority of voters were able to correctly place John Kerry to the left of George Bush on the issue questions asked (92 percent on defense spending, 92 percent on aid to blacks, 82 percent on government services, 66 percent on gun control, 64 percent on environment).

[40] Nie et al., *The Changing American Voter,* 74–95. More recently, Jacoby, "Ideology in the 2000 Election."

[41] Lazarsfeld et al., *The People's Choice,* 69, 27.

[42] See Feldman and Zaller, "A Simple Theory of the Survey Response."

The ambivalence research has generally focused on tensions between political values that underlie a single attitude object, such as opinions toward racial issues or government taxes. For example, citizens will possess ambivalent attitudes toward taxes if they have competing values between a desire for lower taxes and a desire for better government services. This literature has identified a number of different attitudinal and behavioral consequences of ambivalent attitudes, including more moderate attitudinal responses, greater attitude inconsistency and instability, higher levels of survey nonresponse, and less certain attitudes that are more difficult to retrieve from memory.[43]

Although our notion of persuadable voters parallels this literature in many ways, there are subtle but important differences. First, the focus of most ambivalence research has been on a single attitude, while we are interested in a vote decision between two candidates. While an attitude might require no action beyond a mental evaluation, a decision forces individuals to make a choice between competing considerations.[44] When making a mental judgment about an attitude object, competing considerations about that attitude may be easier to ignore (or to avoid by offering a "no opinion" or neutral response). In contrast, when making a decision between alternatives, competing considerations about that decision are explicitly brought to the foreground. Thus, voters cannot help but confront any tensions between their partisan loyalties and the key political issues discussed during a campaign. In presidential elections, in particular, these cross-pressured partisans are more likely to vote than stay home, so they must resolve their conflict in one way or the other.

More importantly, we argue that voters are persuadable when they are ambivalent about the vote decision, *not* the considerations that underlie the decision. Any ambivalent policy attitudes held by an individual should not play a decisive role in the decision-making process.[45] The consequences of cross-pressures as we conceive them are so meaningful precisely because they require voters to simultaneously hold an unambivalent view about a personally important issue and an unambivalent attachment to a political party. It is because both considerations are durable, and yet conflicting, that it creates the opportunity for the campaign to have persuasive effects.

---

[43] Alvarez and Brehm, *Hard Choices, Easy Answers*; McGraw et al., "Ambivalence, Uncertainty, and Processes of Candidate Evaluation."

[44] Lau, "Models of Decision Making," 20.

[45] Because such attitudes are held with ambivalence, we expect they may well be susceptible to influence by the campaign, but do not expect malleable issue attitudes to have an influence on the vote decision. Such attitudes should also be less likely to register as a "personally important" issue.

Our perspective highlights the theoretical distinction between indifference and ambivalence about the vote decision.[46] Our expectation is that individuals ambivalent about their vote decision turn to the campaign for help in sorting through competing considerations, while those who are indifferent should be less inclined to vote at all. Our point is simply that when a voter *does* care about an issue (or issues) that conflicts with that of her party, it opens the door for the issue to be activated during the campaign. In the context of a presidential campaign, ambivalence about the vote decision is more common than often assumed, and it has consequences for both voter behavior and candidate strategy.

This is not to say that political campaigns, even presidential ones, are purely policy-based events. There is a blurry line between policy and pageantry in political campaigns. It is not always clear where vacuous rhetoric ends and policy stances begin. Candidates will reinforce their issue messages with affective appeals, visual symbols, and expressive language, and voters' assessments of character traits and candidate personality are very much intertwined with policy considerations.[47] In 2004, for instance, voters' evaluations of George W. Bush's leadership skills were strongly related to their opinions on the Iraq War, while Bush's campaign communications about his "stay the course" policy in Iraq drew on images and references to September 11, patriotism, and the American flag. Likewise, the direct-mail advertising that identified Bush's opposition to gay marriage discussed his support of traditional family values and included visual images of churches, a Bible, and an "all-American" family. As these examples illustrate, it is difficult for voters (or scholars, for that matter) to untangle value-based appeals from policy-based ones. For all the debate about the role of values in the 2004 presidential election, the reality is that values are *always* important to voters' decisions because policy and values overlap in both the campaign messages of the candidates and the minds of voters. Even with these often implicit and vague policy references, by the end of the campaign, voters are generally aware of the policy differences between the candidates, particularly on the issues that they consider personally important.[48]

[46] For more on the distinction between indifference and ambivalence, see Kaplan, "On the Ambivalence-Indifference Problem in Attitude Theory and Measurement."

[47] Rahn, "The Role of Partisan Stereotypes in Information Processing about Political Candidates." Candidate messages on wedge issues, in particular, often use coded language so that potential supporters receive the intended message but others remain unaware.

[48] Alvarez, *Information and Elections*.

The Challenge of Evaluating Campaign Effects

Theoretically we have identified cross-pressured voters as the group that should be most responsive to campaign information, but empirically linking campaigns to voter behavior is a notoriously difficult task. Questions of measurement, operationalization, and methodological approach are central to campaign effects research, contributing to the persistence of the minimal effects hypothesis.

The first hurdle to capturing campaign effects is simply defining the campaign. Is the presidential campaign the candidates' television advertisements? This definition is not adequate if candidates use different substantive appeals with television than with other media, as we demonstrate in chapter 6. Even if we are able to capture the full array of messages used during the campaign, we would still overlook the fact that voters are most commonly exposed to campaign information indirectly through the media. Yet, the fragmentation of the media today ensures that campaign coverage varies enormously across television, newspapers, radio, and the Internet, as well as within each of these different media. We also cannot forget the influence of information obtained from interpersonal political discussions within social networks, with friends and family, or at the office water cooler.

With all the hoopla surrounding presidential elections it seems hard to imagine that campaigns do not matter, but the broad-scale nature of the campaign is what makes it a difficult task to show how and when campaigns are important. In effect, campaigns are simply information, and presidential campaigns, in particular, are ubiquitous. But it is nearly impossible to identify all the different sources of information during a presidential campaign or to measure the widely varied content of the information received by different respondents.

Only an experiment allows a researcher to know (and control) exactly the source, content, and intensity of the campaign information received by the voters. With an experiment, it is possible to match more clearly a campaign treatment to voter behavior, but experiments have their own limitations. Although controlled environments allow for better isolation of the causal campaign effect, they are often criticized for their poor external validity because they take place under artificial conditions or rely on unrepresentative samples, like college students. Even the gold-standard field experiment "shares the laboratory's limitation: it identifies a potential rather than an actual effect."[49] It is often difficult to know if the experimental effect will hold up in the real world because the more tightly controlled the particular treatment, the more artificial the conditions in which the effects are observed.

---

[49] Brady et al., "The Study of Political Campaigns," 14.

Yet, outside a controlled experimental environment, it is difficult to measure voters' exposure to the campaign. Individual-level measures collected from sample surveys suffer from errors in recall, memory, and selection. Self-reported measures of campaign exposure, in particular, have come under considerable scrutiny because of high levels of measurement error.[50] Simply asking respondents to estimate the number of advertisements they saw in the past week, month, or during the entire campaign is an imprecise measure of campaign exposure. Perhaps most problematic is that the targeted nature of campaign efforts means that it is difficult to separate out cause from effect using self-reported measures of campaign exposure in a cross-sectional survey. Exogenous measures of campaign exposure, such as aggregate measures of campaign spending, television advertising, or candidate visits, however, capture only a very limited aspect of the political campaign and assume equal levels of attention across all individuals.[51]

Because of these difficulties, throughout our investigation, we will use a multimethod approach and will rely on as many different measures of the campaign as possible. Using repeated interviews with the same individuals over the course of a campaign, we are able to directly trace changes in vote choice over the course of the campaign and in response to campaign events. Using panel data across presidential elections, we can look at changes in voter decision making across election years. Using cross-sectional surveys, we evaluate if campaign exposure is related to partisan defections on Election Day. And in measuring campaign exposure, we look at variations across state competitiveness, presidential visits, campaign events, self-reported political attention, and political awareness, as well as variations in campaign content across election years. Finally, we test our theoretical expectations within the context of a survey experiment, allowing us to more precisely isolate the effects of specific issue messages on voter decision making. By combining these various approaches, we attempt not only to isolate the effect of specific campaign messages within a controlled environment, but also to capture the effects associated with the broader issue dialogue of an actual presidential campaign.

A THEORY OF WEDGE CAMPAIGN STRATEGIES

Our expectations about persuadable voters help to explain why candidates might emphasize divisive issues in their campaign agendas. A candidate has the potential to influence the vote of the persuadable

[50] Price and Zaller, "Who Gets the News?"

[51] Ridout et al., "Evaluating Measures of Campaign Advertising Exposure on Political Learning."

voter by highlighting those issues on which she agrees with the candidate and disagrees with the opponent. Perhaps the most obvious example of such a strategy in a presidential campaign is the Republicans' famed southern strategy aimed at winning over southern white Democrats. In developing Reagan's 1984 campaign strategy, advisor Lee Atwater argued that the optimal strategy would "drive a wedge between the liberal (national) Democrats and traditional Southern Democrats. . . . [W]e must assemble coalitions in every Southern state largely based on the country clubbers and the populists."[52]

Although journalists and pundits often talk about the use of "wedge issues" in contemporary elections, campaign scholars, perhaps surprisingly, have not previously explored the nature or influence of wedge campaign strategies.[53] At one time or another, nearly every political issue has been labeled a wedge issue in the media: gun control, abortion, global warming, immigration, affirmative action, school prayer, free trade, gay marriage, stem cell research, welfare reform, education, and Internet taxation to name just a few.[54] One political commentator astutely observed that "wedge issues are—now let me get this straight—things people disagree about."[55] Indeed, any political issue about which there is disagreement within a party coalition has the potential to be used as a wedge issue. But these issues actually become wedges only when raised in an effort to peel away some portion of an opponent's potential supporters.

We define a wedge issue as any policy concern that is used to divide the opposition's potential winning coalition. In using the phrase "potential winning coalition," we acknowledge that an issue does not have to split only existing party loyalists in order for it to be a wedge issue— Independents might also fall into a candidate's expected coalition for one reason or another. This definition also recognizes the divisive nature of such issues, but also does not limit them to a particular policy domain. Moral issues like gay marriage and abortion are widely recog-

[52] Brady, *Bad Boy*, 117–18.

[53] A notable exception is Wilson and Turnbull, "Wedge Politics and Welfare Reform in Australia."

[54] See, for instance, David E. Rosenbaum, "Narrow Issues May Sway Voting," *New York Times*, 27 October 1980, A1; William Safire, "The Double Wedge," *New York Times*, 23 February 1995, A23; Frank Rich, "The War in the Wings," *New York Times*, 9 October 1996, A21; Gerald F. Seib, "Welfare Reform: Hot-Button Issue of New Order," *Wall Street Journal*, 16 November 1994, A30; John Harwood, "Democrats, Courting Swing Voters, Embrace 'Hot-Button' Politics," *Wall Street Journal*, 28 October 1998, A1; John Simons, "Bush Faces Wedge Issue as GOP Rivals Focus on Question of Taxing Internet," *Wall Street Journal*, 6 December 1999, A36.

[55] Jonah Goldberg, "Art, Wedge Issues, and the Virgin Mary," *National Review Online*, posted on 28 September 1999.

nized as wedge issues, but economic and social welfare policies can just as easily be used in a wedge strategy. Wedge issues are typically positional issues, those about which people take different sides and that have different policy-outcome goals. But even consensual issues—those about which most people agree on the goal—can create conflict over a candidate's performance or divergent means for accomplishing the common objective.[56] For example, there have been divisions in the Republican Party over Bush's policy and performance in Iraq. Some use the term *wedge issue* to refer only to that class of issues that both divides the opposition and creates consensus among one's own supporters. Although such issues offer a clear and obvious strategic advantage, we do not require this latter condition because, as we argue later, the contemporary information environment makes it possible for candidates to highlight issues on which there are cleavages in their own camp. By communicating different messages to different audiences, candidates are able to make policy promises that would otherwise exacerbate fractures in their own coalitions.

The limitation of our definition is that it is not possible to identify a wedge issue outside its potential or realized impact on mass behavior. The utility of the concept is that it incorporates the strategic component of a candidate's decision to emphasize a policy position. Returning to the stem cell research example, the issue was raised by the candidates not because the public thought it was the most pressing or important issue facing the nation, but because it was predicted to be an effective way to nibble away at the opposition's potential coalition.

There are, of course, considerable constraints on the candidate's campaign agenda. There will be national-level conditions, such as a failing economy or foreign conflict, that must be addressed; controversies or blunders that reshape the focus of attention; or emerging issues on which candidates will be pressed to take a stance. It is also difficult to imagine that a legitimate candidate could run without addressing the most pressing issues of the day, whether about unemployment, war, education, or health care. In addition to the broader political environment, candidates might also consider the strengths and weaknesses of the opposition, as well as their own voting record, experiences, or reputational advantages. In a study of governors' campaigns, Thomas Carsey quotes a campaign staffer, "The campaign must talk about those issues that matter to people, but you can't stray from what the candidate has a background on. You must meld together the voters'

[56] See Stokes, "Spatial Models of Party Competition," for discussion of positional and valence issues.

concerns and the candidate's qualities. You need to be credible on the issues you discuss."[57]

But within these constraints—where candidates have discretion over their campaign agendas—candidates have an interest in highlighting issues that will help them win over the persuadable voters. This link between candidate position taking and the preferences of the cross-pressured voters is clear in a 1976 campaign strategy memo of President Gerald Ford, on the topic of environmental policy:

> The vast majority of the swing voters who live in the suburbs are conserva-tionists and strongly supportive of a responsible environmental policy. In this issue area, the President is perceived by many as a pro-business, anti-environment candidate. To correct this situation, we must become actively involved in the energy and recreation areas. . . . There are many middle-class conservationists and working-class sportsmen who lean toward the Republi-cans on other issues. We must at least avoid allowing the environmental issue to become so aggravated that environmentalists will vote against Ford on that issue alone. A part of this is going strongly on record in support of a clean environment—with a minimum of modifying conditions. . . . I am told that the environmentalists' current top priorities are: amendments to the Clean Air Act, the toxic substance control bill, and land strip mine regu-lation. . . . [W]herever we can responsibly lean toward them, it would be po-litically helpful.[58]

The success of a particular wedge strategy undoubtedly depends on many factors both internal and external to the campaign. We identify the basic conditions necessary: Individuals must disagree with their party on a policy issue they care about and they must come to believe that their own party candidate will ignore the policy or move it in the wrong direction if elected. Beyond these necessary conditions, how-ever, there are undoubtedly many other factors we have not considered that will influence the success of the strategy, including the broader media dialogue, the incumbent's performance, interest group pres-sures, candidate credibility on the issue, the emotional content of the appeal, the technical difficulty of the issue, and the framing of the mes-sage, among others.[59] Nonetheless, the basic framework provides in-sights into the incentives that push candidates to emphasize particular issues in a presidential campaign.

---

[57] Carsey, *Campaign Dynamics*, 55.

[58] Campaign Strategy Plan, August 1976; folder "Presidential Campaign—Campaign Strategy Program (1)-(3)," box 1, Dorothy E. Downton Files, Gerald R. Ford Library, 48, 21.

[59] See, for instance, Brader, *Campaigning for Hearts and Minds*.

Conventional Wisdom about Campaign Strategy

The classic perspective on candidate position taking is that rational candidates on both sides of the aisle should converge on a centrist campaign agenda in order to appeal to the moderate swing voters. In his seminal work, Anthony Downs concluded that rational, vote-maximizing politicians will be moderate or ambiguous on policy issues in an attempt to vie for the support of the pivotal voter.[60] Downs argues that ambiguity "increases the number of voters to whom a party may appeal. This fact encourages parties in a two-party system to be as equivocal as possible about their stands on each controversial issue. And since both parties find it rational to be ambiguous neither is forced by the other's clarity to take a more precise stand."[61] In other words, candidates should focus on moderate, middle-of-the-road policies rather than taking ideologically extreme positions on divisive issues *because these are the preferences of the median voter.*

Downs' prediction rests on the assumption that the preferences of voters can be aligned along a single ideological dimension ranging from the most liberal to the most conservative.[62] In contrast, we show that persuadable voters are not simply moderate or neutral across policy issues; they are often cross-pressured. Voters have complex belief systems and vary in the issues they care about. The rich literature on "issue publics" documents this variability in the issue concerns of the public.[63] Unfortunately, the term *issue public* often conjures an image of an issue activist, a single-issue voter, or a member of an issue interest group. Yet, an individual need not champion an issue in order for it to be relevant to her decision-making process. Moreover, voters might consider several different issues important, or the concern might even remain dormant until activated during the campaign.[64] In the 2004 election, for instance, citizens who reported that stem cell research was an

[60] The convergence of candidate positions was earlier recognized by Black, "On the Rationale of Group Decision Making"; see also Hotelling, "Stability in Competition."

[61] Downs, *An Economic Theory of Democracy,* 136.

[62] In no way are we questioning the median voter theorem itself, because we focus on voters with complex preferences across multiple policy dimensions. Downs and others have recognized that the median voter theorem does not hold in multiple dimensions. See, for instance, Davis et al., "An Expository Development of a Mathematical Model of the Electoral Process." Others have argued that outcomes tend toward "central" regions of voter distributions even in the absence of equilibria. See, for instance, Kramer, "A Dynamic Model of Political Equilibrium."

[63] Converse, "The Nature of Belief Systems in Mass Publics;" Arnold, *The Logic of Congressional Action.*

[64] Hutchings, *Public Opinion and Democratic Accountability.*

important issue may never have even considered the topic before it was raised during the campaign, but the issue resonated with them for one reason or another. For example, a Republican respondent in our 2004 election survey explained her disagreement with Bush on the issue: "Having had my father suffer from Alzheimer's disease, I feel very strongly that [embryonic stem cell] research should be done." We next consider alternative perspectives on why candidates are willing to take positions on wedge issues.

The Candidate-centered Perspective

The classic thesis explaining why candidates might not take moderate issue positions is that candidates are policy motivated rather than singularly concerned with winning votes.[65] Certainly, politicians insist that their issue agendas reflect personal convictions and principles—what they believe is right and the facts warrant. During the 2000 presidential campaign, George W. Bush insisted that "we take stands without having to run polls and focus groups to tell us where we stand."[66] Perhaps if we are to believe that average Americans have meaningful policy preferences, we should expect the same to be true of political candidates. Certainly, the political process in the United States is structured so that individuals who run for office are more likely to care about policy outcomes than the average citizen.[67] Political candidates are often drawn from the ranks of party activists or are at least vetted by policy-interested elites. Running for office is not an easy or inexpensive task in the United States, so we might expect candidates to care about the work they will do if elected. Examining voting patterns of members of Congress, Barry Burden argues, "Researchers tend to assume that legislators either work only on behalf of their constituents or as foot soldiers for their political parties . . . [but] members routinely reflect on their own interests, expertise, and information in choosing what to do."[68] For example, Republican Senator Norm Coleman says he is an advocate of federal funding for AIDS research because his sister and brother-in-law died of the disease, and Democratic Congress-

---

[65] Wittman, "Candidate Motivation." But others conclude that the candidates will converge even with policy-motivated candidates. See, for instance, Calvert, "Robustness of the Multidimensional Voting Model."

[66] James Carney and John F. Dickerson, "Behind the Rhetoric," *Time Magazine,* 10 October 2000.

[67] Wright, "Policy Voting in the U.S. Senate," 483; Schattschneider, *Party Government.*

[68] Burden, *Personal Roots of Representation,* 14.

man Jim Langevin maintains that a teenage gun accident that left him a quadriplegic led him to oppose euthanasia and abortion.

Yet, if candidates are primarily motivated by policy considerations, we might expect that they would offer a clear and consistent campaign agenda and would communicate the same policy agenda to all voters so that an electoral victory could provide a mandate to implement their policy goals. In order to claim a mandate to implement a particular policy, the issue must have been central to the campaign debate so that the winning candidate can say the policy represents the will of the people.[69] Barry Goldwater, often referred to as an example of a policy-motivated candidate, was known for refusing to tailor his remarks to his audience. Goldwater criticized cotton subsidies in the farmlands of North Dakota, he assailed public power in the home of the Tennessee Valley Authority, and he argued that social security should be made voluntary in St. Petersburg, Florida (the *St. Petersburg Times* headline read "Right City, Wrong Speech").[70]

Of course, electoral and policy goals are not always mutually exclusive. Scholars have argued that electoral considerations can reinforce the selection of issues on which the candidate has a background; in other words, there is an electoral advantage to emphasizing issues on which the candidate is credible. Thus, candidates will be constrained in their policy promises based on their political record, personal experience, or partisan affiliation.[71] Most prominently, the theory of issue ownership contends that candidates benefit from emphasizing those issues on which their affiliated party has a reputational advantage. According to this theory, each of the parties "owns" particular issues about which they have a record of accomplishment. For instance, Republican candidates should emphasize issues like national security and tax cuts, and Democratic candidates should focus on issues such as health care and social security. The implication, in contrast to the median voter theorem, is that candidates will "talk past" each other rather than engaging in campaign dialogue on the same issues.

Although this theory offers an alternative explanation for the issues that candidates will emphasize in the campaign, the focus of this research is on party reputations for handling "problems"—issues for which there is general consensus regarding the policy goal.[72] The the-

---

[69] Conley, *Presidential Mandates*.

[70] Boller, *Presidential Campaigns*, 310.

[71] Sellers, "Strategy and Background in Congressional Campaigns;" Petrocik, "Issue Ownership in Presidential Elections;" Simon, *The Winning Message*.

[72] Recent studies have found that candidates do not focus on "owned" issues in their television advertising, instead largely concentrating on the same consensual issues. See discussion in Kaplan et al., "Dialogue in American Political Campaigns?"; Sides, "The Origins of Campaign Agendas."

ory is silent about why candidates might ever focus on divisive positional issues. Indeed, Petrocik explicitly argues that such issues should be avoided because the pivotal voter conferring the electoral advantage does not care about policy issues:

> The median voter that is assumed by issue ownership is uncertain about what represents a serious problem, lacks a clear preference about social and policy issues, is normally disinclined to impose thematic or ideological consistency on issues, and inclined to view elections as choices about collective goods and resolving problems, and not about the specifics of the resolution. The key fact for this voter is not what *policies* candidates promise to pursue, but what *problems* (medical care needs, high taxes) will be resolved.[73]

In contrast, our expectations rest on the assumption that persuadable voters have meaningful policy preferences, even if they do not add up to a coherent ideology. Similar to the theory of issue ownership, our thesis suggests that candidates will emphasize different issues when talking to the same persuadable voters, but we expect their messages will include appeals on the particular wedge issues about which the voter disagrees with the opposing party candidate.

The Partisan Base Perspective

In contrast to our theoretical expectations, the prevailing popular perception is that candidates take positions on divisive issues to appeal to their partisan base. As one journalist lamented, "As they gear up for the election, Republicans and Democrats are operating on the premise that . . . the outcome will be determined by partisan activists. Consequently, GOP leaders, intent on revving up the party's conservative base, are about to serve up as much red meat as a Kansas City steak house."[74] The 2004 Bush reelection campaign has been characterized as a "base" mobilization strategy, intent on "identifying, learning about, and tailoring policies to meet the political desires of a key group of conservative Republicans."[75]

Why might politicians be more concerned with the preferences of the political base than with the rest of the electorate? Some have ar-

[73] Petrocik, "Issue Ownership in Presidential Elections."

[74] Carroll Doherty, "*Congressional Affairs*: Lots of Inertia, Little lawmaking as Election '98 approaches," *CQ Weekly*, 18 July 1998, 1925–27.

[75] Frontline, PBS Online, "Karl Rove—the Architect," 12 April 2005. http://www.pbs.org /wgbh/pages/frontline/shows/architect/view/.

gued that the primary system in American elections is an institutional factor causing candidates to weight the opinions of their core partisans more heavily than the opinions of the general electorate. Primaries tend to attract fewer voters compared to general elections and these dedicated primary voters are thought to be more ideologically extreme. As a result, candidates might take comparatively extreme policy positions in order to win the nomination of their party, but then may later attempt to moderate their positions during the general election. Although this logic sounds plausible, the hypothesis has found limited empirical support. For instance, candidates who faced competitive primaries are actually more moderate than those who did not.[76] Other work has shown that primary voters are not ideologically distinct from general-election voters.[77] Finally, research on voter decision making in primary elections has shown that primary voters may be more concerned about a candidate's electability and viability than ideological congruence alone because their eyes are on the electoral prize of the general election.[78] This is reflected in the bandwagon phenomenon we observe in the primaries, where voters in states with later primaries rally around the winner of the early primaries. The results from recent presidential primaries are also telling; the successful candidates have not been the most ideologically extreme contenders. Indeed, the more ideologically pure candidates—Howard Dean, Pat Buchanan, Dennis Kucinich, and so on—have typically been on the losing side.

Others have argued that candidate platforms reflect the preferences of party activists because these voters provide the critical resources necessary to run for political office.[79] The base partisans are the ones who volunteer their time and contribute much-needed money. A large rational choice literature has shown that candidates will take divergent positions on policy issues if some voters are more valuable than others.[80] In other words, candidates will make policy promises as a way of motivating their core supporters to give time and money. Lawrence Jacobs and Robbert Shapiro explain that,

> For ambitious politicians, their primary focus is on avoiding the costs associated with compromising the core policy goals that are intensely supported by party activists, campaign contributors, and interest groups. . . . [Politi-

[76] King, "Congress, Polarization, and Fidelity to the Median Voter."
[77] Geer, "Assessing the Representativeness of the Electorate in Presidential Primaries."
[78] Bartels, *Presidential Primaries and the Dynamics of Public Choice.*
[79] Aldrich, "A Downsian Spatial Model with Party Activism."
[80] Miller and Schofield, "Activists and Partisan Realignment in the United States."

cians] face intense pressure from narrow but critical constituents—most notably, party activists who are the "worker bees" in each party's process for selecting candidates and running campaigns. The attitudes and behavior of these activists are a critical influence on ambitious politicians who aspire to a long and successful career in office.[81]

The underlying assumption of this line of work seems to be that citizens outside the partisan base can be ignored because either they are unlikely to vote or they can be swayed with nonideological campaign appeals.[82] As such, it frees up candidates to use their campaign agendas to motivate and mobilize core partisan supporters.

This perspective is also consistent with research that concludes partisan activation is the key dynamic of campaigns.[83] Campaigns are thought to bring home wayward partisans by reinforcing partisan attachments and reminding voters why they affiliate with the party. As one study explains, campaigns activate partisan predispositions by "reaffirming the partisan connection and linking it to the campaign" and the current candidate.[84] And there are clear historical examples of candidates making explicitly partisan appeals. At a campaign strategy meeting with his closest advisors, John F. Kennedy decided that his campaign should "make clear that the two parties are wholly different in goals and pin the Republican label on Nixon as tightly as possible, hammering him as the spiritual descendant of McKinley, Harding, Hoover, Landon, and Dewey."[85]

We are not arguing that candidates should be completely dismissive of their partisan base. To be sure, candidates worry about getting their base supporters to the polls, but their campaign efforts are focused on building a coalition between base supporters and persuadable voters. Ideally, candidates are able to identify issues that will bridge these two groups, but ultimately, candidates choose their issue agendas based on what can sway the persuadable voters (including their own cross-pressured partisans) rather than on what their base supporters necessarily consider a top priority. In the case of Gerald Ford's 1976 presidential-campaign strategy, his advisors recommended targeting his core supporters with a paid television address by Reagan or Connally to be used in base states: "This would be designed to underscore the Presi-

---

[81] Jacobs and Shapiro, "Polling Politics, Media and Election Campaigns," 640. They do argue that candidates become more responsive to constituency pressures as elections approach.

[82] Bartels, "Partisanship and Voting Behavior."

[83] Lazarsfeld et al., *The People's Choice.*

[84] Holbrook and McClurg, "The Mobilization of Core Supporters," 8.

[85] White, *The Making of the President 1960*, 321.

dent's conservative record on the issues and the need for Republican support because of the Carter threat." To appeal to swing voters, Ford's advisors recommended that he "develop positions on specific issues designed to appeal to the voter bloc. . . . Implement new campaign themes aimed at the Independent and ticket splitter. Strive to create the perception of the President as a conservative on social issues and moderate on economic issues . . . [to] portray the President as Presidential and not as a partisan Republican."[86] In developing the issue agenda, it was the persuadable voters who took priority.

Campaign Strategy and the Information Environment

We argue that a candidate's use of a wedge strategy ultimately rests on the information they hold about the policy preferences of the electorate. Staking a position on an issue might win over some voters, but it also has the potential to alienate voters who disagree, so information is critical for calculating the risks and benefits of position taking. Sometimes the policy cleavages within the opposition's traditional coalition are readily apparent—like the racial policy fractures in the Democratic Party in the twentieth century—but oftentimes they may be less evident. Before the campaign begins, political candidates assess the electoral landscape using polls, focus groups, historical voting patterns, and, increasingly, consumer data. Using this information, they divide the voting public into those who are "for them," "against them," and "still available."[87] Across these classifications, candidates look for issues that will bridge their base supporters and the persuadable voters. Describing the growing importance of polling in presidential campaigns, Stephen and Barbara Salmore hint at the link between information about voters and a wedge campaign strategy: "The Eisenhower landslides in the 1950s demonstrated that an appealing presidential candidate could attract large numbers of voters from the opposition party. Campaign organizations needed to know from which groups wavering voters might come, what concerned them, and how they would respond to various candidates and issues."[88] Today's information environment allows candidates to identify not just the groups that are persuadable, but also the individual voters.

[86] Campaign Strategy Plan (drafted by White House aide Michael Raoul-Duval), August 1976; folder "Presidential Campaign—Campaign Strategy Program (1)-(3)," box 1, Dorothy E. Downton Files, Gerald R. Ford Library.

[87] Remarks of Republican consultant Robert Carpenter, Conference on Swing Voters in American Politics, Northeastern University, 10 June 2006.

[88] Salmore and Salmore, Candidates, Parties and Campaigns, 40.

In the few empirical studies that exist, scholars have also found a direct link between the information available about the electorate and politicians' issues agendas. Political elites are more likely to stake out a position on an issue when they are confident about what the public wants.[89] For example, one study finds that "when [Nixon] had data on the public's support for his policy position on an issue, he made statements on that issue 76% of the time, compared to 49% of the time when he lacked such data."[90] To be sure, candidates might be especially likely to poll the electorate on the range of issues that are credibly feasible, but there appears to be a clear link between the preferences of voters and the strategies of the candidates.

While both the electoral landscape and the decision-making processes of individual voters create incentives for candidates to use wedge issues during a campaign, a candidate's decision to emphasize a divisive issue will depend on the extent to which the benefits of doing so outweigh the risks. Thus, the more information candidates have about the preferences of the public, the better able they are to assess the tradeoffs associated with emphasizing a particular issue. And in today's hyperinformation environment, candidates have more information about individual voters than ever before. Critically, the information is no longer simply demographic, it is also psychographic—that is, information about preferences and beliefs. Journalist Dana Milbank writes, "If you're a registered voter, chances are the candidates know not just your name, address, and voting history but also your age and the age of your children, whether you smoke cigars, where you shop, where you attend church, what kind of car you drive, how old it is, whether you're on a diet, and what type of pet you have."[91]

Using this information about voters, contemporary candidates are able to use new campaign tactics to microtarget wedge issues with direct mail, email, text messaging, web advertisements, phone calls, and personal canvassing. By narrowly targeting a message to the voters who are likely to care about an issue, candidates are able to reduce the likelihood that they will be punished by voters on the opposing side of the issue. Although candidates today might not typically take clearly contradictory issue positions to different audiences, candidates will emphasize different issue priorities. The goal is to prime different voters on different issues. For instance, in direct mail to union members in 2004, Democrat John Kerry emphasized issues like minimum wage

---

[89] Geer, *From Tea Leaves to Opinion Polls*; Erikson and Romero, "Candidate Equilibrium and the Behavioral Model of the Vote."

[90] Druckman et al., "Candidate Strategies to Prime Issues and Image," 1193.

[91] Dana Milbank, "Virtual Politics: Candidates' Consultants Create the Customized Campaign," *New Republic* 5 July 1999, 23.

and job creation, while campaign mailings to senior citizens focused on the issues of social security and health care.

The implication of a microtargeted campaign is that candidates are much less likely to emphasize the same policy issues. Even if candidates target many of the same individuals—either to try to pull them into their camp or prevent the other side from doing the same—candidates will talk about those issues on which they have an advantage relative to their opponent. Thus, changes in the information environment may be contributing to the polarization of candidates today compared to the 1950s and 1960s. Candidates had reason to avoid taking a stand on divisive issues when they had only crude information about the preferences of swing voters and when they communicated their issue agendas primarily through broadcast media. In the past, the information available to candidates and parties was typically limited to geographic or demographic characteristics, only weak predictors of issue preferences. Even with the growth of polling, candidates simply did not have the sample size to do anything more than rough demographic breakdowns of general preferences. Today, candidates have databases with information about nearly *every* registered voter, in which they have mapped consumer data, individual party registration, vote history, and other information from voter registration files. Computing and statistical power now allow candidates to target an individual rather than a demographic group, creating incentives for candidates to cherry-pick specific voters on different wedge issues. A recent *Los Angeles Times* article described a suburban African American woman in Ohio who, although she tends to vote Democratic, was deluged with calls, email messages, and other forms of communication by Republican candidates who knew that she was a mother with children in private schools, an active church attendee, an abortion opponent and a golfer.[92]

With microtargeting, swing voters in swing states can be told that the issues he or she cares about are the issues that are a priority to the candidate. In contrast, television advertising, with its broad audience, continues to focus on more generic issue appeals. Our analysis in chapter 6 shows, for instance, that television advertising by both candidates in the 2004 presidential election contained almost no references to the issues of gay marriage or abortion, while these issues were more prominently featured in direct-mail communication. Emphasizing potentially controversial issues through microtargeting, rather that the general media, allows for a "ground war" fought on wedge issues to be run simultaneously with less controversial issues in the traditional "air war."

[92] Peter Wallsten and Tom Hamburger, "The GOP Knows You Don't Like Anchovies," *Los Angeles Times*, 25 June 2006, M1.

Our Strategy For Evaluating Candidate Strategy

To examine the campaign strategy of presidential candidates, we adopt a mixed quantitative and qualitative research design. To uncover the motivations and goals of campaign issue messages, we rely, in part, on archival research about candidate strategy and semistructured interviews with political consultants, campaign operatives, and party leaders. The advantage of these data sources is that relevant players can explain, in their own words, who in the electorate was the target of campaign efforts and why. Unlike other social science phenomena, candidate strategy can be evaluated by simply asking the candidates about their decisions. On the other hand, candidates and consultants might not be fully honest or capable of explaining the motivation behind their behavior. There might be hesitancy in revealing confidential campaign strategy or there could be post-hoc rationalization of actions. Research has long shown that people have a difficult time answering questions about the cognitive processes underlying choices, evaluations, judgments, and behavior.[93] There also are some notable differences in terminology between our key concepts and those used by some practitioners. Consultants' use of terms like partisan identification, ideology, and base voters were often rooted in the available data rather than in a theoretical conception.[94] For example, when consultants talk about "expanding the base," they are often referring to efforts to reach out to Independents and out-partisans who might agree with them on specific issues.

Thus, we look not just at what the campaigns said they were trying to do, but also at what they actually did in their television and direct-mail advertising. Using a unique survey conducted by the Center for the Study of Elections and Democracy at Brigham Young University that captured the specific pieces of campaign mail received by voters, we are able to analyze who received what policy messages. In the next chapter, we talk about our data sources for evaluating both candidate strategy and campaign effects. We also return to square one, considering the measurement of persuadable voters and examining their size and characteristics.

[93] Nisbett and Wilson, "Telling More than We Can Know."
[94] For extended discussion of this issue for the measurement of party identification, see review in next chapter.

Three

Measuring the Persuadable Partisan

> America is divided. . . . The loyalties of American
> voters are now almost perfectly divided be-
> tween the Democrats and Republicans, a
> historical political deadlock that inflames the
> passions of politicians and citizens alike. . . .
> This produced the vivid maps of America,
> divided between the red Republican states and
> the blue Democratic ones.
> —Stanley B. Greenberg, *The Two Americas*

FOLLOWING THE RAZOR-CLOSE presidential elections in 2000 and 2004, many political observers concluded that American voters are deeply divided by ideology and partisanship. The red and blue electoral maps from these elections have been interpreted as a depiction not only of the election outcomes but also of the opinions and attitudes of the American public. As the common stereotype goes, the blue states— won by Democrat John Kerry in 2004—are composed of latte-sipping, NPR-listening, Hollywood-loving liberals who are threatening the fabric of society with their advocacy of gay marriage and abortion rights. In contrast, the red states—won by Republican George Bush—are comprised of gun-totin', NASCAR racin', Bible-thumpin' conservatives who care only about Christian values at the expense of tolerance, equality, and civil liberties. Commentator George Will remarked that the 2004 presidential election "continues—and very nearly completes—the process of producing a perfect overlap of America's ideological and party parameters."[1]

Certainly, ideological polarization is apparent among contemporary partisan elites—Democrats and Republicans in Congress are more consistently opposed to each other on legislation, the party platforms are more ideologically extreme, and party activists are more polarized across a variety of policy issues.[2] There remains considerable scholarly debate about the degree and extent of a culture war in the American

---

[1] George F. Will, "America's Shifting Reality," *Washington Post*, 4 November 2004, A25.
[2] For overview see Layman et al., "Party Polarization in American Politics."

public, but many scholars contend that the mass electorate has similarly polarized along ideological and partisan lines.[3] Alan Abramowitz and Kyle Saunders argue,

> Americans may not be heading to the barricades to do battle over abortion, gay marriage and other emotionally charged issues . . . but there are deep divisions between Democrats and Republicans, between red state voters and blue state voters, and between religious voters and secular voters. These divisions are not confined to a small minority of elected officials and activists—they involve a large segment of the public and they are likely to increase in the future as a result of long-term trends affecting American society.[4]

This portrait of the American public seems difficult to reconcile with our thesis that campaign dynamics in presidential campaigns are shaped in large part by cross-pressured partisans—those who disagree with their party on a policy issue. Our theoretical expectations presuppose that rank-and-file partisans have heterogeneous policy preferences. For a candidate to drive a wedge into the opposition party coalition requires that the party coalitions contain meaningful policy fractures. Yet, are there any cross-pressured partisans to be persuaded in today's polarized environment? If so, what are the salient policy cleavages in the contemporary party coalitions? In subsequent chapters we will examine the impact of cross-pressures on voter and candidate behavior in presidential campaigns, but we first explore the basic extent of policy incongruence in the mass public—a task that requires careful consideration of the many challenges of measurement and operationalization inherent in the study of mass attitudes. In this chapter, we provide careful scrutiny of our measure of cross-pressures and then examine the contours of public opinion in the American public.

Across a variety of different surveys, election years, and policy questions, we show that partisans often are not fully aligned with the policy positions of their affiliated party. There may well be some differences across the *mean* preferences of Democrats and Republicans in the electorate, but there is also considerable *variance* in the preferences of each group. Whatever the trend over time in polarization among political elites, partisans in the electorate are often conflicted between their partisan loyalties and their issue preferences across different policy domains. In a complex and pluralistic society, a two-party system ensures the parties will be coalitional in nature, even in today's political envi-

---

[3] For a general overview of the scholarly debate, see Fiorina, *Culture War?*; Hetherington, "Resurgent Mass Partisanship."

[4] Abramowitz and Saunders, "Why Can't We All Just Get Along?," 1.

ronment. The aggregation of these policy disagreements creates cleavages within the party coalitions, and thus strategic opportunities for the candidates. Indeed, as we discuss at the end of the chapter, conflict *within* the party coalitions on moral issues rather than *across* the party coalitions has created strategic incentives for candidates to try to exploit a "culture war" as part of a wedge campaign strategy. But to get to this descriptive analysis of the contours of policy attitudes in the party coalitions first requires careful consideration of the best way to measure persuadable partisans.

Party and Issues in the Vote Decision

Although we provide a cursory look at persuadable Independents in this chapter, we focus on identifying and measuring persuadable partisans. Party identification has long been viewed as the cornerstone of political decision making, and the relationship between partisan affiliation and vote choice is one of the most robust findings in political science. More than 60 percent of Americans say they think of themselves as a Democrat or Republican (89 percent including Independents who say they lean toward one party or the other). Party identification is an enduring attachment to a political party that creates an initial expectation of support for one candidate over the other. There is debate in political science as to whether party identification is rooted in parental socialization, group attachments, or a "running tally" of government-performance evaluations, but there is a near consensus that it is a politically impactful and generally stable characteristic.[5] As a seventy-five-year-old Democratic respondent to our 2004 Blair Center survey wrote when asked if she disagreed with her party on any policy issues, "Right or wrong I stand by my party! . . . [N]ever in my life have I ever considered being a Republican!"

Some research suggests that the relationship between party identification and vote choice has strengthened in recent decades as the public has realigned along partisan and ideological lines.[6] Although this research offers compelling evidence of temporal changes in the party system, the focus of the literature on aggregate trends across time has potentially overlooked considerable individual-level variation within a given election, which we argue is central to the dynamics of each campaign. Do contemporary partisans disagree with their party on important policy issues or have identifiers so completely aligned them-

[5] For a review, see Green et al., *Partisan Hearts and Minds*.
[6] Abramowitz and Saunders, "Ideological Realignment in the U.S. Electorate."

selves with party mandates that pervasive agreement is now the norm? The key objective of this chapter is to estimate just how many persuadable partisans exist in today's polarized political environment.

Do Citizens Have Policy Attitudes?

One of the key assumptions of our thesis is that partisans will hold consequential disagreements with their affiliated political party. Yet, this assumption is at odds with the traditional perspective of public opinion that citizens are often not sophisticated enough to embrace meaningful policy positions. Phil Converse and others argue that the general public is characterized by "nonattitudes" rather than explicit policy positions. In this view, survey responses about specific policy areas are fleeting and shallow expressions—a sample of "the thoughts that are most accessible in memory at the moment of response."[7] In contrast, we assume that voters, while not necessarily ideologically coherent, do often hold true and meaningful policy preferences. Donald Kinder eloquently explains this revisionist perspective,

> That the original claim of ideological innocence is largely sustained does not mean that the American mind is empty of politics; innocent as typical Americans may be of ideological principles, they are hardly innocent of political ideas. Such ideas, however, defy parsimonious description. Some beliefs are classically liberal, some classically conservative. There are some authentic opinions, tenaciously held; there are some non-attitudes, casually expressed. There are patches of knowledge and expanses of ignorance.[8]

Although we recognize that citizens are far from policy wonks, we argue that when individuals do have real policy preferences inconsistent with their partisan loyalties, it has consequences for how these individuals respond to campaign dialogue on the issue.

We believe that these preferences can be measured using better survey questions and asking about issues that reflect the broader political environment and debate. To be sure, some individuals will answer a survey question even when they do not know or care about an issue, but survey error stems not just from the survey respondent, but also from the survey researcher (asking difficult, vague, or ambiguous questions). In a classic critique of Converse, Chris Achen argued that *"Measurement error is primarily a fault of the instruments, not of the respondent* [emphasis in original]."[9] As Kinder observed, the reality is that

---

[7] Zaller and Feldman, "A Simple Theory of the Survey Response," 580.

[8] Kinder, "Diversity and Complexity in American Public Opinion," 401.

[9] Achen, "Mass Political Attitudes and the Survey Response," 1229.

there are both hazy questions and hazy respondents, and it is the imperative of public opinion scholars to distinguish the two. Surveys can only imperfectly measure respondent attitudes because true attitudes are complex and a survey question provides only the briefest snapshot. Nevertheless, there are ways to improve the accuracy and measurement of respondent attitudes.

Research has found that responses to issue questions are sensitive to question wording, response categories, and the like. Sometimes, even minor differences in the wording of survey questions can have systematic effects on the responses given by individuals. For example, the public reports much greater support for federal spending on "assistance for the poor" than for "welfare."[10] But responses to issue questions more accurately reflect true policy preferences when questions are framed in such a way that both sides of the debate are presented. In recent work, Paul Sniderman and Sean Theriault show that "when citizens are exposed to a complete rather than to an edited version of political debate, they do not succumb to ambivalence or fall into confusion. On the contrary, even though as part of the process of debate they are exposed to an argument at odds with their general orientation, they tend 'to go home,' to pick out the side of the issue that fits their deeper-lying political principles."[11]

Scholars must also take seriously the issue of question interpretation. The more abstract a survey question, the more difficult it is know how a respondent has interpreted its meaning.[12] Respondents do not answer questions in a vacuum, and they provide a context to a question if none is given. Clearly, such a context might differ across respondents. For issues on which candidates stake out opposing positions in the midst of a presidential campaign, we would expect to obtain better measures of policy attitudes because the electoral environment provides a context for the issue, and that context is generally characterized by a two-sided debate. Yet, too often surveys ask questions that in no way reflect the structure of current policy debates. For the sake of continuity over time, or comparability with existing studies, surveys often ask issue questions on which there is actually little disagreement between the contemporary political parties. For instance, the National Election Studies have consistently included questions such as "Should federal spending on

[10] For example, see Smith, "That Which We Call Welfare by Any Other Name Would Smell Sweeter."

[11] Sniderman and Theriault, "The Dynamics of Political Argument and the Logic of Issue Framing," 148.

[12] King et al., "Enhancing the Validity and Cross-cultural Comparability of Measurement in Survey Research."

public schools be increased, decreased, or kept about the same?" Although party distinctions on education policy certainly exist, this question does not measure these differences. Democrats may endorse increased spending for teacher pay or improving urban school districts while Republicans may prefer increased spending on testing and providing financial incentives for merit or performance. Similar problems exist for questions regarding spending on crime, women's role in society, and support for foreign aid, among others. While these are important policy domains, the questions that are often included in leading national surveys are inadequate for measuring the extent to which someone might be incongruent with his or her party on the issue.

In the 2004 Blair Center Survey, we deliberately structured questions to reflect the current debate on salient political issues. By presenting respondents with policy alternatives that more closely represent the actual political environment, the survey should more accurately measure the extent to which respondents might disagree with the position of their party candidate.

It is also the case that while voters might not be fully informed across the spectrum of policy issues, they will be informed on an issue they find personally relevant, so we account for issue importance in our analysis when possible. A large body of research examining "issue publics" demonstrates that people who have personal commitments to particular policy issues will be informed and engaged on that issue.[13] In the classic work *Homestyle*, Richard Fenno quotes one congressman who explained, "[t]here isn't one voter in 20,000 who knows my voting record . . . except on that one thing that affects him."[14] Interest in and knowledge about a policy issue can itself be dynamic depending on the media and campaign context. Vincent Hutchings recently described the electorate as groups of *latent* issue publics—"a loose collection of 'sleeping giants.' . . . When the interests or values of one or more of these giants are at stake in a political contest . . . they can become surprisingly alert."[15] So even if an individual is not an activist on behalf of an issue before the campaign, a particular issue message might be especially resonant, compelling the individual to become informed about the candidates' policy differences on the issue by the end of the election. For instance, over the course of the campaign, senior citizens might become attentive and informed about the candidates' positions on social security, parents with school-age children might learn about

[13] For instance, Krosnick, "Government Policy and Citizen Passion."
[14] Fenno, *Home Style*, 142.
[15] Hutchings, *Public Opinion and Democratic Accountability*, 4.

the candidates' education policy promises, and gun owners might pay special attention to the candidates' positions on gun control policy. Importantly, given the diversity of sources of issue attitudes, we cannot assume that demographics or group identity alone is evidence of attitude importance. At the same time, there are also some issues that capture the interest and attention of nearly all citizens.

Measuring Party-Policy Cross-pressures

Even with better question wording, measuring the extent of internal conflict between party loyalties and issue preferences is still error prone. The task requires comparing the policy positions taken by partisans in the electorate with the positions taken by presidential candidates—yet the measurement of each of these can be difficult. For candidates there will be some issues on which they stake clear and opposing positions, but others on which they are deliberately vague. As Benjamin Page once commented, presidential candidates are "skilled at appearing to say much while actually saying very little."[16] We restrict our estimate of policy incongruence to only those issues on which the candidates take opposing positions, as gauged by party platforms and campaign rhetoric.[17]

For respondents we measure both policy positions and party identification in a conservative manner. First, we limit analysis to those respondents who describe themselves in partisan terms; Independent leaners, self-identified Independents who indicate that they are closer to one party or the other, are not included. If we instead treat leaners as partisans, we find similar results, although leaners, not surprisingly, have somewhat higher levels of policy incongruence, no doubt related to their decision to call themselves Independents in the first place.[18]

In actual campaigns, candidates do not typically have measures of self-identified party identification; rather they must infer party attachments on the basis of party registration, voting history, demographics,

---

[16] Page, *Choices and Echoes in Presidential Elections*, 153.

[17] We first contrasted the party platforms to identify the set of issues on which the parties held divergent positions. We confirmed the issue was salient by looking at campaign coverage of the issue in the *New York Times*. Finally, we excluded any issues for which the majority of both Democrats and Republicans in a given survey shared the same position. By these criteria, for instance, the death penalty, spending on education, and spending on overseas aid were excluded in the 2000 Knowledge Networks survey data.

[18] Carmines and Ensley, "Strengthening and Weakening Mass Partisanship."

and the like. Even when party registration data is available, the electoral rules across states create wide variability in the likelihood that someone will register as a partisan or not. In Alabama, for instance, just 6.5 percent of registered voters in 2004 were classified as Independents; the state's closed primary law means that only partisan identifiers can cast a ballot in the primary race. In contrast, 49 percent of registered voters were Independents in Massachusetts, where Independents are allowed to vote in either party primary without officially registering with the party in advance. In an open-primary state like Michigan, voters do not register with a party at all, so party identification is imputed for most registrants based on previous participation in either the Republican or Democratic primary. The point here is just that a candidate's calculation of the pool of persuadable voters very much depends on the amount and type of data available about the electorate in each state. Our use of a survey-based measure of party identification does not perfectly match the definition used by the political candidates, but it offers the most rigorous test of our theoretical expectations.

Second, in classifying issues as incongruent or congruent, we also err on the side of caution. If the question-response format included a middle, neutral, or don't-know category, individuals selecting these responses were coded as being congruent with their political party, even if they might consider their moderate position incongruent with their party's more extreme position. Thus, to be classified as a cross-pressured partisan, an individual must not only disagree with the position taken by her own party but also agree with the position of the opposition party. Finally, in our analysis using the 2004 Blair Center Survey we coded an issue as incongruent only if an individual also indicated that the issue was "very" or "extremely" important. The resulting measure of cross-pressures has a theoretical range of 0 to 100, capturing the percentage of issues about which a respondent disagrees with her affiliated party candidate in the 2004 presidential campaign. As a robustness check, we examine alternative measures using open-ended data, other surveys, and various subsets of respondents. In the end, though, our analysis still rests on the assumption that we have been able to accurately measure and capture true policy attitudes among ordinary Americans. But to reiterate the three-fold requirement: To be labeled cross-pressured, a weak or strong partisan identifier must disagree with her own party's position on an issue, agree with the opposing party's position on the issue, and consider the issue personally important.

Before turning to our analysis of cross-pressured partisans, we provide an overview of the data sources used throughout the book.

Overview of Data Sources

Throughout this study we will bring to bear a mixed-method approach in looking at the interaction between candidates and voters in presidential campaigns. Each of these research methodologies has its own set of strengths and weaknesses; together, they offer a more comprehensive initial evaluation of our expectations about presidential campaign dynamics.

The analysis in this chapter comes first and foremost from a survey designed to capture the extent of policy incongruence. The 2004 Blair Center Election Survey was a postelection survey of 2,831 respondents fielded by Knowledge Networks (KN) November 5–16, 2004.[19] The KN Internet panel consists of a national random sample of households recruited by random-digit dialing (RDD), who either have been provided Internet access through their own computer or given a WebTV console. Thus, although surveys are conducted over the Internet, respondents are representative of the U.S. population.[20] By using a random probability sample for initial contact and installing Internet access for respondents without it, KN overcomes the most common shortfall of other Web surveys; the Knowledge Networks method eliminates non-Internet coverage bias and allows researchers to accurately gauge the potential for self-selection and nonresponse bias.

Since cross-sectional surveys are limited in their ability to link campaign exposure to individual-level behavior, we turn to a panel survey to more directly examine changes in vote choice over time. Here we use the 2000 Knowledge Networks Election Study panel, a 28,000 repeated-interview survey that allows us to track individual-level changes in vote choice over the course of the campaign. During the 2000 presidential campaign, some seventy-five randomly assigned surveys (with widely varying sample sizes) were sampled from the Knowledge Networks panel, and following the election, there was a postelection survey of more than 12,000 respondents. Since a handful of these surveys included issue questions, we were able to match reported vote choice with issue positions collected before Election Day, thereby allowing us to explore the relationship between issues, party

[19] More information about the survey design and questionnaire is provided in appendix 1.

[20] Independent comparison studies have found that the KN sample is representative of U.S. Census averages. In side-by-side survey comparisons, Krosnick and Chang, "A Comparison of the Random Digit Dialing Telephone Survey Methodology," find the Knowledge Networks survey to be comparable to the RDD telephone survey and representative of the U.S. population across respondent demographics, attitudes, and behaviors.

identification, and the vote. Notably, many of the core political variables were collected before the campaign season even started. These political profile questions were answered without the heightened political context of an electoral campaign and are therefore more likely to be exogenous to candidate support. When looking across election contexts, we rely on the American National Election Studies cumulative data and the 1972–1976 NES panel study.

Finally, we examine the link between policy incongruence and campaign information in a survey experiment conducted as part of the 2006 Cooperative Congressional Election Study (CCES). The CCES was a collaborative survey project conducted by Polimetrix. Polimetrix samples from a volunteer panel of respondents, and then uses statistical matching to create a sample that looks similar to a random sample of adult consumers in the United States across a set of specified characteristics.[21] It is not possible to assess whether the resulting sample is representative across other (unmatched) characteristics, although initial comparisons suggest the sample is similar on some characteristics, but is more politically knowledgeable, more politically active, and more polarized than survey respondents sampled from the general population (e.g., NES surveys). Despite the potential concerns about the generalizability of our results from this data source, the random assignment of respondents to the treatment and control conditions offers internal validity about the effect of the campaign treatment on the sampled respondents.[22]

Shifting gears to our data sources for analyzing candidate strategy, we adopt a mixed quantitative and qualitative research design. We conducted historical and archival research about candidate strategy and interviewed campaign consultants and party strategists. Our quantitative data about the presidential direct mail come from the Campaign Communication Study (CCS) conducted by the Center for the Study of Elections and Democracy at Brigham Young University, which collected data on the phone calls, personal contacts, and actual direct-mail and email pieces received by a national sample of registered voters in the last three weeks of the 2004 campaign.[23] This study offers a picture

[21] More information about the CCES survey and the experimental design is available in appendix 1.

[22] A randomization check found no statistical differences across treatment conditions on a wide range of demographic, political, and attitudinal measures. A multinomial logit model predicting treatment condition as a function of age, race, gender, political sophistication, party identification, ideology, and political interest also found no statistically significant effects.

[23] We are grateful to the CSED scholars and research staff, especially Quin Monson, Jonah Barnes, and Dustin Slade. For more information about the study, see Magleby et

of the specific issue appeals candidates made and to whom. The CCS is a multimode national survey of registered voters who were contacted prior to the 2004 election and asked to collect all political mail and email received and to log all telephone and in-person contact during the last three weeks of the presidential campaign.[24] The final sample included 1,606 respondents who returned 19,297 total pieces of political mail and who logged 9,627 political phone calls and 399 in-person visits. The Social and Economic Sciences Research Center at Washington State University was responsible for recording data from the questionnaire/log booklet as well as the initial coding of the 2,466 unique federal mail pieces. A research team at the Center for the Study of Elections and Democracy then conducted a much more comprehensive coding of the federal mail pieces using a detailed coding instrument (with 100 to 350 coded items depending on the length and complexity of the mail piece) modeled after the Wisconsin Advertising Project.

Analysis of Cross-pressures in 2004

Our key measure of cross-pressures relies on the 2004 Blair survey. In the survey, we asked respondents about issues that were potentially divisive in 2004, both those that had just recently entered the public domain (e.g., stem cell research) and those that represented a historical division between the two major parties (e.g., support for labor unions). Looking at response patterns to these policy questions, we find that the majority of partisans hold positions that agree with the positions taken by their affiliated political party on each issue, but the margins are far from overwhelming. In table 3.1 we show the distribution of issue preferences, ordered from the least incongruent to the most incongruent. Across a variety of policy questions, we find an average of 26 percent of partisans embrace issue positions that are inconsistent with their preferred political party, 20 percent hold neutral or ambivalent positions, and a bare majority (54 percent) completely agree with their affiliated party. Across a variety of different issues, then, there are a sizable number of partisan identifiers who disagree with the national party position of their preferred political party.

---

al., *Dancing without Partners*; and Magleby et al., "Mail Communications in Political Campaigns."

[24] More information about the study design and our coding of direct mail is available in appendix 2.

TABLE 3.1
Policy Congruence among Partisans in 2004

	Percent Incongruent with Party	Percent Neutral	Percent Congruent with Party
Faith-based Initiatives	36	24	40
School Prayer	36	21	43
Abortion	35		65
School Vouchers	35	17	48
Partial-birth Abortion	35		65
Prescription-drug Imports	34	17	49
Education Policy	30	28	42
Gay Marriage	29	16	56
Tort Reform	29	21	50
Gun Control	27	10	62
Environment vs. Oil	27	20	53
Stem Cell Research	26	23	51
Business Regulation	25	31	44
Health Care	25	23	52
Union Support	23	26	51
Social Security Privatization	22	28	50
Government Aid to Poor	22	27	51
Affirmative Action	21	27	52
Tax Cuts vs. Minimum Wage	20	20	61
Multilateralism	15	30	55
Use of Force/Terrorism	14	27	59
Iraq War Evaluation	13	12	75
Economy Evaluation	11	24	65
Average All Issues	26	20	54

Note: Table shows partisans disagree with their party across different policy areas. Reported are the percent of partisans who hold policy attitudes incongruent (or congruent) with those held by the national party on each issue. Data source is the 2004 Blair Center Survey.

Scanning the issues by their level of incongruence, we find social and cultural issues at the top of the list. In contrast, the issues of the Iraq War and the economy found the highest levels of intraparty agreement. On evaluations of the Iraq War, 75 percent of partisans shared the position of their party candidate while 65 percent of partisans were congruent on evaluations of the economy. This no doubt reflects the fact that these evaluative issues are more likely than others to reflect candidate support rather than objective assessments or deep-seated ideological predispositions alone.[25] For instance, Bush supporters may be more likely to give a positive evaluation of the war or economy because they want to show support for the president (and the reverse for Kerry supporters). Although our theoretical arguments certainly apply to evaluative issues, we omit these two measures from our subsequent analysis in an effort to create as conservative as possible a measure of policy incongruence. Indeed, history reveals plenty of cases in which retrospective cross-pressures were likely critical to a particular campaign— for instance, Democrats disappointed with Carter's management of the economy and hostage crisis in 1980 and Republicans unhappy with the recession under George H.W. Bush's tutelage in 1992.

This basic cut of the data also contrasts with the conclusions of scholars who contend that the public is centrist across most policy issues. People were more likely to take a clear stance either for or against a policy than to choose a position in the middle or a neutral category. Although people more often call themselves political moderates than liberals or conservatives, this label can reflect a rather complex set of policy beliefs, not just middle-of-the-road policy attitudes across issue domains.[26] Americans like to think of themselves as moderates (just as we like to call ourselves "middle class"), but this label can represent a broad spectrum of belief systems. Indeed, 60 percent of respondents who call themselves ideological moderates also call themselves Democrats or Republicans, and 85 percent of these moderate partisans are cross-pressured on at least one salient policy issue.

Of course, simply disagreeing with your party on an issue does not necessarily translate into internal conflict or tension. An individual might be closer to the opposition party on an issue, but not really care about the issue. As a way to gauge the importance of a policy disagreement, we included in the survey a question about issue importance for many of the political issues. Issue importance measures "the extent to which attitudes manifest the qualities of durability and impactfulness."[27] Research has found that issues deemed important by respondents are more likely to be stable, resistant to change, and more likely to influence behavior. There is also substantial evidence that if an individual consid-

---

[25] Evans and Andersen, "The Political Conditioning of Economic Perceptions." Because of this, we omit these two attitudes from subsequent analysis. We have replicated the results with controls for evaluations of Iraq with similar effects. Indeed, partisans cross-pressured on these issues were very likely to defect.

[26] Treier and Hillygus, "The Contours of Policy Attitudes in the Mass Public."

[27] Krosnick and Petty, *Attitude Strength*, 3.

ers an issue important, she is more likely to become informed about that issue.[28] Thus, a measure of issue importance helps to ensure that we are distinguishing "real" attitudes from "top of the head" survey responses. Accounting for the importance of an issue reveals some notable differences across issues and parties. For instance, only 33 percent of Democrats who opposed affirmative action said the issue was important to them, while 72 percent of pro-life Democrats considered the abortion issue important. On the Republican side, just 27 percent of Republicans who supported gay marriage considered the issue important, while 82 percent of those who disagreed with Bush on his No Child Left Behind policy indicated that it was an important policy.

Because we have a postelection measure of issue importance, we cannot separate the portion of attitude strength reflecting an individual's inherent interest in a topic from that which was prompted by the campaign. Whatever the origins of importance, we use it here as a simple measure of a meaningful cross-pressure.[29] We then create a scale of policy incongruence from the subset of positional issues (rather than evaluative issues) on which the candidates took publicly opposing positions, issues on which partisans are not in consensus (e.g., support for prescription drugs), *and* issues for which we have a measure of personal importance. This leaves us with ten potential wedge issues from the 2004 presidential election: abortion, gay marriage, stem cell research, gun control, affirmative action, the environment, health care, minimum wage, social security privatization, and aid to the poor. For each self-identified partisan, we determined whether she disagreed with her own party, agreed with the opposing party position, *and* considered the issue personally important. As reported in the first column of table 3.2, we find that 67 percent of partisans disagreed with their political party on at least one issue that they considered personally important in 2004, and 40 percent disagreed with their party on more than one issue.[30] Thus, despite the ideological polarization of party elites in the United States today, most partisans in the electorate experience some degree of tension between their party affiliation and policies they care about. When asked about any policy disagreements with his party,

[28] Gershkoff, "How Issue Interest Can Rescue the American Public."

[29] We have replicated our analysis omitting the issue importance requirement and find similar results.

[30] Among Independent leaners, 67 percent face a least one issue cross-pressure with the "closer" party, 43 percent on more than one issue, and 5 percent on five or more issues. Although a conceptually different measure of cross-pressures, 97 percent of pure Independents held liberal preferences on at least one of the ten policy issues considered here and conservative preferences on at least one (90 percent on more than one).

TABLE 3.2
Summary of Cross-pressures in 2004 Presidential Election

	Percent All Partisans	Percent Strong Partisans	Percent Politically Attentive	Percent College Graduates	Percent Politically Aware
Completely congruent	33	35	38	43	42
Cross-pressured on at least 1 issue	67	65	62	57	58
Cross-pressured on more than 1 issue	40	36	35	30	31
Cross-pressured on 5 or more issues	4	3	5	3	3
Average	1.4	1.3	1.3	1.5	1.2
Sample size	1872	1113	684	450	620

Note: Table shows that the majority of partisans, including the most politically sophisticated, disagree with their affiliated party on a policy issue they care about. A policy cross-pressure is defined as an issue for which an individual (1) disagrees with her own party's position, (2) agrees with the opposing party position, and (3) considers the issue personally important. Data source is the 2004 Blair Center Survey.

one respondent to the Blair Center survey thoughtfully replied, "No party is going to fulfill every citizen's expectations and you have to learn to give and take with the party that benefits as a whole your own needs, the people around you or the area where you live and work."

To be sure, we find that the majority of respondents are aligned with the political party that is closer to their preferences on *most* political issues. Just 4 percent of partisans disagree with their political party on more than half of the ten issues. Generally, then, partisans appear to be correctly sorted into the closest partisan camp. While, the belief systems of the American public are often complex—with respondents liberal on some issues but conservative on others—citizens appear capable of figuring out which of the two major political parties provides the better overall policy fit. Our interest is in identifying the role and influence of any issue disagreements that do exist.

Who are these partisans who disagree with their party on more than half the issues? Perhaps surprisingly, the political knowledge levels of these individuals are not substantially different from those with fewer policy disagreements.[31] Instead, the most highly conflicted partisans

[31] The political knowledge levels of those with at least 50 percent of issues cross-pressured are not statistically different from those with less than 50 percent cross-pressured (p=.23).

appear to be individuals for whom party identification is a closer reflection of socialization than ideological preference. These highly incongruent individuals tend to be older, more likely to share the party
identification of their parents, less likely to have ever affiliated with
the other party, and more likely to be southern Democrats. One highly
incongruent eighty-year-old Republican respondent explained why he
disagreed with his party on so many issues, "I was voting Republican
when young George was an unfertilized egg. The party has changed.
. . . They once believed that the less government intruded into private
affairs, the better. These new [Republicans] want Uncle Sam and the
fifty states to poke their collective noses into the reproductive organs
of the American female."

As a further test of the robustness of our measure, we examine the
extent of cross-pressures among the most politically sophisticated portions of the electorate. According to early research, only a small subset
of the population is capable and motivated to think in ideological
terms, with very few characterized by political belief systems that are
"large, wide-ranging, and highly constrained."[32] Although previous research has long viewed policy incoherence as evidence of political ignorance, we find similar levels of incongruence among the most politically sophisticated respondents. Whether we look only at those who
are self-identified "strong" partisans, college graduates, the politically
attentive, or the most politically aware and informed, we consistently
find that less than half agree with their party on all ten of the issues
considered.

If we construct distinct dimensions of ideology (an economic and a
cultural dimension), instead of analyzing individual policy issues, we
find similar results.[33] Not surprisingly, there is overlap in some policy
conflicts within different domains. Democrats who are opposed to
stem cell research also tend to be opposed to abortion, suggesting that
while voters are often conflicted across issue dimensions they are
somewhat more consistent within issue domains. Combining multiple
measures into broad issue domains is one way to reduce measurement
error, but it would not be theoretically justified for our research questions.[34] We focus on individual policy issues not only because some

---

[32] Luskin, "Measuring Political Sophistication," 860.

[33] In replicating the findings from the next chapter, for instance, we find the effect of
economic cross-pressures increases the probability of defecting by 8.5 percentage points
in nonbattleground states but 29.2 percentage points in battleground states; for the social
cross-pressures, the effects are 9.3 percentage points and 29.5 percent, respectively.

[34] Carmines and Zeller, *Reliability and Validity Assessment.*

issues do not fit as easily within a single dimension (e.g., gun control or the environment), but also because candidates in contemporary elections are attentive to a voter's preferences on individual issues rather than general philosophies. Republican candidates will appeal to a pro-life Democrat even if she is supportive of stem cell research, just as a Democratic candidate will target a member of the Sierra Club with a pro-environmental message irrespective of her position on social security reform.

Finally, we find comparable results using alternative surveys. Although the issue questions from the National Election Studies are less than ideal for measuring policy preferences, they similarly show that partisans often disagree with their party on policy issues.[35] Looking at the 2004 NES, we find that roughly 70 percent of partisans disagreed with their political party on at least one prominent campaign issue. As before, we find similar numbers when looking at various subgroups of politically sophisticated respondents.

Robustness Check: Open-ended Measure

A lingering concern about our measure is that we must infer conflict; it does not tell us whether the individuals themselves actually perceive an inconsistency between their issue position and affiliated party. Although the importance measure might help to alleviate this concern to some extent, we can more directly look at the extent to which people recognize they disagree with their party using an open-ended question. In the Blair survey, we asked partisans if there were any political issues about which they disagreed with their political party. An open-ended question allows respondents to tell us, in their own words, about any issue on which they hold disagreements between their own policy positions and their preferred political party. Many scholars consider open-ended questions the gold standard for gauging attitude strength and importance.[36] At minimum, these open-ended responses indicate that respondents are aware that they have embraced issue positions that are at odds with the issue positions of their chosen political

[35] The issues include gun control, government services, tax cuts, abortion, social security, health care/government insurance, aid to blacks, the environment, and gay marriage. Where available, we limit to "important" cross-pressures (available for gun control, government services, abortion, government health insurance, and aid to blacks).

[36] See, for instance, Geer, "What Do Open-Ended Questions Measure?"

TABLE 3.3
Cross-pressures in 2004 Presidential Election, Open-ended Measure

	Percent All Partisans	Percent Democrats	Percent Republicans
Any Disagreement	46	42	59
Economic Issues	13	9	21
Cultural Issues	20	18	26
Foreign-policy Issues	7	5	10
Non-issue (e.g., Strategy/Person)	4	6	3
Among Issue Disagreements			
Abortion	23	25	21
Gay Marriage	18	24	14
Stem Cell Research	14	9	18
Iraq	10	6	13
Gun Control	9	9	8
Influence of Business/Wealthy	8	3	12
Health Care	6	5	7
Immigration	6	2	9
Welfare/Aid to Poor	6	7	5
Environment	5	2	8
Labor Issues	5	4	6
Separation of Church-State	5	6	5
Education	4	3	5
Race Policy	4	5	2
Social Security	2	1	4

Note: Table shows partisans willing to volunteer a policy disagreement with their political party and on what issues. Data source is the 2004 Blair Center Survey.

party. In table 3.3 we present the coded responses to our open-ended question about policy and party disagreement.[37]

With the open-ended responses, we find slightly fewer partisans who disagree with their affiliated party on a policy issue than with the closed-ended items, but still 46 percent volunteered a policy disagreement. Republicans were more likely than Democrats to offer a policy disagreement (59 percent versus 46 percent), perhaps reflecting the

[37] Percentages reported for partisans who responded to the open-ended question. Among partisans in the survey, 35 percent skipped the open-ended question, 32 percent offered a policy disagreement, and 33 percent indicated they had no policy disagreements. In terms of political knowledge, partisans who skipped the question were as able to identify the candidates' positions as liberal or conservative as those who offered an open-ended response. Their average number of incongruent issues was in between that of individuals who answered that they had no policy disagreements and those who offered a policy disagreement.

fact that an incumbent president offers a clearer policy reference point. Categorizing the issue responses, we find, similar to our earlier results, that partisans were particularly likely to mention that they disagreed with their party on cultural issues more than on economic- or foreign-policy issues. Republicans were also more likely than Democrats to say they disagreed with an economic-policy issue or a foreign-policy issue, accounting for the higher overall levels of cross-pressures among Republicans.

Looking more closely at the specific policy conflicts, we find that Republicans who offered a policy disagreement were most likely to mention being incongruent on abortion, stem cell research, gay marriage, Iraq, and policy toward business/the wealthy. A fifty-one-year-old Republican offered the following response about her disagreement with the Republican Party, "They just make the rich richer and the poor poorer." Another Republican explained his opposition to his party's stance on gay marriage: "While I'm a Christian, I believe a lot of these things are personal and it's very dangerous to start mixing religion and government." Among Democrats volunteering issue disagreements, the top policy disagreements were about abortion and gay marriage, followed by stem cell research and gun control. A seventy-three-year-old Democrat volunteered that she disagreed with her party on "the abortion issue, stem cell research, and gay marriage—don't agree with these issues at all and never will."

Reflecting the limitation of open-ended questions, 14 percent of respondents gave responses that were not actually a policy issue, most frequently providing a comment about party strategy or the party nominee. For instance, a fifty-eight-year-old Democrat complained that the Democratic Party "didn't work hard enough to get rid of that terrible man before he ruins our country," while a seventy-four-year-old Republican offered simply, "The only thing I can say is I believe in this President." These numbers are perhaps smaller than we would have expected given the findings of early research using open-ended questions. The focus of the early research, however, was on finding the "holy grail" of ideology so that policy mentions were not considered separately from other levels of conceptualization. In contrast, our intention is simply to identify any issue-based tensions with partisan loyalties.

Reassuringly, we find a strong relationship between the open-ended responses and closed-ended responses. On the issue of stem cell research, for instance, we find that 84 percent of those who volunteered they disagreed with their party on stem cell research were also coded as incongruent based on the closed-ended question (compared to just 24 percent of those who did not volunteer stem cell research). And 62

percent of those who volunteered the environment as a policy disagreement in the open-ended question were also coded as incongruent
based on their closed-ended responses. The correlation between the
open-ended and closed-ended measures is positive and statistically
significant (p<.01). Thus, although each type of question has its own
set of strengths and weaknesses, either way we find consistent evidence of a significant number of cross-pressured partisans in the contemporary electorate.

How Many Persuadable Voters?

Based on our measure of cross-pressures summarized in table 3.2, we
calculate a rough estimate of the proportion of individuals in the electorate who have the potential to be persuaded. Reported in table 3.4
are the percentage of persuadable partisan identifiers, Independent
leaners, and pure Independents in the full citizenry and the voting
public in 2004.[38] Clearly, it is a simplification to label someone as persuadable or not—persuadability is undoubtedly a continuum—but
this gives us a rough estimate of how much of the electorate had some
potential to be influenced by campaign dialogue. In the last column,
we offer the most conservative estimate in that we count an individual
as persuadable only if the respondent is also able to identify the Republican Party position as being more conservative than the Democratic Party position. Notably, this additional requirement does not
change the proportion of cross-pressured partisans in the electorate
(because the cross-pressures measure is already restricted to personally
important issues), but it reduces considerably our estimate of the percentage of persuadable Independents in the electorate. Using this most
conservative measure, we estimate that 25 percent of the voting public
is composed of persuadable partisans, another 5 percent are persuadable Independent leaners, and 4 percent are persuadable pure Independents, resulting in roughly one-third of the electorate being potentially
persuadable by policy appeals in the 2004 presidential election. These
estimates are based on a postelection survey, so the electorate is more
likely to be informed about the issues and may consider them more

---

[38] Partisan identifiers and leaners are defined as cross-pressured if they disagree with
their affiliated (or leaning) party on more than one policy issue, if they agree with the
opposing party position on those issues, and if they consider the incongruent issues personally important. Independents are defined as policy conflicted if they hold liberal positions on more than one issue and conservative positions on more than one issue.

TABLE 3.4
Persuadable Voters in 2004 Presidential Election

	Percent of Citizenry	Percent of Electorate	Percent of Electorate (Politically Aware)
Cross-pressured Partisans	26	27	25
Cross-pressured Independent Leaners	8	9	5
Policy-conflicted Pure Independents	13	9	4
Total Persuadable	46	46	34

Note: Table shows that a sizeable segment of the electorate was potentially persuadable in 2004 because of cross-pressures between their party affiliation and important policy preferences or, in the case of pure Independents, between different policy attitudes. Restricting coding of persuadability based on awareness of candidates' positions on the issues only reduces the percentage of persuadable Independents in the electorate. Data source is the 2004 Blair Center Survey.

important than earlier in the campaign.[39] But even if we are to code a partisan as cross-pressured based on the open-ended responses (cross-checked by closed-ended responses), we still find that 24 percent of the electorate is composed of persuadable partisans. So, whether looking at the general citizenry or the voting public, we find that a substantial portion of the electorate has at least a toe in each camp.

Reassuringly, our estimate of the percentage of persuadable votes matches quite closely other estimates. In *Applebee's America*, Matthew Dowd, Ron Fournier, and Douglas Sosnick reached a similar prediction:

> Conventional wisdom suggests that 2004 was the first of what will be a series of "base elections," with both parties catering only to their core voters. . . . Wrong. . . . [A] closer look at the numbers reveals a much higher percentage of voters—as much as 35 percent—who don't feel at home in either party. . . . By casting all-Republican or all-Democratic votes in 2004, these people created a false impression that the U.S. electorate is permanently polarized.[40]

Similarly, our estimate closely approximates the number of respondents in the 2004 Campaign Communication Study who received direct mail communications from both the Democratic and Republican candidates, another indication of perceived persuadability. In battle-

---

[39] Across issues, roughly 88 percent of voters on average were able to correctly identify the Republican Party as holding a more conservative position than the Democratic Party. Independents were defined as politically aware if they were able to correctly identify the Democratic Party position as more liberal than the Republican Party position on seven of eight issues.

[40] Sosnik et al., *Applebee's America*, 57–58.

ground states, nearly 40 percent of respondents received mail from both candidates.

Of course, being incongruent also does not necessarily mean that these individuals will be persuaded to vote one way or the other. Their final vote will depend on how the voters weigh different considerations in their decision-making process, which we suggest is dependent on the campaign environment, an analysis that we take up in the next chapter.

Tracing Cross-pressures over Time

To ensure that our measure is not simply reflecting something unique about one election, we look at changes over time in policy incongruence. Given the prevailing conventional wisdom about polarization, we might expect, if anything, that the extent of cross-pressures would have dramatically declined in recent decades. We should note that we approach this analysis with particular caution. Given changes in the available issue questions, question wording, and even survey modes, these comparisons are best viewed as blunt estimates of the presence of policy cross-pressures. As a rough gauge, we identified issues in the 1972–2004 ANES cumulative file that distinguished the party candidates in these presidential elections. Although many issues do not span the entire time series, we included in our analysis those issue questions that were consistently asked in several consecutive years and represented policy areas in which the parties took divergent stands. Unfortunately, we are not able to restrict the analysis to personally important issues, resulting in slightly higher overall levels of policy incongruence compared to prior estimates. The issue positions included for each year are listed in appendix 1.

Figure 3.1 illustrates the percentage of partisans since 1972 who report at least one issue on which they disagree with their affiliated party. Through nearly three decades of NES data, we find similar proportions of partisans who are incongruent on at least one issue. As before, policy incongruence is not limited to the unsophisticated, inattentive, nonvoters, or weak partisans. Also listed in figure 3.1 are the percentages of people who report disliking something about their preferred political party from an open-ended question included in the NES surveys. Here again, we find substantial stability in responses with around 50 percent of respondents volunteering that they dislike something about the political party to which they belong.

Looking carefully at the patterns over time, we see a hint of a decline in policy incongruence between 1992 and 2004. Even still, the percentages of party and policy disagreements presented in this figure are far from a picture of complete ideological and partisan polarization in the

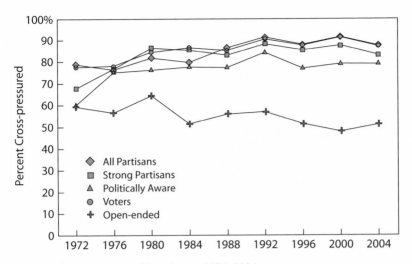

Figure 3.1: Cross-pressured Partisans, 1972–2004
Note: Figure shows percent of partisans who disagree with their affiliated party on at least one issue or volunteered any party dislike in the open-ended question. Data source is the American National Election Study cumulative file.

mass public that is so often portrayed in the media and popular discussions of contemporary politics. The relatively flat trend line stands in contrast, for instance, to the strengthening relationship between self-reported ideology and party identification. The percentage of Democrats who call themselves liberal and the percentage of Republicans who call themselves conservative have increased in recent decades, but our brief analysis here suggests that these trends are more likely to reflect symbolic uses of ideological labels than meaningful changes in policy preferences.[41]

In figure 3.2, we graph the individual issues that have been included in the NES cumulative file for several electoral cycles. Looking at policy incongruence on these individual issues over time, we again see a small decline in the prevalence of some issues in recent years, but the clearest pattern is one of overall stability. Again, these findings indicate much greater stability in policy disagreements than we might expect given theories of ideological and partisan realignments. These data hardly show a picture of partisans "hardening into uncompromising ideological camps."[42] Some scholars have argued that partisans will gradually bring their views in line with those of their party or switch

[41] DiMaggio et al., "Have Americans' Social Attitudes Become More Polarized?"
[42] David Von Drehle, "Political Split Is Pervasive: Clash of Cultures Is Driven by Targeted Appeals and Reinforced by Geography," *Washington Post*, 25 April 2004, A1.

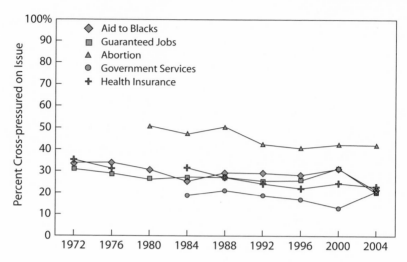

Figure 3.2: Cross-pressures on Specific Policy Issues, 1972–2004
Note: Figure illustrates percent of partisans incongruent on each specific issue. Data source is the American National Election Study cumulative file.

identification to the other party.[43] Yet, we find only minimal change in the average percentage of partisans who are incongruent on each of these issues. Our analysis also shows that policy incongruence is not limited to new issues or "hard" issues; partisans are also incongruent on the long-standing issues that have historically differentiated the two parties. Although there is some evidence that the party coalitions grew more homogenous in the 2004 presidential election, it would be easy to overstate the extent of issue agreement among partisans.

Estimates of the absolute level of cross-pressures in the American electorate will of course depend on the particular data sets employed, the particular issues examined, and the wording of the questions asked. Nonetheless, across different national surveys, conducted at different times by different investigators, we consistently find that a substantial portion of partisans are conflicted between their party affiliation and policy issues. Whatever the extent of ideological and partisan realignment that may be occurring over time, our results indicate that *within a given election*, many partisans face substantial policy disagreements with their party's nominee. Next, we take a step back to consider the implications of these conflicts for the composition of the party coalitions.

[43] Abramowitz and Saunders, "Ideological Realignment in the U.S. Electorate;" Layman et al., "Party Polarization in American Politics."

Cleavages in the Party Coalitions

Thus far, our findings highlight the coalitional nature of contemporary American political parties. The patterns suggest that even in the highly polarized environment of the 2004 presidential election, partisans often faced tensions between partisan loyalties and policy preferences. And in contrast to perceptions that the majority of Americans are moderate or neutral across most policies, we find that voters generally take a stand on policy issues, but that the stand might not be the one held by their affiliated political party. Certainly, any single survey question or set of questions will only imperfectly measure the extent to which an individual experiences real policy tensions with the party. But across different measures, we consistently find that cross-pressures remain prevalent in the American public. So, despite the familiar theme of polarization in the American public, the party coalitions can still perhaps be described as "vast, gaudy, friendly umbrellas under which all Americans, whoever and whatever and however-minded they may be, are invited to stand for the sake of being counted in the next election."[44] In a complex and pluralistic society, political parties will always be coalitions of diverse individuals. The choice of only two major parties ensures that some partisans will be cross-pressured on some issues, creating policy cleavages within the party coalitions.

The policy disagreements we have identified are reminiscent of the findings of early research showing the American public as "ideologically innocent." But whereas this early research took similar patterns as evidence of nonattitudes, more recent research recognizes that heterogeneity in issue preferences largely reflects the diverse sources of the public's policy attitudes. As Donald Kinder summarizes, Americans' policy attitudes are rooted in pluralistic sources, so that preferences can be organized in any number of ways, including by "personal needs, by self-interest, by group identifications, by core values, and by inferences from history."[45] Once we acknowledge the multiple sources of political beliefs, the observed patterns of policy incongruence are less surprising. After all, the same core value might underlie a "conservative" position on one issue but a "liberal" position on another. Most classically, the individual who is opposed to government intervention will rationally find himself closer to the Republican Party on economic issues but to the Democratic Party on social issues. Or we might expect policy disagreements when an individual's sociodemographic charac-

[44] Rossiter, *Parties and Politics in America*, 11–12.
[45] Kinder, "Diversity and Complexity in American Public Opinion," 390.

teristics are cross-cutting. As Benjamin Page and Robert Shapiro point out, "Differences in people's social and economic surroundings, conditions of life, historical experiences, knowledge, and cognitive abilities all give rise to group-related differences in policy preferences."[46]

In many respects, then, our expectations bring us back to the original cross-pressures theory of Lazarsfeld and his colleagues. Their sociological perspective held that conflicts in group membership would shape voter decision making. Although we offer a psychological perspective in which issue tensions provide the critical link between candidates, voters, and campaigns, these issue tensions may well be rooted in group identities, among other sources. Highlighting the bridge between these sociological and psychological perspectives, we conduct a cursory analysis of policy cross-pressures along religious, economic, and racial lines to see the extant cleavages within the party coalitions. This analysis is not meant to be exhaustive—we do not report across the full spectrum of relevant characteristics (for instance, we might also consider differences by gender or region) and we report only the top three issues about which we find notable variation in the extent of policy incongruence—but it offers an initial view of the policy fractures within the party coalitions in the electorate in the 2004 election.[47]

We first examine the relationship between policy incongruence on moral issues and religiosity, illustrated in figure 3.3. Religiosity has been considered one of the key sources of tension between Democrats and Republicans in recent years. Yet, looking at policy incongruence on moral issues among Democrats and Republicans we find that it also creates tension *within* the party coalitions. For instance, among the Democrats who believe in the inerrancy of the Bible, 62 percent are incongruent on gay marriage, compared to just 14 percent of those who believe the Bible is the work of men. On the other side of the aisle, just 12 percent of Republicans who believe in the inerrancy of the Bible disagree with the party's pro-life stance, compared to more than 70 percent of Republicans who believe the Bible is the work of men. Following the 2004 election, much was made of the fact that religious individuals were more likely to vote Republican than Democratic. Critical to candidate strategy is not just the likelihood that a group supports one party over the other, but also the size of the group in its party coalition. For instance, the distributions of religiosity within the two parties are not as different as is often portrayed. Looking at respon-

---

[46] Page and Shapiro, *The Rational Public*, 318.

[47] This exercise also offers an assessment of construct validity by examining how our measure of policy incongruence is related to demographic variables that we expect to be related to conflicting issue predispositions.

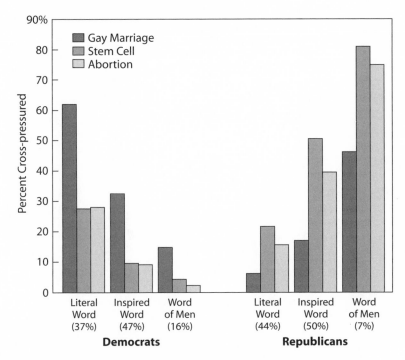

Figure 3.3: Religious Cleavages in Party Coalitions, 2004
Note: Figure shows cross-pressures on moral issues by respondents' interpretation of the Bible. Reported in parentheses is the percent of party coalition in each belief category. Data source is the 2004 Blair Center Survey.

dents' views of the Bible, slightly more Republicans view the Bible as the literal word of God (44 percent of Republicans and 37 percent of Democrats), but a large plurality of both Democrats and Republicans view the Bible as the inspired word of God (50 percent of Republicans and 47 percent of Democrats). So, despite the substantial media attention to religious differences between the two political parties, it is clear that religious diversity in the electrate leads to policy disagreements both across and within the party coalitions.

In figure 3.4, we look at variations in issue preferences by income levels—the historic division between parties. We find that income levels are also a source of variation in policy preferences within the parties.[48] On the economic issues of social security privatization, government-provided health care, and support for taxes versus a minimum-wage

---

[48] Our measure of income quartile adjusts for differences in the standard of living across states. As one of the authors frequently complains, an equivalent salary translates to a much lower standard of living in Massachusetts than in Arkansas.

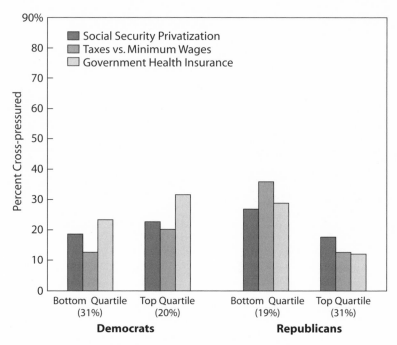

Figure 3.4: Economic Cleavages in Party Coalitions, 2004
Note: Figure shows cross-pressures on economic issues by income level. Reported in parentheses are percent of party coalition in each income category. Data source is the 2004 Blair Center Survey.

increase, we find predictable divisions between the wealthiest and poorest partisans in both parties. Poor Republicans are somewhat more likely to share the stance of the Democratic Party on these issues, while wealthy Democrats are closer to the stance of the Republican Party on these issues. Similar to our earlier findings, we see less within-party disagreement on these issues than we saw with the moral issues.

Finally, we examine racial divides within the parties in figure 3.5. For Democrats, there is a large split on the issue of affirmative action, with 46 percent of white Democrats opposed compared to just 12 percent of nonwhites. Likewise, minority Republicans are more supportive of affirmative action than are white Republicans, although the difference is nowhere near as stark as the division found among Democrats. Reflecting the diverse sources of policy cross-pressures, we find that race is related to policy incongruence on moral issues as well, with minorities more often conservative on gay marriage and stem cell research. Given the composition of the political parties, with just 11 percent of Republicans identified as nonwhites compared to 40 percent

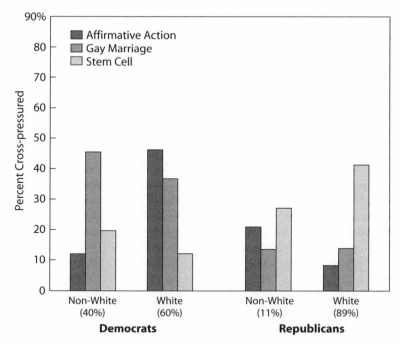

Figure 3.5: Racial Cleavages in Party Coalitions, 2004
Note: Figure shows cross-pressures on racial and moral issues by race. Reported in parentheses are percent of party coalition in each racial category. Data source is the 2004 Blair Center Survey.

of Democrats, racial divisions have much more pronounced implications for the Democratic Party than for the Republican Party, an asymmetry we explore further in chapter 5 where we explore the Republicans' "southern strategy."

Although not shown, we find other issue cleavages when we look at other individual-level characteristics. For instance, older Republicans are more likely to be incongruent on the issue of social security privatization than are younger Republicans, while younger Democrats are much more supportive than older Democrats. There are also regional differences, with Democrats in the South and Midwest more likely to be incongruent on social issues like abortion and gay marriage while Republicans in the West and Northeast are more likely to disagree with their national party on these issues.

While far from a comprehensive examination of the sources of cleavages within the Democratic and Republican parties, these breakdowns highlight some important basic points. Most fundamentally, partisans have heterogeneous policy preferences ensuring that political parties remain coalitional organizations. With this diversity comes susceptibility to wedge issues.

Scholars and journalists have long recognized this as a characteristic of the Democratic Party. Through its historical development, the Democratic Party has brought together very different demographic and social groups with various policy interests and priorities and has attempted to keep these competing interests under a single tent. In response to accusations that he divided the Democrats, Eugene McCarthy replied, "Have you ever tried to split sawdust?" And half a century earlier, journalist Finley Peter Dunne's Mr. Dooley observed, "Th' dimmycratic party ain't on speakin' terms with itself."[49] In the book *The Divided Democrats*, William Mayer shows that the fractures in the Democratic Party are fundamentally rooted in policy differences among different groups in the Democratic coalition.[50]

But our findings also highlight the extent of cleavages within the contemporary Republican Party. With electoral success, the Republican Party has grown larger and more diverse. Mayer observes that "Even the smallest and most doctrinate parties inevitably encounter disagreements: about issues, tactics, and personalities; over matters of longstanding incompatibility as well as new issues that were not part of whatever original consensus brought the party together."[51] As a party grows, it brings greater variation in the policy goals and priorities of its adherents. If we consider the sheer number of different policies on which elected officials must stake out a position in contemporary American politics, it should be of no surprise that partisans often encounter a policy disagreement with their national party, even in today's more polarized environment. Political elites may have become increasingly ideological during the previous few election cycles, but the structure of American politics guarantees that the parties in the electorate will remain heterogeneous coalitions. In 1960 Clinton Rossiter observed that the American political parties are "creatures of compromise, coalitions of interest. . . . It would be hard to imagine a political association more motley than the Democratic Party of the United States. The Republicans, for all their apparently sterner commitment to principle and respectability, are not much less of an army with a hundred different banners. They, like the Democrats, are a vast enterprise in 'group diplomacy.' "[52] It appears that little has changed.

---

[49] Mayer, *Divided Democrats*, 1.

[50] The key competing explanation is that the Democratic Party has an inherently more divisive nomination process. Mayer, *Divided Democrats*, 8.

[51] Mayer, *Divided Democrats*, 6.

[52] Rossiter, *Parties and Politics in America*, 11–12.

Conclusion: A New Take on the Culture War?

We have proposed a fundamental shift in existing perceptions about persuadable voters. Voters have complex belief systems, and it is not sufficient to simply classify someone as a swing voter based on whether she is an Independent versus a partisan or a moderate versus an ideologue. Partisan identification and policy preferences are related, but distinct, considerations that contribute to candidate selection, and frequently these considerations pull the voter in opposite directions. Our expectation is that these incongruent voters will be responsive to campaign information.

In this chapter, we have shown that cross-pressures are typically limited in scope—people tend to agree with their affiliated political party on *most* issues—but they are also extremely common. The majority of partisans disagree with their affiliated party on at least one policy issue, and roughly one-third are cross-pressured on more than one salient policy issue. There will always be questions and qualms about the existence and measurement of policy attitudes in the American public. In light of such inherent skepticism, we have approached our measure with caution and with multiple robustness checks. Across different surveys, different question types, and different respondents, we consistently find considerable policy incongruence among contemporary partisans, opening the door for campaign persuasion.

Whatever the trend over time between self-reported ideology and partisanship, the results here indicate that contemporary American voters are hardly extremists who have wholeheartedly followed elites to opposite ends of the ideological continuum. Partisans are generally aligned with the party that is closer to them on most policy issues, but they nonetheless disagree with some aspect of their party's platform. At the same time, the American public is not simply moderate across policy issues; it holds heterogeneous policy preferences.

Across different measures, we also find that self-identified partisans are more likely to disagree with their party's stance on moral or cultural issues than on the economic issues that have historically divided the political parties. If more voters are incongruent on cultural issues than economic issues, why have candidates given so much attention and focus to such issues in recent years? Our perspective provides a new take on the so-called culture war. Since cultural issues create cleavages *within* party coalitions, candidates have an incentive to emphasize these issues in their targeted campaign appeals even as economic issues remain the primary division *across* party coalitions. Thus, the focus on cultural issues in contemporary political campaigns may not be as much a reflection of the policy priorities of the public, but a consequence of the strategic opportunities available to the candidates. Candidates emphasize cultural issues exactly because these issues divide the opposition. By emphasizing those issues about which an individual disagrees with the opposing party candidate, the campaign increases the likelihood that the individual's issue preference will outweigh party loyalties in her vote decision. To be sure, we are not arguing that party identification is inconsequential to the decision-making process—it remains the single best predictor of candidate choice. But even as most individuals cast their ballot for their party's nominee, those who do defect (or have some potential to defect) play an especially important role in shaping the dynamics of a presidential campaign.

In many ways, our arguments parallel those found in the party realignment literature. Conflicts between issues and party identification are at the heart of classic research on mass realignments, as parties look for policy cleavages to exploit. According to this literature, the introduction of a new wedge issue serves as the catalyst for individual-level changes in partisan affiliation.[53] One difference between our and the realignment research is that the latter literature typically assumes that politics is conducted along a single policy domain at a time.[54] As James Sundquist argues, "*the* characteristic that identifies a party realignment [is] . . . the displacement of one conflict by another."[55] E. E. Schattschneider similarly assumes that "the old cleavage must be played down if the new conflict is to be exploited."[56] Yet, in the contemporary political environment, political debate crosses a wide variety of different issues. Political elites have taken opposing positions on issues as divergent as foreign-policy interventions, social security, affirmative action, stem cell research, education reform, same-sex marriage, minimum-wage policy, and so on. Geoffrey Laymen and Thomas Carsey have labeled this process "conflict extension" reflecting the limited mass response to the growth in elite-level polarization along multiple issue dimensions.[57] Yet, they expect that, as party elite take divergent positions on multiple issue domains, strong partisan identifiers will

[53] Key, "Secular Realignment and the Party System"; Sundquist, *Dynamics of the Party System.*

[54] Schattschneider, *Semisovereign People*; Stimson, *Tides of Consent*; Carmines and Stimson, *Issue Evolution*. A notable exception is Layman and Carsey, "Party Polarizations and 'Conflict Extension' in the American Electorate."

[55] Sundquist, *Dynamics of the Party System,* 13 (emphasis in the original).

[56] Schattschneider, *Semisovereign People*, 63.

[57] Layman and Carsey, "Party Polarizations and 'Conflict Extension' in the American Electorate."

bring their views in line with party elites—a conclusion that does not appear in our aggregate trends. Strong partisans are nearly as likely as weak identifiers to disagree with their affiliated party. Indeed, in an environment in which there is a wide and fragmented issue dialogue, party identification might be less impervious to a single-issue conflict because the diversity of issue dialogue makes clear that neither party offers a perfect policy match.

More critically, the realignment literature is focused on policy incongruence as part of a slow transition in the political system over time. In this literature, there is a gradual, path-dependent—some say, evolutionary—change in the party coalitions over the course of many electoral cycles, irrespective of the particular dynamics of a single campaign.[58] In contrast, we argue that policy incongruence shapes the strategic incentives and opportunities of candidates within a given electoral context, and that the campaign environment helps determine the link between policy incongruence and voter decision making. To be sure, individuals who vote against their party in one election might be more likely to change their party identification in the future;[59] even still, we suggest that the degree of tension between partisan loyalties and issue preferences within a given campaign shapes how individuals respond to information in that campaign. In the next chapter, we explicitly evaluate this link to determine if the persuadable voters identified are in fact responsive to campaign appeals.

[58] Carmines and Stimson, *Issue Evolution.*

[59] Markus and Converse, "A Dynamic Simultaneous Equation Model of Electoral Choice."

Four

Capturing Campaign Persuasion

MACOMB COUNTY, MICHIGAN, a suburban county just north of Detroit, was the most Democratic suburban county in the nation in 1960, voting 63 percent for John F. Kennedy. In 1984, the county gave 67 percent of its votes to the Republican candidate Ronald Reagan. Pollster Stanley Greenberg conducted a study of Macomb County to figure out why so many traditional Democrats had begun to cast their ballots for a Republican presidential candidate.[1]

What Greenberg found was widespread sentiment among white blue-collar men that they were "getting a raw deal" from the Democratic Party, which they viewed as beholden to minority interests and caught up in the civil rights movement. Most of the disaffected Democrats Greenberg spoke to were unionized auto workers who were supportive of Democratic policies on social security, education, and health care, but were conservative on issues like busing and welfare, and hawkish on foreign policy.

Reagan appealed to these working-class Democrats by emphasizing patriotism, anticommunism, religion and family values, as with his 1984 campaign commercial that scrolls through images of rolling farms, steel mills, coal miners, and churches to the tune of Lee Greenwood's "I'm Proud to Be an American." In nearly every campaign stump speech, Reagan promised to cut taxes, strengthen the military, and reduce regulation, and then he would explicitly reach out to Democrats in the crowd, "To all those Democrats who have been loyal to the party of FDR, Harry Truman, and JFK, but who believe that its current leaders have changed that party, that they no longer stand firmly for America's responsibilities in the world, that they no longer protect the working people of this country, we say to them, 'Join us. Come walk with us down the new path of hope and opportunity.' "[2]

In this chapter, we examine the influence of campaign efforts on the vote decisions of the electorate to evaluate whether cross-pressured partisans and Independents are more responsive to campaign appeals.

---

[1] Greenberg, *Middle Class Dreams*.

[2] Stump speech, Endicott, New York, 12 September 1984, Annenberg/Pew Archive of Presidential Campaign Discourse.

We test our theoretical expectations using multiple tests and across multiple data sources, including a cross-sectional survey, a panel survey, and a survey experiment, resulting in a flood of empirical evidence. This chapter will cover a wide span of different analyses, but we attempt to navigate the results in a way that highlights the key substantive findings, relegating the full set of statistical details to appendix 3. Through these many cuts of data, the findings will challenge prevailing views about campaign effects in presidential campaigns. Campaigns not only have more than "minimal effects" on the public, but these effects reflect the activation of issues at the expense of partisan loyalties, especially among those most exposed to campaign dialogue.

Policy Incongruence and Vote Choice

Partisans who are ideologically conflicted with their party are more likely to defect, as the Reagan Democrats of Macomb County illustrate. And we might expect that the more an individual disagrees with her political party, the more likely she should be to defect.[3] We trace the relationship between cross-pressures and vote defection in figure 4.1 using our measure of policy incongruence described in the last chapter—the percentage of issues for which a partisan disagrees with her own party's position, agrees with the opposition party position, and considers the issue personally important.[4] Not surprisingly, defection rates are higher among those individuals with higher levels of policy cross-pressures.[5] Among partisans completely congruent (i.e., no policy disagreements with their political party) fewer than 5 percent defected to the opposition candidate. At the other extreme, more than one-third of the partisans defected among the small percentage of respondents who disagreed with their party on at least 60 percent of the issues surveyed.[6] Of course, our key argument is that the relationship between policy incongruence and defection depends on the campaign context. In other words, we expect that policy incongruence interacts with the campaign dialogue to shape voter decision making, with cross-pressured partisans more susceptible to influence.

[3] Boyd, "Presidential Elections;" Macaluso, "Parameters of 'Rational' Voting."

[4] See appendix 1 for the issues included in this measure, and chapter 3 for discussion of coding.

[5] The 2004 relationship is likely stronger because the measure is restricted to personally salient issues, while we were not able to make such a distinction with the 2000 data.

[6] If we include Independent leaners in the analysis, we find an even more dramatic relationship, with defection ranging from 4 percent to 49 percent in the 2000 election and from 2 percent to 52 percent in the 2004 election.

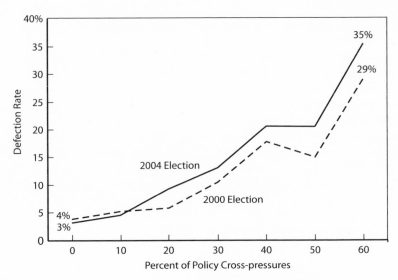

Figure 4.1: Defection by Policy Cross-pressures, 2000 and 2004
Note: Graph shows that partisans are more likely to defect to opposing party candidate at higher levels of policy cross-pressures. Data from 2000 Knowledge Networks Postelection Survey and 2004 Blair Center Survey.

Cross-pressures and Campaign Persuasion

Research in psychology has long recognized a link between internal conflict and susceptibility to persuasion. As a textbook on persuasion explains, "By regulating the degree of conflict experienced, the persuader can make it more likely that the persuadee will choose the option desired by the persuader."[7] When the underlying structure of an attitude is less consistent, that attitude is more responsive to new information.[8] Psychologists Christopher Armitage and Mark Conner, for instance, found that hospital workers who were ambivalent about low-fat diets were less resistant to persuasive communication promoting low-fat diets.[9] Other research has found that individuals who are internally conflicted are more motivated to seek out new information and to carefully process any information they receive.[10] In looking at attitudes

    [7] Okeefe, *Persuasion*, 81.

    [8] Eagly and Chaiken, "Attitude Strength, Attitude Structure, and Resistance to Change."

    [9] Armitage and Conner, "Attitudinal Ambivalence."

    [10] Hodson et al., "The Role of Attitudinal Ambivalence in Susceptibility to Consensus Information"; Wood, "Access to Attitude-Relevant Information in Memory as a Determinant of Persuasion."

toward immigration policy, for instance, one recent study finds that "people who are ambivalent toward a particular group more thoughtfully consider the merits of messages about the group."[11] Although this research has focused primarily on persuasion effects on a single attitude, we would expect parallels in our search for persuasive effects on the vote decision.

In the context of presidential elections, we have argued that individuals conflicted by the considerations underlying their vote decision should be open to campaign persuasion. This internal tension is most apparent among cross-pressured partisans, but should also be present among Independents who are conflicted about competing policy issues, core values, or other considerations.[12] We have argued that the campaign helps shape the salience of various considerations by defining what is at stake in the election. For persuadable partisans, the campaign is critical in determining whether the conflict is exacerbated or assuaged by altering the salience of the incongruent issue relative to partisan loyalties.[13] When the campaign discussion is focused on a conflicting issue, these cross-pressured partisans should be more likely to abandon their party at the ballot box. In the absence of campaign attention to a cross-pressuring issue, these voters should rely on their partisan predisposition or the broad performance components of the election.

Some partisans might know from the beginning of an electoral campaign that their party's nominee will not perfectly match their policy preferences, and the only question is whether the incongruent issue will become salient to their vote decision. Other partisans only come to learn of their issue disagreements as the campaign progresses, so that campaign learning might precede issue priming.[14] As a consequence, we expect that cross-pressured partisans not only will be more likely to defect, but also be more likely to be undecided early in the campaign and to change their mind during the campaign. In contrast, congruent partisans—those who share the policy positions of their party—should quickly converge to support their party's candidate. Congruent partisans should be able to "vote correctly" even before the campaign gets under way, and new information will do little beyond reinforcing that decision.

[11] Maio, "Ambivalence and Persuasion," 514.

[12] Given that 90–97 percent of Independents are cross-pressured by different issue preferences, and thus persuadable by our definition, we simply report results for all Independents.

[13] One mechanism of priming might also be simple learning of issue positions—voters must have knowlege of an issue to evaluate a candidate on the basis of that issue. See Lenz, "Learning, Not Priming."

[14] Michael Alvarez, *Information and Elections*.

Our expectations predict a pattern of campaign dynamics that is quite different from what we would expect if partisan activation is the primary campaign effect. Early research concluded that campaign messages strengthen the connection between partisanship and vote choice by giving voters a reason to support their party's nominee and by restoring partisan unity after a fractious nomination campaign. Our analysis will allow us to test between these competing expectations.

Smoking-gun Evidence

We take an initial look at our hypothesis that cross-pressured partisans and Independents are persuadable with a simple descriptive analysis of vote choice responses to a panel survey from the 2000 election. In table 4.1, we compare the vote choice dynamics of congruent partisans, cross-pressured partisans, and political Independents.[15] We see that Independents and cross-pressured partisans are much more likely to be undecided early in the electoral season and much more likely to change their candidate selection during the campaign than are congruent partisans. It also takes longer for Independents and persuadable partisans to reach a final vote decision. Two-thirds of congruent partisans report choosing a preferred candidate before their party had formally selected its nominee. In contrast, only 43 percent of Independents and just over half of persuadable partisans report making up their mind that early in the campaign. Also striking is the simple extent of volatility in vote choice observed over the course of the campaign. Some 45 percent of the electorate changed their vote choice (including moving from undecided to a decision) at some point during the campaign. Although this number may be higher in 2000 because it was an open seat election, it is also markedly higher than one might expect given the "minimal effects" conventional wisdom.[16]

Finally, cross-pressured partisans are more likely to defect on Election Day than are congruent partisans. Much of our subsequent analysis will focus on partisan defection as the dependent variable. How an

[15] Cross-pressured partisans are defined as individuals who disagree with their party on more than the average number of policies. If we include Independent leaners as partisans, we find that 23 percent of cross-pressured partisans were undecided in the first interview, 44 percent changed their vote choice during the campaign, 44 percent settled on a final vote decision after the conventions, and 20 percent defected on Election Day.

[16] It is worth noting that while the extent of vote instability is perhaps higher than often assumed, it is actually not that different from the numbers observed by Lazarsfeld and his colleagues in the classic *Voting* study, where they found that roughly 40 percent of respondents changed their mind at some point during the campaign.

TABLE 4.1
Vote Dynamics in the 2000 Presidential Election

	Percent Undecided in 1st Interview	Percent Changed Mind during Campaign	Percent Final Vote Decision after Conventions	Percent Election-day Defection
Congruent Partisans	13	23	30	3.7
Cross-pressured Partisans	20	40	41	19.0
Independents	40	57	53	
All Respondents	29	45	42	

Note: Table shows that cross-pressured partisans and Independents were more volatile in the vote choice during the campaign. An ANOVA allows us to reject the null hypothesis of equal percentages for each of the measures. Data source is the 2000 Knowledge Networks Election Study.

individual casts her ballot is, after all, what the candidates care about. This focus also allows us to test our expectations with cross-sectional surveys as well as within a panel survey design.

Although these dynamics are not explicitly linked to campaign activities, they offer some "smoking gun" evidence highlighting which voters had the potential to be influenced by the campaign. Those holding the same vote choice every time they were interviewed throughout the race were unlikely to have been influenced much by the information encountered during the campaign. These descriptives alone suggest that previous research has painted too simplistic a picture of campaign effects since it appears that some individuals are resistant to campaign effects, but others may be open to persuasion. We should also emphasize that these cross-pressured partisans are more susceptible to influence by the campaign, but it's still entirely possible that they will ultimately cast a ballot for their party's candidate on Election Day. Issue incongruence is a necessary, but not sufficient, condition for campaigns to have a persuasive effect on partisans.

Evaluating Campaign Persuasion: Statistical Results

To more explicitly evaluate campaign persuasion, we estimate a series of logit models predicting defection in the 2004 presidential election to evaluate the relationship between policy incongruence and defection across different levels of campaign exposure. Measuring campaign exposure is notoriously error-prone. Our approach to measuring campaign exposure is to capture it in as many different ways as possible. Thus, we consider differences in the campaign environment that might result from living in a state where the campaign is intensely fought compared to a less competitive state. Battleground states not only have more television advertising, they also have more personal canvassing, higher levels of political discussion, and more coverage of the campaign in the media.[17] We also consider differences in candidate exposure resulting from a candidate visiting a state—whether the travel is motivated by campaigning or fund-raising. But we also recognize that the presidential campaign is a national event that generates interest and attention across the nation. Those in uncompetitive states can ob-

---

[17] For review, see Holbrook, *Do Campaigns Matter?* Battleground-state definitions are based on Shaw, *The Race to 270*, and include seven states that were considered battleground by both candidates: Florida, Iowa, New Hampshire, New Mexico, Ohio, Pennsylvania, Wisconsin; and another nine were thought to be a battleground state by at least one of the candidates: Maine, Michigan, Minnesota, Oregon, Washington, Missouri, Nevada, West Virginia, Colorado.

viously still tune in to the campaign through national newspapers, television, or the Internet. Voters might require a bit more self-motivation to follow the campaign closely in an uncompetitive state, but there are nonetheless millions who do so. Thus, we also measure campaign exposure with two individual-level measures: attention to the campaign and political awareness, often considered the best measure of campaign exposure.[18] In other analyses, we measure the campaign with time—comparing candidate preferences before and after campaign events, and looking at changes in vote choice over time.

In looking at the relationship between cross-pressures and defection, we assume that those most exposed to the campaign receive more information about the policy priorities of the candidates than those least exposed. The campaign is able to activate the incongruent issue only to the extent that an individual receives the campaign message. In predicting defection, we also account for other factors that might influence an individual's decision to vote for the opposing party candidate, including demographic characteristics (age, race, gender, and education), strength of partisanship, and general political knowledge. These controls are necessary to account for the alternative hypothesis that partisan defection and vote instability might be an artifact of political ignorance or weak attachments to a party. In replicating our analysis in the 2000 presidential campaign, however, some of our measures are less than ideal. In the 2000 data, some individuals were asked more issue questions than others and we are unable to capture the personal salience of the issue, so our measure of policy incongruence is necessarily less precise.[19] We also do not have a measure of general political knowledge for the entire sample, so we use education as a proxy for political information.[20] On the other hand, the panel design provides some unique opportunities to look at individual-level dynamics, and our measures of issue preferences and party identification were collected long before our measure of candidate choice, reducing concerns about endogeneity. For the ease of presentation, we present the key results graphically and report the full set of results (including coefficients, standard errors, model fit, and Wald estimates for cross-pressures effect) in appendix 3.

[18] Price and Zaller, "Who Gets the News?" See appendix 1 for question wording and coding information.

[19] The issues include abortion, defense spending, environment, gun control, affirmative action, school prayer, social security, tax cuts, and school vouchers.

[20] We have replicated many of the results on the smaller subset of respondents for whom we have an imperfect political-knowledge measure, the ability to correctly identify the party and incumbency status of the candidate supported in the U.S. Senate race in the state. Including this control did not change any of the key findings.

Results: Campaign Persuasion in 2000 and 2004

As shown in figure 4.2, the effect of cross-pressures on the likelihood of defection is conditional on exposure to the presidential campaign. Whether comparing across state competitiveness, campaign visits, self-reported attentiveness, or political awareness, we consistently find that the substantive impact of policy incongruence is much greater among those most exposed to the 2004 campaign.[21] For instance, highly conflicted partisans are 18 percentage points more likely to defect than congruent partisans in nonbattleground states, but the difference in predicted defection is 34 percentage points in battleground states. Similarly, when exposure is measured with self-reported attention to politics, we find a stronger effect among those most attentive. Among the most attentive partisans, those who are highly cross-pressured have a probability of defecting that is 42 percentage points higher than those who are congruent, compared to just a 9 percent difference in the probability of defection among those less attentive to the campaign. So, we find a similar pattern whether we use an external measure of campaign exposure that captures differences in the opportunity to receive campaign messages or we use an individual-level measure that captures variation in individuals' motivation to receive campaign information. This pattern of findings suggests that campaign information serves to activate policy cross-pressures, leading to partisan defection at the ballot box. When exposed to presidential campaign dialogue, voters give incongruent issues greater weight in their vote decision, whereas those who avoid the swirl of campaign debate are more likely to remain loyal to their affiliated party despite any policy disagreements.

We replicate our results using data from the 2000 presidential election to ensure that the results are not confined to a single election. Using a distinct data set and alternative election year, we find the same pattern of results (figure 4.3). The impact of cross-pressures on partisan defection is much stronger among those respondents most exposed to campaign dialogue. Partisans who disagreed with their party nominee on a campaign issue were more likely to vote for the opposing party candidate when they lived in a battleground state, lived in a state that received a lot of campaign visits, were politically aware, or were politically attentive. In contrast, cross-pressured partisans were more likely

---

[21] Throughout the presentation of results, we report the change in the predicted probability of defecting between a highly conflicted partisan (95th percentile: 67 percent of issues incongruent) and a completely congruent partisan, for the different levels of campaign exposure. All other variables are held at their global means or modes, so that estimates are calculated for a white male, age 45–54, with some college education, who is a weak partisan able to answer two of three factual political questions.

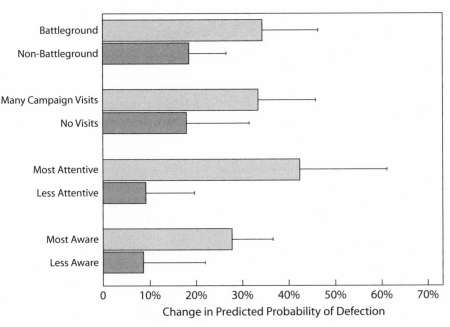

Figure 4.2: Campaign Exposure and Impact of Cross-pressures on Predicted Probability of Defection, 2004

Note: Graph shows the impact of cross-pressures on defection is larger among these highly exposed to the campaign. Reported is change in the predicted probability of defection between highly conflicted and completely congruent partisans, holding constant all other variables in the model. Upper bound of 90 percent confidence interval shown. Data source is the 2004 Blair Center Survey.

to remain loyal to their party's nominee if they were not exposed to intense campaign dialogue.

These findings have a number of important implications for our understanding of the role and influence of presidential campaigns. First, campaigns do not appear to serve to automatically activate partisanship—whether a partisan remains loyal depends on the messages received during the campaign. Likewise, in contrast to much of the rational choice literature that assumes a static relationship between issue preferences and vote choice, the effect of issue preferences on vote choice depends on the campaign environment. In this respect, our findings reinforce the conclusions of earlier research that shows political context helps to shape how voters make up their minds.[22] And the results fit nicely with recent research finding that individuals who are

[22] Kahn and Kenney, *The Spectacle of U.S. Senate Campaigns*; Franklin, "Eschewing Obfuscation?"

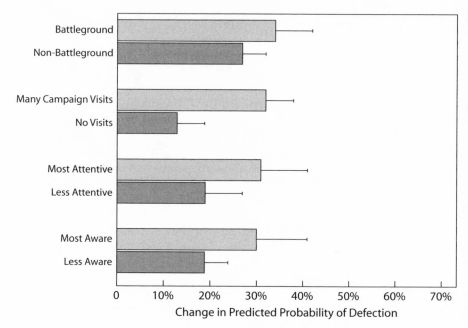

Figure 4.3: Campaign Exposure and Impact of Cross-pressures on Predicted Probability of Defection, 2000

Note: Graph shows that impact of cross-pressures on defection is greater among those highly exposed to the campaign. Reported is change in the predicted probability of defection between highly conflicted and completely congruent partisans, holding constant all other variables in model. Upper bound of 90 percent confidence interval shown. Data source is the 2000 Knowledge Networks Election Study.

ambivalent about their party are less likely to use partisan cues when casting their ballots in competitive races, instead relying on information about issues and ideology they receive from the campaign.[23]

These results also challenge previous expectations that partisans will be resistant to messages that conflict with partisan predispositions. To the contrary, compared to congruent partisans, cross-pressured partisans appeared quite responsive to messages from the opposing party candidate, with the most politically aware and attentive especially likely to defect.[24] John Zaller has argued that the most politically sophisticated voters are "rigid, moralistic, and partisan," and are resistant

---

[23] Basinger and Lavine, "Ambivalence, Information and Electoral Choice."

[24] A similar pattern is observed among minor party supporters—with partisans and policy-motivated voters most inclined to change their vote choice to vote strategically. Hillygus, "The Dynamics of Voter Decision Making Among Minor Party Supporters."

to new information that might conflict with their partisan predispositions.[25] Our analysis offers an important clarification. Partisans are not simply bull-headed ideologues. Rather, cross-pressured partisans are quite responsive to information from the opposition party, while partisans who share the policy views of their candidate are rationally loyal.

Thus, similar to V. O. Key's conclusions many years ago, our findings suggest that changes in vote choice are not simply the by-product of an ill-informed segment of the electorate responding randomly to survey questions. Voters appear to judge the policy positions of the candidates and to support the candidate that most closely matches their preferences on the salient issues of the campaign, even when that candidate is not their party's nominee.

The Impact of the Campaign on 2004 Election Outcomes

These results so far indicate that persuadable partisans are responsive to campaign dialogue, but it is difficult to translate that finding into a prediction about the impact of this campaign effect on election outcomes. Can the campaign convince enough partisans to defect such that it actually influences who wins or loses the election? In order to make a rough estimate of total impact, we classify voters as cross-pressured or not, and reestimate the 2004 model.[26] The results, reported in appendix 3, are remarkably similar to those found with the continuous measure. For instance, we predict that 10 percent of persuadable partisans defected in nonbattleground states, compared to 33 percent in battleground states, suggesting that the campaign increased the defection rate among persuadable partisans in the electorate by more than 22 percentage points.

Given the proportion of persuadable partisans in the electorate and the proportion of the U.S. voting public living in battleground and nonbattleground states, our model predicts that 2.8 million more partisans defected (6.4 percent of voters in these states; 2.4 percent of national electorate) in battleground states than we would have expected had those states seen the same campaign activity of battleground states. It is worth noting that Bush beat Kerry by less than 200,000 voters in those battleground states (and just over 3 million votes nation-

---

[25] Zaller, "Perversities in the Ideal of the Informed Citizenry." Paper presented at conference on "The Transformation of Civic Life," Middle Tennessee State University, Murfreesboro and Nashville, 12–13 November 1999.

[26] A respondent is coded as cross-pressured if she disagrees with her affiliated party on more than one policy issue, agrees with the opposing party on those issues, and considers them personally important.

wide). If we instead consider the hypothetical case in which the entire country received the same campaign efforts as the battleground states, our analysis predicts that an additional 4.4 million voters (3.6 percent of the electorate) would have switched their vote to the opposing party candidate. Clearly, the observed campaign effects have potentially pivotal consequences for the election outcomes—even among partisan identifiers alone.

Another Test: Cross-pressures and Vote Dynamics

For an alternative test of the campaign's ability to shape the decision making of persuadable partisans, we turn to a temporal analysis. We consider changes in the relationship between predispositions over the course of the campaign and then we explore reactions to specific campaign events. If campaigns work by priming incongruent issues, then the relationship between policy incongruence and defection should strengthen over the course of the campaign as voters become more "enlightened" about the candidates' policy priorities. As earlier discussed, voters may not be informed about the policy alternatives offered by the political candidates before the campaign begins, but as the campaign progresses, voters are better able to incorporate information learned about the candidates into their decision-making process.[27] As the issue positions of the candidates are clarified and highlighted over the course of the campaign, we should find that persuadable partisans become increasingly likely to defect. In contrast, if campaigns serve primarily to activate partisanship, we might expect that weak partisan identifiers would come to look increasingly like strong partisans as Election Day approaches.

In figure 4.4, we plot the predicted effect of policy incongruence and partisan strength over the course of the campaign.[28] While the effect of strength of partisanship remains flat over the course of the campaign, the effect of our cross-pressures measure sharply increases. Thus, in contrast to expectations that the campaigns serve primarily to "bring home" partisans, these findings suggest that policy considerations are given greater weight over the course of the campaign, even at the ex-

[27] Gelman and King, "Why Are American Presidential Election Campaign Polls So Variable."

[28] This is the same logic underlying ibid. Reported is the difference between the predicted probability of defecting for a weak and strong partisan or between a highly incongruent (67 percent of issues incongruent) and a completely congruent partisan, holding other variable constant at its global mean.

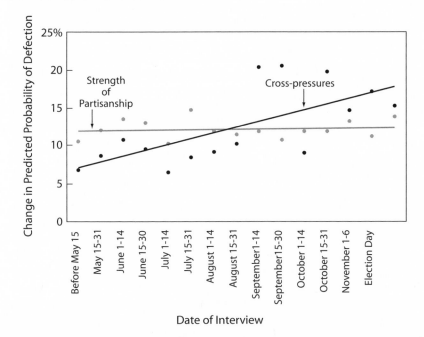

Figure 4.4: Change over Time in Impact of Cross-pressures and Strength of Partisanship on Predicted Probability of Defection, 2000

Note: Graph shows that the effect of cross-pressures increases, while the effect of partisan strength remains flat over the course of the campaign. Also shown is the linear trend in the relationship. Data source is the 2000 Knowledge Networks Election Study.

pense of party loyalties.[29] Interestingly, early in the campaign, strength of partisanship had a larger effect than policy incongruence on the likelihood of defection. Strong partisans were 12 percentage points less likely to support the opposing-party candidate than weak partisans, while highly conflicted partisans were just 6 percentage points less likely than congruent partisans to support the opposition. By the end of the campaign, however, the effect of partisan strength had not changed, but the effect of policy incongruence grew such that highly conflicted partisans became 18 percentage points more likely to defect by Election Day.

When partisan affiliation and issue attitudes reinforce each other, it is difficult to separate which one has the greater influence on decision making. When these two conflict, however, it gives us leverage to identify the conditions under which partisanship is outweighed. These

[29] Lazarsfeld et al., *The People's Choice*.

findings again indicate that campaigns can induce voters to reassess initial expected support for a candidate. These results also suggest that both priming and learning contribute to the persuasive effects of campaigns on vote choice. Party identification provides the starting value or initial expectation of support for one candidate over the other, but that does not prevent partisans from being influenced by the swirl of issue-based dialogue during the campaign.

Campaign Events

As a final evaluation of the temporal dynamics of campaign effects, we turn to an analysis of voter reactions to specific campaign events. Conventions and debates are the most high-profile and high-information events of the presidential campaign, so we examine whether reactions to these events follow our hypothesized patterns. Before turning to the results, we briefly provide background on nominating conventions and debates.

The conventions, more than any other event during the campaign, are about providing information to the voters. Except for during the final week of the campaign, the spike in newspaper coverage of the candidates is higher during the conventions than at any other point in the campaign.[30] Conventions provide the opportunity for a candidate to dominate the news for several days and, to a great extent, control the flow of information about their policy priorities. Though party conventions are no longer important for nominating the party candidates, they do provide an opportunity for each candidate to dominate the flow of information, and, as such, they tend to produce a "bump" in public support for the candidate.[31] Scholars have pointed to the rally function of presidential conventions, suggesting that they are especially likely to activate partisans.[32] While we certainly agree that conventions have the potential to rally the rank-and-file, our expectation is that the individuals most likely to use the information they receive about the candidates and parties following the nominating conventions will be political Independents and cross-pressured partisans. Voters who disagree with their party will be reminded of that fact if the nominee focuses on incongruent issues in these public appearances. For instance, Ron Reagan's impassioned speech in support of stem cell

[30] Holbrook, *Do Campaigns Matter?*

[31] Shaw, "A Study of Presidential Campaign Event Effects from 1952 to 1992"; Holbrook, *Do Campaigns Matter?*

[32] For example, Campbell et al., "The Convention Bump."

research at the 2004 Democratic National Convention was targeted to incongruent Republicans, but it also may have increased the salience of the issue for Democrats who disagreed with Kerry's support of stem cell research.

We expect a similar pattern following the presidential debates, although we expect a somewhat smaller effect since these events occur much later in the campaign. Presidential debates draw a larger audience than any other campaign event, and they allow the audience to assess and compare the issue positions and personal qualities of the candidates without the media gatekeepers, but the principle of diminishing returns is applicable—not only because information provided by the debates is less likely to be new information but also because as people make up their minds, it is more difficult to get them to change.[33]

We measure the effect of conventions and debates on voter decision making by comparing an individual's candidate preference before and just after each of these events, allowing us to characterize individual-level movements in vote intention.[34] In other words, we treat the conventions and debates as intervening events. Because we do not have a controlled experiment, we cannot rule out the possibility that the observed movements in vote preferences are caused by something other than the events themselves. For instance, the respondents may have been exposed to other stimuli such as television advertising, political discussions, or news coverage between interviews. These other sources of information may have caused voters to change their vote choice during this same time period. Yet, many of these alternate sources of information are likely to reflect the events themselves (e.g., media coverage of events). Moreover, individual survey questions gauging reactions to the conventions and debates also show evidence of responsiveness to the events. Following the Republican Convention, 46 percent of interviewed respondents reported that the convention had an effect on their vote. In response to the individual debates, 13 to 15 percent gave an affirmative response to the question, "Has anything you have learned from, or about, the debates made you change your mind about whom to vote for?" Finally, transitions in vote choice are much higher during

[33] Holbrook, *Do Campaigns Matter?*, 63.

[34] For each event, we compare the last interview prior to the event and the first interview following the event (no more than ten days after). This cutoff date is consistent with the campaign effects research, which has found in the aggregate that campaign effects may be strongest three to ten days after an event. Shaw, "A Study of Presidential Campaign Event Effects from 1952–1992."

these event periods than at other points during the campaign, suggesting that changes in attitudes may be attributable to the events.[35]

The pattern of candidate choice before the events offers some initial support for our expectations. Before the conventions, just 12 percent of congruent partisans were still undecided, compared to 22 percent of cross-pressured partisans and 37 percent of Independents. Before the debates, just 8 percent of congruent partisans are undecided, compared to 10 percent of cross-pressured partisans and 23 percent of Independents. But our interest is in transitions in vote choice following these events. The full set of results from the models predicting vote transitions and defection is reported in appendix 3, with the key findings reported in figures 4.5 and 4.6. Reported in figure 4.5 is the predicted probability that congruent partisans, Independents, and highly cross-pressured partisans would change their vote choice following the campaign events. As expected, our model predicts that voters are less likely to change their vote after the debates than after the conventions, but the general patterns are the same for both events. Congruent partisans are not very likely to change their vote choice, while highly cross-pressured partisans and Independents are much more likely to change their vote. For the partisans alone, we predict the probability of defection in response to the events, reported in figure 4.6. Once again, we find that persuadable partisans are more likely than congruent partisans to change their support to the opposing-party candidate following these events.

These findings suggest that the patterns identified in the temporal and final vote dynamics are also observed in reactions to high-profile events. To be sure, an open-seat election such as the 2000 campaign might have greater levels of vote instability during the campaign than we would expect to find if an incumbent were in the race. Nevertheless, the nominating conventions and presidential debates have previously been identified as the campaign events most clearly linked to voter learning. The large number of individuals who transition from being undecided to being able to make a candidate selection following these events offers additional evidence of such learning effects. But our analysis also shows that persuadable partisans were receptive to messages from the opposition, in contrast to the conventional wisdom that Democrats and Republicans view the debates through a purely parti-

[35] See Hillygus and Jackman, "Voter Decision Making in Election 2000." To ensure that the changes in vote choice were not simply picking up sophistication levels, we also replicated the analysis among only the most politically attentive respondents with almost identical results.

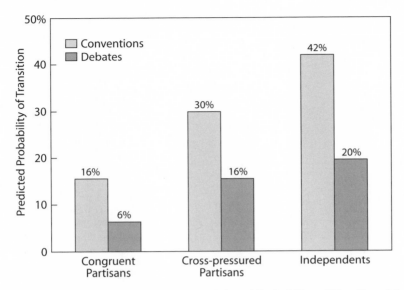

Figure 4.5: Effect of Cross-pressures on Predicted Probability of Vote Transition following Campaign Events
Note: Figure shows that cross-pressured partisans and Independents were more likely than congruent partisans to change their vote choice following the campaign events (compared to vote choice before the event), holding constant all other variables in the model. Data source is the 2000 Knowledge Networks Election Study.

san lens. These events were able to activate issue preferences at the expense of partisan activation. Thus, the results again suggest that the individuals responding to campaign information are those who are imperfectly matched to their party's nominee.

Possible Alternative Explanations

Although our set of survey results—across different surveys and different measures of the campaign—provides consistent evidence that the persuadable voters in the electorate include cross-pressured partisans who use campaign information as part of a deliberative process of decision making, there are potential alternative explanations for our observed findings that must be considered. As Gabriel Lenz most clearly articulates, a prominent alternative hypothesis is that "exposure to [campaign] messages can strengthen issue-vote consistency by causing individuals to change their opinions on the issue to be more

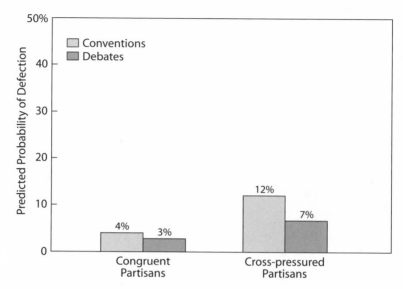

Figure 4.6: Effect of Cross-pressures on Predicted Probability of Defection following Campaign Events
Note: Figure shows that highly cross-pressured partisans were more likely than congruent partisans to change their vote choice following the campaign events (compared to their vote choice before the event), holding constant all other variables in model. Data source is the 2000 Knowledge Networks Election Study.

consistent with their preferred candidate's position."[36] In other words, the stronger relationship between vote choice and policy preferences might be attributed to voters changing their policy positions to match those taken by their preferred candidate, rather than the other way around. Certainly, scholars have offered compelling evidence of such empirical effects among some voters during a campaign, especially among the least politically sophisticated and on new or emerging policy issues.[37] The question is whether we have identified an additional pattern of movement or our results are an artifact of this process.

On the face of it, it seems less likely that this alternative explanation accounts for our findings. This perspective typically assumes that there are some voters who select their candidate on the basis of party attach-

[36] Lenz, "Learning, Not Priming"; Zaller, *The Nature and Origins of Mass Opinion.*
[37] See, for instance, Brody and Page, "Comment: The Assessment of Policy Voting"; Markus and Converse, "A Dynamic Simultaneous Equation Model of Electoral Choice"; Page and Jones, "Reciprocal Effects of Policy Preferences, Party Loyalties and the Vote"; Layman and Carsey, "Changing Sides or Changing Minds?"

ments, and then will adopt the policy preferences of that candidate. But we are explicitly looking at the effect of policy disagreements with partisanship, so party clearly is not driving the relationship. We have also looked only at issues on which the candidates have taken clear stands and that voters indicate are personally important to them. It seems less likely that individuals are changing their opinions on divisive issues like abortion, affirmative action, and so on, compared to less controversial issues or issues considered less important.

In the 2000 survey data, policy preferences and party identification were measured early in the campaign, often before voters had selected a candidate. As a robustness check, we replicated our 2000 model for only those respondents who were undecided early in the campaign (results reported in appendix 3). For this subset of the sample, it is especially difficult to believe that their support for a candidate is shaping issue preferences. Consistent with our previous findings, the analysis finds that the substantive impact of cross-pressures is much larger among those most exposed to the campaign. The first difference, or change in the predicted probability of defecting between highly incongruent partisans and completely congruent partisans, is 25 percentage points in nonbattleground states but 56 percentage points in battleground states. As a robustness check in the 2004 cross-sectional analysis, we replicate our analysis for the most politically aware subset of voters on the premise that they should be more likely to hold durable issue positions. We again find that the effects of cross-pressures are higher in battleground states than in nonbattleground states.[38] Finally, we conducted a survey experiment to test for our expected effects within a controlled context, to which we now turn.

Final Robustness Check: A Survey Experiment

As a final test of our hypothesis we conducted a survey experiment, which allows us to precisely evaluate the effects of priming specific policy conflicts. The benefit of an experiment is that we are able to control the specific information voters receive, so we do not have to assume that respondents were exposed to information about an incongruent issue. In the experiment, we randomly assigned survey participants to one of three "campaign" conditions: (1) control group, (2) stem cell research treatment, or (3) social security reform treatment.

[38] In nonbattleground states, the highly incongruent are 10.2 percentage points more likely to defect than the congruent, while the difference is 17.0 percentage points in battleground states.

Respondents assigned to the control group were provided basic information about two potential presidential candidates, a Democratic and a Republican senator, with similar backgrounds, characteristics, and experiences.[39] Respondents assigned to the stem cell treatment condition received the candidate information as well as a vignette that highlighted the candidates' contrasting positions on stem cell research and included a political analyst's prediction that stem cell research would be an important issue in the upcoming campaign. Consistent with the stated positions of the two senators, the Democratic candidate favored federal funding of stem cell research and the Republican candidate opposed it. A parallel treatment was given on the issue of social security reform for the third set of randomly assigned respondents. To reiterate our key hypothesis, we expected that persuadable partisans would be more likely to defect to the opposition candidate when they received campaign information about their incongruent issue. In contrast, congruent partisans would behave similarly irrespective of the particular campaign information received.

In figure 4.7 we present the percentage of defecting incongruent and congruent partisans across the different conditions.[40] First, as expected, cross-pressured partisans were always more likely than congruent partisans to indicate that they would vote for the opposing party candidate.[41] In the control group, 28 percent of respondents conflicted on

[39] See appendix 1 for vignette and question wording. The two hypothetical candidates were Democrat Tim Johnson and Republican Larry Craig. These two senators were selected because they were similar across a set of demographic characteristics (notably both were from the Midwest), they were relatively low-profile senators (at the time of survey) so respondents were unlikely to hold preexisting opinions, and they held positions on stem cell research and social security reform that were congruent with their national party. Senator Johnson was cast into the national spotlight in December 2006 when he had a brain hemorrhage, raising questions about the balance of power in the U.S. Senate if he were unable to serve his term. Larry Craig became a nationally recognized figure following a scandal in 2007. The survey was completed before these events and, incidentally, before any candidates but Tom Vilsack had formally announced their candidacies.

[40] The sample contained fewer partisans cross-pressured on social security or stem cell research than have been found by other surveys (10 percent and 13.4 percent, respectively, compared to 26 percent and 22 percent in the 2004 Blair Survey). With the random assignment across three different conditions, we were left with eighty-four persuadable partisans receiving a campaign treatment on their incongruent issue and eighty-seven in the control group.

[41] Roughly one-third of respondents indicated that they would not vote if these two candidates were running for president. Comparing across groups, we find that abstention was 9 percentage points higher among cross-pressured partisans in the treatment group compared to the control group, offering suggestive evidence that policy incongruence might also have an influence on turnout.

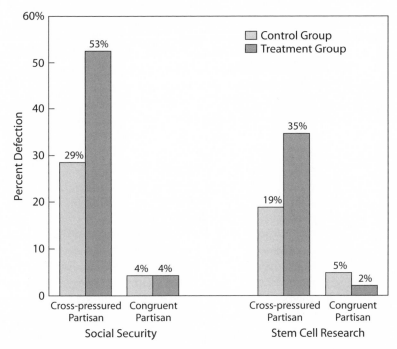

Figure 4.7: Cross-pressured Partisans More Persuadable in Survey Experiment
Note: Graph shows that cross-pressured partisans were more likely to defect when exposed to a campaign treatment about their incongruent issue. The differences in defection rate are statistically significant at $p < .05$ for the cross-pressured partisans. Data source is the 2006 Cooperative Congressional Election Study.

social security and 19 percent of respondents conflicted on stem cell research said they would vote for the candidate from the opposing political party—compared to approximately 4 percent of respondents who were consistent on these issues and also assigned to the control group.[42] More notably, when cross-pressured partisans were exposed to campaign information about their incongruent issue and told the

---

[42] At the suggestion of Gabe Lenz, we also looked at the subset of respondents who had the same issue position as measured in an earlier wave of the CCES study. The question wordings are slightly different, but we find similar results if we restrict our analysis to those with stable attitudes: 49 percent of those who were cross-pressured on social security or stem cell research and received the campaign treatment on the cross-pressured issue indicated that they would defect, compared to 22 percent of those in the control group. Among the consistently congruent partisans, fewer than 5 percent indicated they would defect in both the control or treatment conditions.

issue would be important in the campaign, they were significantly more likely to defect. Nearly 53 percent of those cross-pressured on social security and nearly 35 percent of respondents incongruent on stem cell research indicated that they would vote for the opposition-party candidate when exposed to a campaign message about these issues.[43] In contrast, among partisans embracing consistent issue positions, we find a high level of party voting irrespective of the particular experimental condition. Campaign information might reinforce party loyalties for these congruent partisans—which might account for the slight drop in defections among congruent partisans in the treatment groups—but given their low baseline level of defections, there is little room for much movement in the vote decision among this group.

The higher percentage of defections among cross-pressured partisans who received information about their incongruent issue again suggests that campaign information can shape the decision making of these voters.[44] To be sure, we must be careful about generalizing these results to the real-world campaign context. Our results do not account, for instance, for the possibility that the experimental effect might decay over time.[45] More importantly, in order to narrowly identify the treatment effect, we have grossly oversimplified the information environment and the decision-making process. Contemporary presidential campaigns do not emphasize just a single issue; rather, campaign dialogue covers a wide range of different issues. So, voters undoubtedly encounter some campaign messages that reinforce attachments to the party candidate and others that exacerbate tensions with partisan loyalties. Nonetheless, the experimental results offer compelling evidence of the potential for large campaign effects when individuals are exposed to and think about an issue about which they disagree with their party's nominee.

[43] We find some evidence of a "spillover" effect in which the campaign treatment activates issue policy incongruence *not* mentioned by the treatment, perhaps by encouraging respondents to give greater thought to their vote decisions. Since the candidates held positions consistent with the national party positions, it was not unreasonable for respondents to assume that they might disagree with candidate on *other* issues. Among those in the treatment conditions who disagreed with their party on a different issue, the defection rate was 29 percent, still significantly lower than the average 43 percent defection rate among those who were cross-pressured on the issue mentioned in the campaign treatment.

[44] Although other factors could be ignored because of random assignment (analysis shows randomization was successful), we find similar results in a logit model of defection that also controls for gender, race/ethnicity, age, income, political sophistication, strength of partisanship, and ideological extremity.

[45] Gaines et al., "The Logic of the Survey Experiment Reexamined."

Conclusions

The findings presented here have implications for several areas of political science, including campaign effects, issue voting, and political persuasion. At the most general level, our analysis demonstrates substantial campaign effects among at least a subset of the populace—cross-pressured partisans. Beyond showing that "campaigns matter," these results highlight the fact that campaigns do not have a single effect on all voters. Responsiveness to campaign information depends on the strength and consistency of partisan and policy predispositions. In contrast to research suggesting that campaigns work to predictably bring home wayward partisans, our findings indicate that campaigns serve to bring vote decisions in line with policy preferences, even when it comes at the expense of partisan loyalties. To be sure, voters are still much more likely to vote for their party's nominee than against. Party identification remains the single most important predictor of voting behavior. But our findings suggest that partisans are willing to defect if the campaign is able to increase the salience of an issue on which they disagree with their affiliated party.

Research using in-depth interviews and focus groups has reached a similar conclusion about voter reactions to presidential campaigns:

> When people talk about the candidates, both those they favor and those they oppose, they talk about them as persons with a mixture of positive and negative qualities, and they talk about the candidates in the here and now, not in terms of their past accomplishments or future possibilities. . . . Citizens during a campaign apparently feel comfortable considering new information about their candidates, including negative aspects of the candidates they prefer and positive news about the candidates they do not. Certainly, they do not approach the campaign with blank slates; yet it is impressive how willing people are to consider (if often only to rebut and reject) dissonant information, particularly at early stages of the campaign.[46]

Early campaign research, motivated by anxieties about the apparent influence of propaganda in World War II, had been concerned that presidential campaigns might induce voters to act against their preferences. This early research largely concluded that such concerns were unfounded because campaigns primarily served to predictably "bring home" partisans. Our analysis shows that campaigns do have a direct persuasive effect, able to induce partisans to vote against their partisan loyalties. Notably, however, campaigns are not manipulating prefer-

---

[46] Marion et al., *Crosstalk: Citizens, Candidates, and the Media in a Presidential Campaign*, 229.

ences; campaigns are able to persuade voters because of the *complexity* of voter preferences. Campaigns help voters sort through a diversity of predispositions, shaping which preferences voters bring to bear in selecting a preferred candidate. In the next chapter, we turn to an additional test of campaign persuasion that looks across election years, and we focus attention on the implications of our findings about persuadable voters for the campaign strategies of the candidates.

Five

The Republican Southern Strategy:
A Case Study of the Reciprocal Campaign

DURING THE SECOND televised debate in the 1960 presidential election, moderator Alvin Spivlak asked Republican presidential nominee Richard Nixon, "Mr. Vice President, you have accused Senator Kennedy of avoiding the civil rights issue when he has been in the South, and he has accused you of the same thing. With both North and South listening and watching, would you sum up your intentions in the field of civil rights if you become president." Nixon responded with a lengthy defense of civil rights, including his support of government action to ensure fair treatment in employment and education and offering his support for lunch-counter sit-ins:

> I have talked to Negro mothers, I've heard them explain—try to explain—how they tell their children how they can go into a store and buy a loaf of bread but then can't go into that store and sit at the counter and get a Coca Cola. This is wrong and we have to do something about it. . . . Why do I talk every time I'm in the South on civil rights? Not because I'm preaching to the people of the South because this isn't just a Southern problem. It's a Northern problem and a Western problem. It's a problem for all of us.[1]

Nixon's pro–civil rights response is especially notable because he is more frequently remembered for promising to slow the pace of civil rights as part of the Republican "southern strategy" to recruit southern white Democrats to the Republican Party. In a 1968 televised interview in the South, for instance, Nixon argued that federal efforts to enforce school desegregation "are going too far. . . . and in many cases . . . should be rescinded."[2] Did Nixon change his rhetoric on racial issues as a deliberate campaign strategy aimed at driving a wedge in the traditional Democratic coalition? Moreover, did this change in campaign rhetoric influence voter decision making?

In this chapter, we examine the Republican southern strategy as a case study of our expectations about the interaction of candidates, vot-

---

[1] The full text of debate, nomination speeches, and party platforms cited in this chapter are available online through the American Presidency Project (www.presidency .ucsb.edu).

[2] Ambrose, *Nixon: The Triumph of a Politician*, 187.

ers, and campaign dynamics. The Republican use of racial issues to appeal to conservative white Democrats is perhaps the most widely recognized example of a wedge campaign tactic, thus making it a natural case for closer examination of our theoretical arguments. With qualitative analysis of candidate strategy, we are able to explore the link between the preferences of swing voters and the candidates' decision to use wedge issues. In addition, a quantitative analysis of voter behavior allows us to evaluate the role of the campaign in shaping when and if persuadable partisans were willing to defect to the opposing candidate at the ballot box.

This chapter also offers a careful look at the use of wedge issues prior to the contemporary hyperinformation environment examined in the next chapter. Compared to the information available to campaign strategists today, candidates in the 1960s and 1970s largely had to infer the policy preferences of voters based on region, race, or other broad characteristics, so that strategic policy decisions were made on this rather imprecise information. Likewise, candidates' campaign messages were primarily communicated through broadcast television or stump speeches, so that message targeting was much less precise than we see today. And stump speeches were often covered by the national press, making it more difficult to communicate unique messages to different audiences and inevitably making wedge issues part of the national campaign dialogue. Thus, given the blunt nature of campaign targeting during this era, candidates faced clear electoral tradeoffs in staking a particular position on a divisive policy, and such tradeoffs were often explicitly discussed as part of the candidates' strategic planning during the campaign.

A great deal has been written about the Republican southern strategy and we make no attempt to provide a complete chronology here.[3] We begin this chapter with a brief historical examination of the origins of and motivations behind the southern strategy, but then focus our attention on empirically evaluating how changes in GOP campaign rhetoric influenced white Democratic voters, and particularly white Democrats who embraced issue positions at odds with their national party. Thus, we analyze both the extent to which Republican campaign strategies were based on reaching cross-pressured Democratic voters and the effect of emphasizing wedge issues on their voting behavior.

By most accounts, the Republican southern strategy was successful. After losing nearly all of the southern states to the Democrats in 1960,

---

[3] For a more complete account of the Republican southern strategy, see Black and Black, *The Rise of the Southern Republicans*; Edsall and Edsall, *Chain Reaction*; Aistrup, *The Southern Strategy Revisited*.

Richard Nixon returned to carry five of eleven southern states in 1968 and won each and every Confederate state in his lopsided 1972 presidential victory. The Republicans' improved showing across the South is often taken as evidence that the southern strategy was effective at winning over southern Democrats. For many observers, the twelve years between Nixon's loss in 1960 and his landslide victory in 1972 represented the beginning and end of the transformation of the once solidly Democratic South to the current GOP stronghold.[4] Much of the rich literature on southern politics focuses on the partisan realignment of the South during this time period, as the conservative South switched allegiances from the Democratic to the Republican Party.[5] But even as the South gradually realigned partisan loyalties, Republican candidates still encountered many yellow-dog Democrats (voters who would rather vote for an old yellow dog than a Republican). And many of these otherwise strong Democratic supporters held positions on issues of race that were inconsistent with the policy positions of the Democratic Party. Our analysis leverages changes in campaign content across election years to examine how these inconsistencies between party affiliation and issue attitudes interacted with the campaign environment to shape voter decision making.

We also consider changes in candidate strategy over time. One of the perverse realities of American politics is that once a group's vote becomes predictable, candidates have less incentive to offer policy rewards to win them over.[6] The policy interests of groups fully aligned with one party are more likely to be taken for granted as candidates focus attention on the persuadable voters. Once racially conservative Democrats realigned to the Republican Party, the Republicans shifted their focus to a new group of potential swing voters: socially conservative Democrats.[7] Thus, we also trace this transition in the changing rhetoric of the Republican presidential campaigns as well as in the behavior of the electorate.

At the outset, we want to recognize some of the limitations of our analysis. While our interest is in tracing the relative effect of racial and cultural issues over time, racial issues were not the only, or even the most important, issue in the presidential elections covered by our anal-

---

[4] Carmines and Stimson, *Issue Evolution.*

[5] There is debate about how much of the aggregate realignment was attributable to individual-level party switching versus generational differences among new partisan identifiers. For a review, see Green et al., *Partisan Hearts and Minds.*

[6] An outcome Frymer and Skrentny call being "electorally captured." See Frymer and Skrentny, "Coalition-building and the Politics of Electoral Capture during the Nixon Administration."

[7] Black and Black, *The Rise of Southern Republicans.*

ysis. General economic- and foreign-policy issues, in particular, are almost always the centerpiece of presidential campaigns. By focusing on
the patterns and trends over time, we necessarily lose a more complete
picture of each individual presidential contest. Also, because our analysis is focused on the attitudes and behaviors of white Democrats, we
give only cursory attention to the vote decisions of Republicans and
Independents (the results for these groups are mentioned briefly in
footnotes). Our analysis also does not touch on the rich public opinion
literature examining the nuances of racial attitudes. For instance, we
measure the extent to which white Democrats are cross-pressured on
racial policies, but do not consider whether those policy conflicts are
rooted in antiblack prejudices, group identities, or conservative ideologies.[8] In addition, when we examine the ability of presidential campaigns to prime racial cross-pressures, we do not consider the possible
difference in the effects of implicit and explicit racial campaign messages.[9] During this time period, the line between implicit and explicit
messages is especially blurry. While many scholars argue that campaign communications about crime and welfare contain implicit racial
messages, we focus here on explicitly racial policies, such as segregation, busing, affirmative action, and the like.

Finally, our analysis in this chapter is not meant to suggest that
Republicans alone use wedge issues. Democrats have a long history
of emphasizing issues for strategic reasons as well. In our view, all
candidates are rational actors seeking electoral victory, so the policy
promises of candidates of both parties are shaped by the preferences
of voters considered pivotal in building a winning electoral coalition. Indeed, a brief historical look challenges any notion that Democrats took a pro–civil rights position by dint of moral superiority;
rather, their position taking on civil rights is also traceable to electoral considerations.

Democrats Set the Stage on Civil Rights

After the end of Reconstruction, southern white hostility toward the
Republican Party translated into a cohesive and consistent Democratic
voting pattern that continued for nearly a century. In 1928 Herbert
Hoover was the first Republican presidential candidate to make inroads in the South, winning Florida, Texas, North Carolina, Virginia,

---

[8] There is a long-standing debate about explanations for intergroup conflict and attitudes. Classic works include Allport, *The Nature of Prejudice*; Kinder and Sanders, *Divided
by Color*; Sniderman and Piazza, *The Scar of Race*; Sears et al., *Racialized Politics*.

[9] See Mendelberg, *The Race Card*.

and Tennessee by campaigning on prohibition and anti-Catholic senti-ment.[10] Looking to expand the Republican presence in the South, Hoo-ver pushed to make a "lily-white" GOP by replacing black patronage hires with white Protestants, but these expansion efforts were derailed by the Great Depression.[11] The Great Depression solidified the Demo-cratic stronghold among southern whites, but it also brought northern enfranchised African Americans into Roosevelt's New Deal coalition, breaking their long-standing loyalty to the "Party of Lincoln." Before the 1936 election, Pittsburgh publisher Robert Vann advised fellow black voters, "My friends, go turn Lincoln's picture to the wall. That debt has been paid in full."[12]

Yet, as the 1948 election approached, it was unclear if Truman could hold together this uneasy Democratic coalition. Truman's approval rat-ings were at an all-time low and Republicans had captured control of both houses of Congress in the midterm election. As Truman devel-oped his campaign strategy, his advisors concluded that black voters could prove pivotal in the election. One of Truman's advisors, special counsel Clark Clifford, argued forcefully that the African American vote would be crucial to the ultimate success of the Truman campaign:

A theory of many professional politicians is that the northern Negro voter today holds the balance of power in Presidential elections for the simple ar-ithmetical reason that the Negroes not only vote in a bloc but are geographi-cally concentrated in the pivotal, large and closely contested electoral states such as New York, Illinois, Pennsylvania, Ohio and Michigan. . . . [The Negro] is just about convinced today that he can better his present economic lot by swinging his vote in a solid bloc to the Republicans. . . . To counteract this trend, the Democratic Party can point only to the obvious—that the re-ally great improvement in the economic lot of the Negro of the North has come in the last sixteen years only because of the sympathy and policies of a Democratic Administration. The trouble is that this has worn a bit thin with the passage of the years. . . . Unless there are new and real efforts . . . the Negro bloc, which, certainly in Illinois and probably in New York and Ohio, does hold the balance of power, will go Republican.[13]

[10] Protestant churches became very involved in the presidential campaign, pro-claiming that "The plain duty of every churchman is to work and pray and vote for the election of Herbert Hoover." "For Christ and Church," *Time Magazine*, 1 October 1928.

[11] Hoover transferred patronage away from blacks and toward white Protestant busi-nessmen because he believed that the GOP could not make inroads with the existing "Negro's domination of Southern Republican politics." See "G.O.P., South," *Time Maga-zine*, 18 February 1929.

[12] *Pittsburgh Courier*, 17 September 1932, I1.

[13] Memo, dated 19 November 1947, from Clark M. Clifford, Special Counsel to Presi-dent Harry S. Truman, to President Harry S. Truman. Truman Presidential Library.

The campaign strategy memo went on to predict that Republicans would use legislation to appeal to the black swing voters,

> In all probability, Republican strategy at the next session will be to offer a [Fair Employment Practices Commission], an anti-poll tax bill, and an anti-lynching bill. This will be accompanied by a flourish of oratory devoted to the Civil Rights of various groups of our citizens. The Administration would make a grave error if we permitted the Republicans to get away with this. It would appear to be sound strategy to have the President go as far as he feels he must possibly go in recommending measures to protect the rights of minority groups. This course of action would obviously cause difficulty with our Southern friends but that is the lesser of two evils.[14]

It seems that a clear strategic calculation was made on the basis of electoral interests to stake a pro–civil rights stance. Truman's advisors assumed that southern whites would remain loyal to the Democratic Party even if their presidential candidate appealed to black voters. The strategy memo bluntly declared, "As always, the South can be considered safely Democratic. And in formulating national policy, it can be safely ignored."

President Truman appeared to follow the strategy laid out by his advisor. On February 2, 1948, Truman sent a message to Congress asking for civil rights legislation and outlined a specific list of policy objectives. On July 26 he issued two executive orders. One instituted fair employment practices in the civilian agencies of the federal government; the other provided for "equality of treatment and opportunity in the armed forces without regard to race, color, religion, or national origin."

In hindsight, it was a political miscalculation to take the South for granted. In protest of the pro–civil rights agenda, Strom Thurmond walked out of the 1948 Democratic convention and ran for the presidency as a segregationist. Truman narrowly won the White House, but he laid bare the deep fractures in the Democratic Party coalition over the issue of civil rights. Many years later, presidential advisor Clark Clifford acknowledged this miscalculation, "We did not realize how

[14] Memo, dated 19 November 1947, from Clark M. Clifford, Special Counsel to President Harry S. Truman, to President Harry S. Truman. Truman Presidential Library. (Memo was initially drafted by James Rowe Jr. on 18 September 1947, but would not receive presidential attention until relayed to the president through Clifford, see pages 12–13, 39–40). The Fair Employment Practices Commission was created by President Roosevelt and was designed to help African Americans obtain jobs. For a detailed discussion of African Americans as a homogeneous voting bloc see Dawson, *Behind the Mule*; or Tate, *From Protest to Politics*.

quickly Southern whites would abandon the President if he supported equal civil rights for all Americans."[15]

Truman's campaign strategy for the 1948 presidential election highlights the importance of pivotal voters in shaping the policy agenda of presidential candidates. His decision also placed the national Democratic Party squarely in the pro–civil rights camp. In making the first move on this divisive issue, Democrats placed the ball in the Republicans' court. They now had the choice either to exacerbate the fracture in the Democratic Party by taking the polar position of the Democrats, or to neutralize the issue by taking the same position.

Republican Position Taking on Civil Rights

As the minority party, Republicans had little choice but to appeal to traditional Democratic voters if they wanted to capture the White House. Since the New Deal, the majority of the American public has affiliated with the Democratic Party. Measures of party identification from the NES cumulative file finds as few as 29 percent of the public identified themselves as Republicans during the mid-twentieth century. The Eisenhower victories of the 1950s, however, demonstrated that it was possible for a Republican candidate to pull voters away from the New Deal coalition, and Republican Party leaders openly debated how they could best attract voters from the Democratic camp. During the late 1950s and early 1960s, northeastern Republicans, led by Nelson Rockefeller, pushed for a "city strategy" that included appealing to northern blacks and the growing numbers of registered black voters in the South. Opposing this strategy were western Republicans who argued that gains could be made among white southern Democrats.[16]

Throughout the 1950s, candidates from both parties battled for the black vote. Before the 1956 election, Democrat Hubert Humphrey warned, "Unless we do something constructive and take a firm forward step [on civil rights] our party is going to suffer at the ballot boxes. . . . Our Republican friends know they are not going to get votes in the South, so they're pushing hard for [black] voters in the North."[17] Eisenhower attracted 39 percent of the black vote in 1956, and there were projections that Republicans could improve on that share in the 1960 election. It was, after all, a Republican Supreme Court that struck

---

[15] Clifford, *Counsel to the President.*

[16] See, for instance, Frymer, *Uneasy Alliances.*

[17] Quoted in Klinker, *The Losing Parties,* 34.

down the separate-but-equal doctrine and a Republican president who mobilized federal troops against a Democratic governor in Little Rock. Republicans had also routinely cosponsored pro–civil rights legislation in Congress.

Thus, in the run-up to the 1960 presidential election, two things were clear. First, there was a divisive racial cleavage between northern and southern Democrats that was ripe for exploiting. Second, the number and political importance of enfranchised blacks had increased. As Journalist Theodore White explained, "Since the northward migration of the Negro from the south, the Negro vote, in any close election, has become critical in carrying six of the eight most populous states of the union. To ignore the Negro vote and Negro insistence on civil rights must either be an act of absolute folly—or one of absolute calculation."[18]

Some scholars have argued that Republicans' decision to take a conservative position on civil rights in the 1960s was driven not by electoral concerns, but rather, by an ideological struggle between conservative and liberal party leaders.[19] After all, there had long been clashes between northeastern liberal Republicans like Nelson Rockefeller and western conservative Republicans like Barry Goldwater across a number of policy domains. Since Richard Nixon was the Republican nominee in 1960, 1968, and 1972, we have the opportunity to look for changes in campaign strategy and rhetoric used by the same individual, reducing the likelihood that any changes were due to pure ideological considerations. We thus compare the party platforms, campaign speeches, and campaign strategy memos across these election years to determine if Nixon's position taking on racial issues was grounded in electoral or ideological considerations.

Nixon's Strategy in the 1960 Election

With the Democratic Party wedded to a pro–civil rights position, the question facing Richard Nixon was whether his campaign strategy would appeal to southern whites or northern blacks. In *The Making of the President 1960*, Theodore White concludes that "it lay in Nixon's power to reorient the Republican Party toward an axis of Northern-Southern conservatives. His alone was the choice. . . . Nixon made his choice, I believe, more out of conscience than out of strategy."[20] Although it is of course difficult to directly assess the motivations behind

[18] White, *The Making of the President 1960*, 203.
[19] Rea, *The Decline and Fall of the Liberal Republicans*, 198.
[20] White, *The Making of the President 1960*, 204.

a candidate's decision making on policy issues, there were also indications that Nixon believed the civil rights actions of the late 1950s would lead to higher levels of black enfranchisement that would benefit the Republican Party.[21] In a letter to Richard Nixon, Martin Luther King Jr. estimated that the Civil Rights Act of 1957 would create 2 million new black voters who would vote Republican if the GOP continued to support civil rights.[22] The 1960 Republican Party platform made reference to this expected growth in black voters in the South, stating, "The new law will soon make it possible for thousands and thousands of Negroes previously disenfranchised to vote." Incidentally, the 1960 election also corresponded to the decennial population census, which had documented a tremendous growth in the number of northern blacks.

Nixon's pro–civil rights rhetoric was particularly pronounced early in the campaign. During the 1960 Republican National Convention, it was Nixon who personally pushed hard to court northern blacks by being indistinguishable from the Democratic Party on civil rights policies. According to Theodore White's firsthand account,

> The original draft plank prepared by the platform committee was a moderate one: it avoided any outright declaration of support for Negro sit-in strikes and Southern lunch counters and omitted any promise of federal intervention to secure Negroes full job equality—both of which the Democrats, at Los Angeles had promised. . . . On Monday, July 25th, it is almost certain, it lay in Nixon's power to reorient the Republican Party toward an axis of Northern-Southern conservatives. Nixon insisted that the platform committee substitute for the moderate position on civil rights (which probably would have won him the election) the advanced Rockefeller position on civil rights.[23]

In his nomination acceptance speech, Nixon went further, proclaiming that "for those millions of Americans who are still denied equality of rights and opportunity, I say there shall be the greatest progress in human rights since the days of Lincoln, 100 years ago." As he campaigned in the South, Nixon began his stump speeches with a defense of his civil rights position, "I have my convictions, you have yours, but together, we must move forward to solve it. . . . We must not continue

[21] Stanley and Niemi, *Vital Statistics on American Politics*, 98. Black voters overwhelmingly supported the Republican Party until becoming part of the New Deal coalition following the Great Depression.

[22] Mayer, *Running on Race*, 16. In 1960, Martin Luther King Jr. did not endorse either candidate for president.

[23] White, *The Making of the President 1960*, 204.

to have a situation exist where Mr. Khrushchev . . . is able to point the finger at us and say that we are denying rights to our people."[24]

Nixon had credibility on civil rights issues—he was a member of the NAACP and as vice-president had been the administration spokesperson on civil rights.[25] One journalist commented that Nixon was the "spearhead of the Republican efforts to capture a larger share of the Negro vote in 1958 and 1960."[26] Indeed, Nixon's pro–civil rights background was not lost on the Kennedy campaign, which in its *Counterattack Sourcebook*, a confidential campaign strategy book, listed Nixon's NAACP membership as a point for attacking Nixon in the South.[27]

Nixon's policy agenda on civil rights appeared to reflect those votes Nixon considered pivotal to the election outcome and in 1960, those votes included northern blacks. Theodore White reports that both candidates decided that the "swing states" were California, New York, Illinois, Ohio, Pennsylvania, Texas, and Michigan (with Kennedy also considering Massachusetts and New Jersey pivotal states). In each case, these swing states had sizable black populations.[28] Nixon's campaign strategy was also reflected in his vice-presidential selection of Henry Cabot Lodge Jr., a former Massachusetts senator with a liberal record on civil rights. The first African American to serve in a White House administration, E. Frederick Morrow, was among a select group of advisors who attended a secret midnight caucus at the Republican National Convention in 1960 to discuss Nixon's vice-presidential selection. When asked his choice, Morrow recommended Lodge because he felt "not even the NAACP can be against his superb liberal record."[29]

To be sure, Nixon still tried to appeal to southern voters on other issues, especially later in the campaign when he realized Kennedy did not have a lock on the South, but Nixon's campaign agenda on civil rights in 1960 appeared to be particularly concerned with appealing to (or at least retaining support of) black voters.[30]

[24] Campaign stump speech, 3 October 1960, Charlotte, North Carolina. Annenberg/ Pew Archive of Presidential Campaign Discourse.

[25] In August 1954, President Eisenhower established, by an Executive Order, the President's Committee on Government Contracts. The committee, chaired by Vice President Richard Nixon, was created to enforce mandated nondiscriminatory hiring practices by private industries receiving federal funding.

[26] Schlesinger, *Kennedy or Nixon*.

[27] Counterattack Sourcebook, Kennedy Campaign Materials, JFK Library.

[28] White, *The Making of the President 1960*, 241, 267–68.

[29] Morrow, *Black Man in the White House*, 294. In his memoirs, Nixon mentions that Lodge was also the favorite selection of Eisenhower, Senator Thruston Morton, and Congressman Walter Judd.

[30] White, *The Making of the President 1960*, 204.

The Strategic Shift

Nixon lost the 1960 election in one of the closest presidential contests in American history. Moreover, despite Nixon's efforts to reach African American voters, he received less support from the black community than Eisenhower only four years earlier.[31] With this loss, many Republicans, including Nixon, appeared to reassess their electoral strategy. In a 1961 speech to southern GOP leaders in Atlanta, Republican Senator Barry Goldwater verbalized what would come to be known as the "southern strategy"—"We're not going to get the Negro vote as a bloc in 1964 and 1968, so we ought to go hunting where the ducks are." Theodore White summed up this perspective: "[L]et us give the Northern Negro vote to the Democrats, and we shall take the Old South for ourselves."[32]

The Republican National Committee initiated "Operation Dixie" in 1957 to build on Eisenhower's gains in the South, but they stepped up those efforts after Nixon's loss. Conservative journalist Robert Novak reported his observations from a conference of state party chairmen in 1963, "A good many, perhaps a majority of the party's leaders, envisioned substantial political gold to be mined in the racial crisis by becoming in fact, though not in name, the White Man's Party. 'Remember,' one astute party worker said quietly over the breakfast table one morning, 'this isn't South Africa. The white man outnumbers the Negro 9 to 1 in this country.' "[33]

Goldwater's extreme conservatism and states' rights platform in 1964 contributed to a thumping at the polls, but it also highlighted the fact that southern whites were willing not only to abstain from voting for the Democratic candidate (as they did in 1948), but were also willing to vote Republican. The 1964 election made clear that southern whites would go to the Republicans if the candidate offered a conservative policy position on civil rights. In South Carolina, political strategist Harry S. Dent, then political advisor to Senator Strom Thurmond, reportedly rejoiced following Goldwater's defeat in 1964, "In the next two years, the seeds of the Republican southern strategy began to sprout and grow. . . . The Tree was bearing fruit. . . . We South Carolina Republicans were now getting ready for the big coup—the White

[31] Key, *The Responsible Electorate.*

[32] White, *The Making of the President 1960,* 203. It was assumed that only these two groups cared about civil rights policy—an assumption that seems borne out by data.

[33] Novak, *The Agony of the GOP,* 179.

House—with this new Southern Strategy."[34] It wasn't just the Republicans who foresaw the electoral playing field shifting. President Johnson lamented to one of his aides that the Civil Rights Act had probably "delivered the South to the Republican Party for a long time to come."[35]

In the run-up to the 1968 election, debate continued about the Republican Party position on civil rights. The Ripon Society, founded in 1962 and named after Ripon, Wisconsin, the birthplace of the Republican Party, continued to push for a pro–civil rights position. Throughout the 1960s and early 1970s, the Ripon Society produced several strategy reports outlining how they believed the GOP could become the majority party by reaching out to minority voters. For example, a 1968 report argued that the GOP should explicitly denounce policy positions that might alienate moderates and minority voters: "This is the direction the party must take if it is to win the confidence of the 'new Americans' who are not at home in the politics of another generation . . . [like] the moderate of the new South—who represent the hope for peaceful racial adjustment and who are insulted by a racist appeal more fitting another generation. These [policies] and others like them hold the key to the future of our politics."[36]

In 1968 Nixon would once again win the Republican presidential nomination. Given his previous pro–civil rights platform, it was initially unclear how Nixon would position himself on racial issues. A *Time* magazine article predicted that "Ronald Reagan is probably the only Republican capable of consolidating his party's arduous—and still tenuous—risorgimento in Dixie."[37] Yet, as soon became clear, Nixon shifted his electoral strategy from a northern, urban focus to one concentrated on the South (especially the rim South). In his memoirs, Nixon writes,

> I would not concede the Carolinas, Florida, Virginia, or any of the states of the rim of the South. These states became the foundation of my strategy; added to the states that I expected to win in the Midwest, the Great Plains, the Rocky Mountains, and the Far West, they would put me over the top and into the White House. My polls showed that Wallace's vote was overwhelmingly Democratic but that when his name was not included in the poll sampling, his votes came to me on more than a two-to-one basis, espe-

[34] Dent, *The Prodigal South Returns to Power*, 67–70.

[35] Johnson's remark to Bill Moyers quoted in Michael Oreskes, "Civil Rights Act Leaves Deep Mark on the American Political Landscape," *New York Times*, 2 July 1989, A16.

[36] http://www.riponsociety.org/history.htm.

[37] "Enigma in the South," *Time Magazine*, Friday, 12 May 1967.

cially in the South. . . . A major theme that we used very effectively in key states such as Florida, North Carolina, Tennessee, Kentucky, and Virginia was that Wallace couldn't win.[38]

And the calculation was that the southern voters were particularly concerned about racial policies. A memo from advisor Harry Dent to the newly elected Nixon made clear, "So far as Southern politics is concerned, the Nixon administration will be judged from the beginning on the manner in which the school desegregation guidelines problem is handled. Other issues are important in the South but are dwarfed somewhat by comparison."[39]

Some historians have traced Nixon's decision to switch from courting northern blacks to southern whites to a meeting with Strom Thurmond in an Atlanta hotel room in early 1968. According to Reg Murphy and Hal Guliver, authors of *The Southern Strategy*, Nixon made a deal:

> The essential Nixon bargain was simply this: *If I'm president of the United States, I'll find a way to ease up on the federal pressures forcing school desegregation—or any other kind of desegregation.* Whatever the exact words or phrasing, this was how the Nixon commitment was understood by Thurmond and other southern GOP strategists. In 1968 Strom Thurmond, once the darling of the third-party Dixiecrat movement of two decades before, would campaign for Nixon in the Deep South, doing all he could to undercut the third-party movement of former Alabama Governor George Corley Wallace, the most successful third-party presidential drive in more than half a century. Wallace simply could not win, Thurmond insisted, as attractive as Wallace's segregationist views might seem. But Nixon—that was something else again. Nixon, Thurmond suggested, really held views much closer to Wallace than it might appear.[40]

The seeds of change for Nixon's 1968 position shift on racial issues, however, were planted during his failed 1960 presidential bid. In a December 15, 1960, meeting following his narrow defeat, Vice President Nixon, outgoing President Dwight Eisenhower, and GOP chairman Thruston Morton discussed the lessons of the 1960 presidential election. Hinting at the southern strategy to come, Nixon commented that Lodge's campaign promise to appoint a Negro to a Nixon cabinet "just killed us in the South." On the subject at hand, Eisenhower pointed

[38] Nixon, *RN: The Memoirs of Richard Nixon*, 316–17.
[39] Memo dated 23 January 1969 from Harry Dent. Quoted in Genovese, *The Nixon Presidency*, 85.
[40] Murphy and Guliver, *The Southern Strategy*, 2.

out that "we have made civil rights a main part of our effort these past eight years but have lost Negro support instead of increasing it." Nixon responded that "we discovered as far as this particular vote is concerned it is a bought vote, and it isn't bought by civil rights." To this, Senator Morton offers his full agreement "and, as far as he was concerned, 'the hell with them.' " [41] In 1968 and 1972 we see this strategic shift in civil rights position taking in Nixon's campaign rhetoric.

Nixon Strategy in 1968 and 1972

With Nixon's shift in perspective from viewing northern blacks as the critical swing voters to viewing southern whites as necessary for victory, Nixon's rhetoric on civil rights also underwent a substantial transformation.

In 1960 Nixon had fought to insert a 1,250-word civil rights plank in the party platform declaring that "civil rights is a responsibility not only of states and localities; it is a national problem and a national responsibility. . . . We favor the enactment and just enforcement of such Federal legislation as may be necessary to maintain this right at all times in every part of this Republic." Such language directly addressed the "states' rights" argument of civil rights opponents. In contrast, the 1968 platform made little reference to civil rights and promised "decisive action to quell civil disorder, relying primarily on state and local governments to deal with these conditions." In contrast to the explicit support expressed for counter sit-ins and the "vigorous support of court orders for school desegregation" found in the 1960 Republican Party platform, the 1968 platform asserted that "America has adequate peaceful and lawful means for achieving even fundamental social change if the people wish it." Whereas Nixon's 1960 platform pledged "vigorous support of court orders for school desegregation," in the 1968 (and 1972) campaign Nixon made clear his opposition to "forced integration," school busing, and affirmative action.

As was also the case in 1960, Nixon's electoral calculation about the strategically important persuadable voters was reflected in his selection of a vice-presidential running mate. In 1968 Nixon selected Maryland governor Spiro Agnew, who was recognized for his appeal to Democrats. Nixon explained that "Agnew fit the bill perfectly with the strategy we had devised for the November election. With George Wallace in the race, I could not hope to sweep the South. It was absolutely

---

[41] Meeting notes taken by Bryce Harlow. "Staff Notes December 1960," box 55, DDE Diary Series, Dwight D. Eisenhower's Papers as President (Ann Whitman File).

necessary, therefore, to win the entire rimland of the South."[42] Journalists called Agnew the "chief agent of the President's Southern Strategy" in the 1968 campaign. At an event in Mississippi, for instance, Agnew declared, "The principles of most of the people of Mississippi are the principles of the Republican Party."[43]

Nixon's change in campaign rhetoric from 1960 to 1968 is also apparent in his stump speeches in the South. Not only did Nixon spend more of his time campaigning in the South and border states, he also now emphasized his affection for and allegiance to the region:

> [M]ore than any recent American presidents I perhaps have a closer affinity to the South because of my education. I took my law degree at Duke University. . . . I learned a lot about law and I learned also a lot about this nation's background, and the differences, and I learned some of the things I had thought were right when I got there might not be right. . . . [W]hen I went to Duke University in 1934, after a very good college education at Whittier in California, I was utterly convinced that Ulysses S. Grant was the best general produced on either side in the Civil War. After rooming for years with Bill Perdue of Macon, Georgia, I found, and was almost convinced by Bill Perdue's constant hammering on it, that Ulysses S. Grant would be lucky to be about fourth behind Robert E. Lee, Joseph Johnston, and Stonewall Jackson.[44]

Nixon's switch on racial policies is also apparent in the reactions of political elites to his candidacy and campaign promises. In 1960 Nixon garnered the praise of Roy Wilkins, executive secretary of the NAACP, for his "good record on civil rights."[45] By 1972 Nixon's campaign positions earned the scorn of the very same NAACP leader. The *New York Times* reported, "In some of the strongest language he has ever used in referring to any President, Roy Wilkins yesterday condemned Richard Nixon as one who is 'with the enemies of little black children' . . . Mr. Wilkins accused President Nixon of turning back the clock on integration."[46]

These changes in Nixon's rhetoric on issues related to race and his change in targeted voters, suggest that his campaign strategy reflected a switch from viewing blacks as an important electoral voting bloc in 1960 to viewing racially conservative white Democrats as the more critical swing vote in 1968 and 1972. Nixon presidential advisor Kevin

---

[42] Nixon, *RN: The Memoirs of Richard Nixon*, 312.

[43] "Spiro Agnew: The King's Taster," *Time Magazine*, 14 November 1969.

[44] Campaign stump speech 12 October 1972, Atlanta, GA.

[45] Farnsworth Fowler, "Wilkins Praises Nixon on Rights," *New York Times*, 21 June 1960, 28. C. Gerald Fraser, "Wilkins Puts Nixon with Foes of Blacks," *New York Times*, 26 May 1972, 10.

[46] Phillips, *The Emerging Republican Majority*, 108.

Phillips argued in *The Emerging Republican Majority*, a book that *Newsweek* called the "political bible of the Nixon era," that GOP efforts to reach minority voters were not reaping rewards and greater benefits would be secured by reaching out to persuadable Democrats. According to Phillips, "for all their advocacy of programs aimed at the Negro vote, liberal establishment Republicans, like Nelson Rockefeller, Jacob Javitts, and John Lindsay proved unable to induce sizable numbers of Negros to vote for them."[47] The Republican's electoral fortunes rested on "turning [the South] into an important presidential base of the Republican Party."[48]

Thus, rather than focusing Republican campaign efforts heavily in northeastern states, as they did in 1960, Nixon and the GOP shifted efforts South. In notes from a meeting with the president, Nixon chief of staff H. R. Haldeman makes clear the new focus on the South: "South terribly important . . . look at whole spectrum of So[uth] gains [in] '60 vs. '70, <u>that's</u> where the ducks are. Sh[ou]ld give <u>NO</u> credence to Ripon Society bull. . . . Ducks are in the mountains and the So[uth]" (emphasis in original).[49] Similarly, in a memo titled "The President's Developing Image in the South" sent from Harry Dent shortly after the 1968 election, Dent referenced Nixon's efforts in the South stating,

> I digested every word the president said in the [1968] campaign. This was used, after editing by the New York office, to effectively assist in carrying five crucial states—Tennessee, North Carolina, South Carolina, Florida, and Virginia—in addition to countering the Wallace vote in other states. . . . I also believe we must look to the South politically to further develop the two-party system, get new Congressmen and Congressional control, win Southern Congressional support for the Nixon program, and to insure re-election in 1972.

Nixon's handwriting on the memo requested that it be circulated to John Mitchell, Nixon's campaign manager.[50]

Critically, Nixon was targeting not the hard-core Republicans, but the persuadable Democrats and Independents—those who disagreed with the Democratic Party's position on racial policies. In 1972 cam-

---

[47] Ibid., 22. Phillips clearly points out that he was writing about his own perspective, not necessarily that of Nixon or the administration, and that he did not think that the realignment of the South would come from racial policies alone.

[48] James O'Toole, "RNC, Expecting Tough Elections, Mobilizes Troops," *Pittsburgh Post-Gazette*, 7 August 2005.

[49] Nixon Presidential Materials Staff. White House Staff Member and Office Files. H. R. Haldeman. Haldeman notes, box 42. July–September to October–December 1970.

[50] See Nixon Presidential Materials Project National Archives. President's Office Files. President's Handwriting, White House Notes. Handwriting 1968–April 1969, box 1.

paign advisor Patrick Buchanan argued in a memo sent to President Nixon and other campaign advisors:

> [W]e should schedule RN into the "undecided" arenas, union halls, Columbus Day activities, Knights of Columbus meetings, etc. We should keep in mind that there is only—at most—20 percent of the electorate that will decide this, not who wins, but whether or not it is a landslide, and quite frankly, that 20 percent is not a principally Republican vote. Perhaps RN has to make appearances at GOP rallies—but when he does, he is not going where the ducks are.[51]

Referencing southern Democrats, in particular, Harry Dent sent news of the Nixon administration's policy goals and its potential impact on the persuadable Democrats, "The administration is moving toward reform, decentralization, and reorganization as per the campaign statements of 1968. . . . The President's new welfare reform program should prove to be quite a political boon to the South. . . . If this is handled properly, you ought to be able to get some traditional Democrat votes loosened up."[52]

In 1972 the Nixon campaign actively sought the support of Democratic voters who had supported segregationist George Wallace. While working on plans to publicize the number of "Democrats for Nixon," GOP campaign worker Mickey Gardner wrote to Pat Buchanan on July 17, 1972, about an important development in their plans for courting southern Democrats:

> Bill Franz, President of NASCAR, and a key Wallace supporter . . . feels that the time is right for a nearly "complete" defection of the Wallace Campaign structure to the re-election effort of Richard Nixon. This defection would be, in fact, simply a shift from Wallace to Nixon. . . . [P]rompt action could result in a pro-Nixon re-election resolution coming out of the Independent Party convention in a few weeks.[53]

By no means are we the first to observe that Nixon's campaign agenda reflected a strategic decision to appeal to policy-conflicted Democrats. An impressive historical analysis by Paul Frymer and John David

[51] Nixon Presidential Material Staff. White House Special Files. Staff Members and Office Files. Patrick J. Buchanan. Chronological Files 1971–1972. January 1972, box 2. Memorandum, to the President (per H. R. Haldeman). 5 July 1972.

[52] Nixon Presidential Material Project National Archives. White House Special Files. Staff Member and Office Files. Harry S. Dent. 1969 Southern GOP, box 8.

[53] White House Special Files. Staff Member and Office Files. Charles W. Colson. D.C. Health and Welfare Council. Democrats For Nixon, box 55. Memorandum to Chuck Colson from Mickey Gardner, "Possible 'Complete' Defection of Wallace Campaign Effort to 'Democrats for Nixon.' " 17 July 1972.

Skrentny similarly concludes that "the decision making process [of the Nixon administration] was . . . directly shaped by the ability of various groups to claim themselves as potential swing-voters and for the party to find these groups compatible with both important elements of the existing electoral coalition and with other crucial swing groups in national elections."[54] Historian James Reichley writes

> To what extent was Nixon motivated by conviction in his handling of the busing issue, and to what extent by political expediency? . . . Nixon dug in hard against any remedy that would cause even mild concern among the southern, suburban and white working class constituencies that he aimed to win by large majorities in 1972. It would be hard not to conclude that his judgment was heavily influenced by his immediate political interests.[55]

It seems clear that Nixon's position taking on racial policy issues reflected strategic considerations about the potentially persuadable voters in the electorate rather than his ideological convictions alone. The remaining question is whether or not these campaign efforts to prime racial issues influenced voter decision making.

The Influence of the Southern Strategy on Voters

While Nixon clearly changed his racial campaign rhetoric from 1960 to 1968, it is not clear if such changes were successful in attracting southern white Democrats. Certainly, aggregate vote returns suggest that Nixon's southern strategy was successful. In 1960 Nixon won only Florida and the border states of Tennessee, Virginia, and Kentucky. In 1972 he won every southern state and in most cases he won by overwhelming margins—exceeding the victory margins of nearly any other state in the country. Of course, aggregate voting returns do not conclusively demonstrate that Nixon was successful at priming racial policy preferences among the targeted voters. To gain a better view of the individual-level dynamics of the southern strategy, we turn to an evaluation of racial priming efforts on the decision-making process of indi-

---

[54] See Frymer and Skrentny, "Coalition-Building and the Politics of Electoral Capture during the Nixon Administration," 141.

[55] Riechley, *Conservatives in an Age of Change*, 204. Beyond his positioning on racial issues, Nixon's targeting of cross-pressured Democrats was also evident in his change in rhetoric about labor policy. As a member of Congress, Nixon helped draft the Taft-Hartley Act, which severely restricted the activities and power of labor unions, but in 1968 and 1972 Nixon tried to court union members who might feel part of the "silent majority."

vidual voters, especially those cross-pressured Democrats who were the target of Nixon's racially conservative appeals.

In order to compare the effects of this wedge strategy, we examine the influence of racial policy incongruence on the presidential vote choice of white Democrats across different campaign contexts.[56] We expect that Democrats who were incongruent on racial issues would be more likely to defect when the campaign emphasized the racial policy differences between the candidates. We first compare individual-level behavior in 1960 and 1968—years in which the Republican candidate was constant but campaign rhetoric on racial issues was quite different—using the open-ended likes/dislikes questions from the American National Election Studies. We then take advantage of the NES 1972–76 panel study to evaluate changes in decision making among the same respondents in two very different campaign contexts. Finally, we use the NES cumulative file to trace the evolution and influence of changing GOP electoral strategies from 1964 through 2004, as they transitioned from a focus on racial policies to the contemporary emphasis on "moral" wedge issues.

A content analysis of *New York Times* campaign coverage shows that racial issues constituted roughly 16 percent of news coverage of domestic policy issues in 1960 and 22 percent in 1968.[57] Similarly, a content analysis of Nixon's campaign speeches in 1960 reveals that just over 10.3 percent of his stump speeches referenced racial issues compared to 22.4 percent of his speeches in 1968.[58] More importantly, the candidates not only increased attention to racial policies, they offered distinct alternatives in 1968 compared to 1960. A wedge strategy can work only to the extent that the candidates take different policy positions. When the campaign highlights the key differences between the candidates, the voters are able to vote on the basis of those differences.[59] To be sure, things on the ground were also changing during this time period. In 1960 the civil rights movement was relatively new;

[56] Breaking down the national-level data into not only white Democrats, but also southern white Democrats who are cross-pressured on issues related to race stretches the data very thin—a problem long recognized by scholars (see, for instance, Prysby, "A Note on Regional Subsamples from National Sample Surveys"). Throughout our analysis, Independents who leaned toward the Democratic Party are included with partisan identifiers.

[57] During this time, national security topped the list of campaign issues, followed by crime (often thought to hold implicit racial implications), then civil rights and other explicitly racial issues. See Sigelman and Buell, "Avoidance or Engagement?" for more information about the coding of *New York Times* campaign coverage.

[58] Estimated from speeches in the Annenberg/Pew Archive of Campaign Discourse. See appendix 2 for included topics.

[59] Kahn and Kenney, *The Spectacle of Senate Campaigns.*

by 1968 Martin Luther King Jr. had been assassinated, urban riots had erupted across the country, and tensions were high both within the black community and between whites and blacks. Nixon's change in rhetoric on racial issues between 1960 and 1968 reflected a change in the group of voters he viewed as persuadable, a calculation that no doubt was influenced by this changing political environment.

In order to evaluate whether there was a corresponding change in the effect of racial cross-pressures on voting behavior, we rely on the NES open-ended questions that asked respondents if there was anything they liked/disliked about the political parties and candidates.[60] The advantage of this measure is that a volunteered response is more likely to capture an important issue preference and, therefore, a meaningful tension between party affiliation and issue preference.[61] The disadvantage is that there are somewhat higher levels of nonresponse, so that the sample sizes for some subgroups (especially white southerners) are quite small. Even more regrettably, the open-ended questions were asked of only half of the NES sample in 1972, preventing a comparable analysis of the open-ended questions in the 1972 presidential election.

Looking first at the extent of racial policy incongruence in these two election years, we see in table 5.1 that the majority of surveyed Democrats volunteered that they disliked something about the Democratic Party (or the candidate), although relatively few mentioned racial policy issues. As a percentage of the policy issues mentioned, however, racial policies accounted for more than one-third of the issue-based disagreements volunteered.[62] Interestingly, in the South, the percentage of white Democrats mentioning a racial cross-pressure was actually higher in 1960 than in 1968. At the 1960 Democratic convention, southern Democrats had strongly opposed the national Democratic Party's platform on civil and voting rights. Critically, though, we do not expect that this opposition should influence defection because Nixon matched the Democrat's position in 1960. In her diary about the Democratic National Convention in 1960, Eleanor Roosevelt wrote about the South's opposition to the civil rights plank: "As usual, the Southern people threatened that the Democratic Party would lose their states in the No-

---

[60] The measure includes mentions of dislikes about the Democratic Party or candidate as well as mentions of likes about the Republican Party or candidate.

[61] See, for instance, Gershkoff. "*The Importance of Properly Measuring Importance.*" Paper Presented at the American Association of Public Opinion Research Annual Conference. Again, we are unable to untangle the extent to which the campaign itself shapes this measurement.

[62] Republicans were much less likely to be cross-pressured on racial issues (22 of 513 Republican respondents volunteered a racial policy dislike). And among those Republicans who were cross-pressured on racial issues, it was not related to their vote choice.

TABLE 5.1
Volunteered Racial Cross-pressures among White Democrats in 1960 and 1968

	Percent All		*Percent Non-South*		*Percent South*	
	1960	1968	1960	1968	1960	1968
Any Cross-pressure	67.4	75.1	62.6	74.0	78.9	77.8
Racial Cross-pressure	5.4	5.4	1.0	4.3	15.6	8.4

Note: Table shows that southern white Democrats were more likely to volunteer a racial policy dislike about their party than northern white Democrats. Data source is the American National Election Study cumulative file.

vember election. One wonders where these states will go if they leave the Democratic Party."[63] Indeed, in Mississippi and Alabama, fourteen unpledged Democratic electors won election from the voters. By 1968 it became clear that those unhappy southern Democrats would go to the Republican camp if the candidate took a more favorable position on the issue. The proportion of Democrats in the South had also declined from 66 percent of the southern populace in 1960 to 58 percent by 1968, suggesting some of those racially cross-pressured Democrats may have changed their partisan affiliation by 1968.

The key question, however, is whether or not there is a relationship between racial policy incongruence and an individual's decision to defect. We estimate the effect of racial cross-pressures on a white Democrat's decision to vote for the Republican nominee, controlling for other factors that may influence the likelihood of defection, including age, education, gender, and strength of party identification.[64] The model results, including coefficients, standard errors, model fit, and Wald estimates for the cross-pressure variable are reported in appendix 3.

To evaluate the priming effects, we compare the effect of racial cross-pressures across years. In figure 5.1, we see that racial cross-pressures among white Democrats predicted support for Nixon in 1968, but not 1960. In 1960 Democrats who disagreed with the national party position on civil rights and other racial issues were no more likely to support Nixon than those not cross-pressured. In 1968, in contrast, these cross-pressured Democrats had a 58 percent probability of defecting to Nixon. In other words, racially conservative Democrats were more

[63] 14 July 1960. *Eleanor Roosevelt, John Kennedy, and the Election of 1960: A Project of the Eleanor Roosevelt Papers*, ed. by Allida Black, June Hopkins, John Sears, Chris Alhambra, Mary Jo Binker, Christopher Brick, John S. Emrich, Eugenia Gusev, Kristen E. Gwinn, and Bryan D. Peery (Columbia, S.C.: Model Editions Partnership, 2003). Electronic version based on unpublished letters. http://adh.sc.edu (Accessed 29 April 2007).

[64] Given the small number of cases for southern white Democratic voters (fifty-eight cases in 1968), we include only age, education, and gender as additional controls in 1968. Using a similar model specification for 1960 does not change the results.

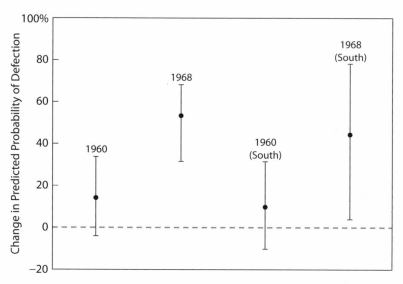

Figure 5.1: Effect of Racial Cross-pressures on Predicted Probability of Defection, 1960 and 1968

Note: Figure shows racial cross-pressures were related to Democratic defections to Nixon in 1968, but not 1960. Shown is the difference in the predicted probability of defection for a racially cross-pressured white Democrat compared to a racially consistent, white Democrat, holding constant other variables in the model. A Wald test rejects the null hypothesis of equal coefficients across elections for the national sample. Data source is the American National Election Study cumulative file.

likely to vote Republican than Democratic.[65] These findings are supportive of our expectation that the decision for a persuadable partisan to defect depends on the issue content of the campaign. When candidates offered distinct issue positions on racial issues in 1968 and the issue was emphasized in the campaign, racial policy conflicts weighed more heavily in the vote decisions of incongruent Democrats. This is true even though the extent of policy incongruence remained stable or even declined (among southern Democrats) from 1960 to 1968.

Without considering variation in candidate positions and campaign dialogue across elections, existing research may provide an incomplete picture of the relationships between campaigns, issues, and voting behavior. For instance, pooling elections into a single decade, Byron Shafer and Richard Johnston find very little change in the relationship between racial attitudes and presidential voting between the 1950s and

---

[65] Results hold whether or not we code a vote for Wallace as a defection.

1960s.[66] Yet, our analysis suggests that this relationship varies across different election years depending on the extent to which racial attitudes were central to the campaign. By ignoring the fact that voters' conflicting predispositions shape responsiveness to political campaigns, studies of campaign influence miss the ways in which campaigns affect the decision to defect. If elites take divergent positions on issues and emphasize those issues in their campaigns, cross-pressured partisans are likely to weigh these inconsistent positions more heavily in their vote choice.

A potential alternative explanation for our conclusion is that the direction of causality is reversed. That is, support for a candidate, in this case for Nixon in 1968, influenced the policy position that voters adopted, rather than the other way around. As discussed in the previous chapter, some scholars have argued that voters may bring their policy preferences in line with those held by their preferred political candidate.[67] The standard argument is that policy preferences are fleeting reflections of candidate preference and that candidate choice is determined by more long-standing party attachments. But our focus on policy preferences that conflict with party attachments belies this logic—clearly, party identification was not the determinant of vote choice among those who voted for the opposition party candidate. In addition, the use of volunteered policy disagreements makes it more likely that we have captured genuine policy attitudes that are in disagreement with voters' preferred political party.

Moreover, by most indications conservative preferences of racial policies predated elite campaign efforts, especially in the South.[68] In the 1956 NES, 19 percent of white southerners volunteered a racial issue as something they disliked about one of the two major parties in contrast to just 3 percent of white northerners. In 1958, 33 percent of white southerners disagreed with the statement, "If Negroes are not getting fair treatment in jobs and housing, the government should see to it that they do" (compared to 16 percent of white northerners). These conservative racial preferences came at a time when the parties were not taking appreciably different positions on racial issues, suggesting that these preferences were more likely to be the determinant of, not the result of, candidate preferences. To more directly address this potential concern, we turn to an additional test of our hypothesis using the National Election Study's 1972–1976 panel study. With repeated inter-

---

[66] Shafer and Johnston, *The End of Southern Exceptionalism*, 76.

[67] See review in Achen and Bartels, "*It Feels Like We're Thinking: The Rationalizing Voter and Electoral Democracy.*"

[68] Carmines and Stimson, *Issue Evolution*.

views of the same individuals in two distinct campaign contexts, we are able to examine the extent to which racial attitudes—in this case, opinions on school busing—remain stable during this four-year time period. We can then evaluate the influence of being incongruent on this issue in an election in which the issue was a source of considerable debate in the campaign, compared to one in which it was not.

Comparing the Effects of the Busing Issue in 1972 and 1976

In contrast to his 1960 campaign efforts, Nixon attempted to prime racially conservative attitudes among white Democrats during the 1968 and 1972 campaigns. In 1972 his rhetoric was particularly focused on the issue of busing to achieve racial integration of public schools. According to Joseph Aistrup, Nixon's "plans were to structure his appeal around support for the idea of civil rights, but opposition to its active enforcement. . . . Nixon's metaphor symbolizing this struggle over the intermediate color line was the battle over busing."[69] In developing his campaign strategy for the 1972 campaign, his advisors viewed busing as a potential wedge issue because Democrat George McGovern was supportive of busing, while many rank-and-file Democrats were opposed. In a campaign strategy memo titled the "Assault Book," Nixon advisor Patrick Buchanan wrote, "It can be stated, flatly, that George McGovern supports both 'forced busing' and the concept of racial balance (a statistical quota system) in every public school in the United States. . . . This entire albatross, either as a whole or independently, can be publicly hung around the neck of the Democratic candidate."[70]

To establish his opposition to busing, early in the 1972 campaign season—corresponding with George Wallace's announcement that he would seek the Democratic nomination—Nixon placed the issue center stage by requesting that Congress place a moratorium on busing. The Republican platform also emphasized the issue, stating that "we are irrevocably opposed to busing. . . . [W]e regard it as unnecessary, counter productive and wrong." Reinforcing our contention that candidate position taking is shaped by information about the preferences of the public, Nixon referenced his efforts to gauge public opinion on the issue during the 1972 election. Campaigning in the South, Nixon noted,

[69] Aistrup, *The Southern Strategy Revisited*, 33.

[70] Nixon Presidential Materials Staff. White House and Central Files. Staff Member and Office Files. Patrick J. Buchanan. 1972 Election File. Assault Book, box 10.

I was looking at some polls recently. . . . [D]id you know that busing is a much hotter issue in Michigan today than it is in Alabama? Now, what does that mean? It does not mean that the majority of the people in Michigan are racist, any more than the majority of the people of Alabama, because they happen to be opposed to busing. It simply means this: it means parents in Michigan, like parents in Alabama and parents in Georgia and parents all over this country, want better education for their children, and that better education is going to come in the schools that are closer to home and not those clear across town.[71]

In contrast, four years later presidential candidate Gerald Ford mentioned busing only once in his stump speeches.[72] Following President Nixon's resignation in 1974 in the wake of the Watergate scandal, the 1976 presidential campaign focused on issues of government reform rather than racial policies. Indeed, racial issues were mentioned in less than 4 percent of Ford's campaign speeches compared to more than 10 percent of Nixon's speeches in 1972.[73] A comparison of *New York Times* campaign coverage indicates that there were 610 articles referencing the busing debate from January 1 through Election Day in 1972 compared to just 244 articles during the same time period in 1976. Compared to Nixon's presidential campaign rhetoric in 1972, Ford did very little to appeal to racially cross-pressured Democrats in 1976.

Why did the issue of busing drop out of campaign rhetoric from 1972 to 1976? Some scholars have attributed the change to Ford's lack of "southern political acumen." From this perspective, Ford was simply unwilling to exploit racial issues for electoral gain. Joseph Aistrup concludes that "Gerald Ford, whose Republican roots were firmly within the Rockefeller-Scranton wing of the party, did not possess the political will to politicize racial issues in the 1976 presidential contest. . . . Rather, Ford ran a campaign against federal spending and reminded voters that he had restored integrity to the White House."[74]

Although we cannot speak to Ford's personal convictions on racial issues, we would expect the change in his campaign agenda if the candidate determined a different group of voters would be pivotal. Inter-

---

[71] Stump speech, 12 October 1972 Atlanta Georgia. Annenberg/Pew Archive of Presidential Campaign Discourse.

[72] Annenberg/Pew Archive of Campaign Discourse.

[73] The exact estimates were 10.2 percent in 1972, 13.8 percent in 1968, 10.3 percent in 1960. If we include general references to civil disobedience, the percentage in 1968 spikes to 22.4 percent. General campaign coverage from the *New York Times* shows an across-the-board decline in the discussion of all policy issues, with racial issues accounting for less than 9 percent of domestic policy topics in 1976. See appendix 2 for included topics.

[74] Aistrup, *The Southern Strategy Revisited*, 38.

nal memos from Ford's campaign suggest that Ford made a strategic decision to try to build a winning coalition outside the South. After a lunch with conservative journalist George Will, a staff assistant sent a note to President Ford mentioning that "Will suggested that Ford might write-off the South and capitalize on the anti-Carter feeling [in] the West and Northeast."[75] Similarly, in a lengthy memo from campaign advisor Michael Duval, the Ford campaign reached the same conclusion, recommending that Ford target "maximum" resources to the large swing states in the northern industrial belt. According to the report, "The *first* decision is whether to concentrate total effort on the northern industrial states from New Jersey to Wisconsin, plus California, or to devote some effort to peripheral southern states, plus California. . . . *We recommend concentration on the northern industrial states*" (italics added).[76] These calculations were no doubt made based on the strengths and weaknesses of both Ford and Carter and the broader political environment. Either way, they had implications for Ford's issue agenda.

Although the particular policy messages were different, Ford's strategy continued to appeal to cross-pressured partisans and Independents on wedge issues. Duval's memo offers a clear link between the preferences of persuadable Democrats and Independents and the campaign agenda:

> To build a winning coalition in the swing states, the president must build on his base of rural and small town majorities with suburban independents and ticket splitters. . . . In very general terms, the target constituency in the suburbs for the President is the upper blue collar and white collar workers. . . . These are independent minded voters, many of whom are Catholic. In addition, there is a weakness in Carter's support among Catholics and also among Jews. . . . Jewish skepticism of Carter as a Southern fundamentalist provides an opportunity to strip away part of the traditional Democratic coalition.

The memo goes on to recommend a specific policy agenda designed to appeal to these persuadable voters (italicized phrases are those President Ford highlighted with marks in the margin):

> The swing constituency is concerned about the following issues: 1. National Defense—This group favors national defense. . . . *The president is well positioned on these issues, but the articulation of his policies has been insufficient. . . .*

---

[75] Memo, Stef Halper to David Gergen, 11 June 1976; folder "Strategy/Planning," box 5, James Reichley Files, Gerald R. Ford Library.

[76] Emphasis added. Campaign Strategy Plan, August 1976; folder "Presidential Campaign—Campaign Strategy Program (1)-(3)," box 1, Dorothy E. Downton Files, Gerald R. Ford Library, 35.

2. Morality . . . *This group also wants to feel that the country is moving again, after Vietnam, Watergate, and the recession.* . . . 3. Economy and Taxes—These issues are of major concern and the President's record is excellent. *But public awareness of the President's policy on tax reduction and the effect on the taxpayer of the Democrat's economic policy need more effective communication.* . . . 4. Crime . . . the President must come down hard on the issue. His programs will work and they make sense. (However, we must be careful not to turn the gun lobby against us. . . .) 5. Education . . . The President must show awareness and concern on this issue above and beyond the busing question. . . . 6. Quality of life—The vast majority of the swing voters who live in the suburbs are conservationists and strongly supportive of a responsible environmental policy. In this issue area, the President is perceived by many as a pro-business, anti-environment candidate. *To correct this situation, we must become actively involved in the energy and recreation areas.*[77]

In nearly two hundred pages of campaign strategy documents, busing received only a cursory mention—other issues were clearly believed to be more critical for winning over persuadable voters in targeted states. Once the campaign decided to focus on swing voters in northeastern states, the media strategy presented by Bailey, Deardourff, and Eyre, Inc., made a similar recommendation about the campaign issue agenda:

> In many of the target States, where Democrats and Independents are needed to win, the most serious problem a Republican candidate has is the perception of Republicans in general as hard-nosed, big-business types—against the working people, against the poor people, against minorities. President Ford has to break the Republican stereotype. . . . One way to show compassion is in his treatment of the issues. . . . [I]t is important that he express strong feelings, and take a leadership position, on such matters as the Equal Rights Amendment, black opportunity, the plight of the Indians, and the hardships of older people. In the northern industrial States, Republicans are seldom successful unless their words and a few strong "people" stands make them more popular than their Party.[78]

Late in the campaign, after polling found that Ford might have a shot at picking up states in the South, Ford added some southern stops on the campaign trail. But advisors David Gergen and Jerry Jones reminded Ford that his appeals in the South must still keep his target constituency in mind, "You do not want to appear to be kowtowing

[77] Campaign Strategy Plan, August 1976; folder "Presidential Campaign—Campaign Strategy Program (1)-(3)," box 1, Dorothy E. Downton Files, Gerald R. Ford Library, 42.

[78] Preliminary Media Plan, 21 August 1976; folder "Presidential Campaign—Preliminary Media Plan," box 1, Dorothy E. Downton Files, Gerald R. Ford Library, 10.

to the South and especially to perceived Southern prejudices. If your supporters in Philadelphia find you stressing very conservative Southern themes, they could easily be alienated. Instead of identifying yourself with strictly Southern interests, what you want to do is identify interests of the South with the interests of the entire nation—interests that you deeply share."[79] The memo continued on to recommend that Ford focus on holding down government spending, the size of government, taxes, costs of living, and maintaining a strong national defense.

So, whereas President Nixon strategically chose to emphasize the issue of busing to appeal to incongruent Democrats in the South in 1972, President Ford focused on other issues in appealing to a different subset of incongruent Democrats in the Northeast in 1976. The positions of the candidates were also somewhat less distinct in 1976 than in 1972. Although the 1976 Republican Party platform affirmed that "we oppose forced busing" and the Democratic Party platform endorsed "mandatory transportation," Jimmy Carter generally tried to avoid talking about the issue. The contrasting campaign agendas in the two election years allow us again to compare the effects of racial cross-pressures in 1972 when the issue was highlighted and in 1976 when the issue was not emphasized.[80]

Despite the variation in attention to racial issues during these campaigns, it is important to note that the extent of policy incongruence among white Democrats did not dramatically change during this time. Polls found that, in the aggregate, the majority of white Democrats were opposed to busing in both 1972 and in 1976. More importantly, individual-level attitudes on the issue were quite stable. Looking at respondent opinions in the NES panel, we find that 85 percent of white Democrats had consistent attitudes on busing—either supportive of busing or opposed to busing in both waves of the study.[81] As shown in figure 5.2, 57 percent of white Democrats and 70 percent of southern white Democrats indicated that they preferred to "keep children in neighborhood schools," rather than support busing

[79] Memo, David Gergen and Jerry Jones to Gerald Ford, 24 September 1976; folder "9/24–27/76," box 93, Presidential Handwriting File, Gerald R. Ford Library.

[80] Among participants in the NES 1972–76 panel study, the difference in candidate placement on the issue of busing was 1.8 points on a 7-point scale in 1972 but just 0.4 points in 1976.

[81] Among white Democrats in the panel, just 6 percent changed the direction of their response during the four-year time frame of the panel, while the other 9 percent switched from holding an opinion in one wave to saying "Don't Know" or selecting the middle category in the other wave. Our logit analysis includes only white Democrats who kept their party identification in both waves of the panel and who remained directionally consistent in their support or opposition to busing across the survey.

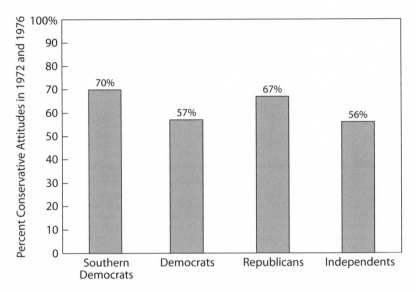

Figure 5.2: Attitudes toward School Busing in 1972 and 1976
Note: Figure shows that the majority of white respondents held stable, conservative attitudes on the issue of busing in both 1972 and 1976. Data source is the American National Election Study 1972–1976 panel.

in both waves of the 1972–76 panel study.[82] On the other side of the aisle, Republicans in the electorate also opposed busing, so it was a particularly attractive wedge issue: 67 percent of Republicans and 56 percent of Independents indicated that they preferred to "keep children in neighborhood schools" in both waves of the survey. Clearly, Nixon could emphasize his opposition to busing among Democrats without fear of generating substantial opposition among his own party members or among Independents.

Restricting our analysis to only those individuals with stable opinions (and stable partisan identification) allows us to compare the influence of these attitudes on presidential vote choice in 1972 and 1976 with less concern that the observed relationship reflects projection or learning effects. Reported in figure 5.3 are the substantive effects of being conflicted about the busing issue on the probability of defecting

[82] These percentages are based on panel respondents indicating that they were Democrats (including Independents leaning toward the Democratic Party) in both waves of the study. Approximately 14 percent of respondents who indicated that they were Democrats in 1972 changed party identification by 1976, with many of these party switchers indicating that they were "pure Independents" or Independents that "leaned" Republican; 86 percent of Democratic panel respondents maintained consistent party identification.

to the Republican candidate in 1972 and in 1976. Reported is the difference in the predicted probability of defecting to the Republican president between cross-pressured Democrats and those congruent on the
busing issue.[83] In 1972 a cross-pressured Democrat was 35 percentage
points more likely to defect than a congruent Democrat, but in 1976
there was no difference in the probability of defection between these
two groups. These results suggest that racial cross-pressures played a
much greater role in voters' decision making in 1972 when it was a
focus of the campaign discourse, compared to 1976 when, although
the candidates' positions and the public attitudes had not changed, the
campaign no longer made the issue salient.[84]

So, whether we use open-ended responses from 1960 and 1968, or
closed-ended questions and panel respondents from 1972 and 1976, we
find that the effect of racial cross-pressures on voter decision making
depends on campaign context. Although we cannot conclusively state
that results are attributable directly or exclusively to campaign messages alone, the evidence is supportive of our hypothesis that the effect
of cross-pressures on vote choice very much depends on the candidates' campaign agendas.

Of course, our analysis cannot untangle the candidates' efforts from
the broader political context and media dialogue. There is little doubt
that the external environment shapes both the campaign strategy of
the candidates, and the voters' priorities, and that it shapes the extent
to which a campaign message will resonate or not.[85] Even still, the historical evidence suggests that both Nixon and Ford were responsive to
the attitudes of targeted voters in developing their issue agendas.

Racial and Moral Issues in the Evolution of the "Southern Strategy"

Next we turn to a broader longitudinal analysis that considers the evolution of the original GOP "southern strategy," as it moved to incorporate cultural or moral issues. Using the closed-ended questions from

---

[83] The model also controls for the effects of education, age, and gender. A Wald statistic comparing the coefficients in the two years is significant at the .05 level. The 1972
effect is statistically significant while the effect in 1976 does not reach even generous
levels of statistical significance. Full results are in appendix.

[84] The difference in effect is not attributable to Democrats switching party affiliation by
1976. Rerunning the analysis using only 1972 party identification (so that Democrats who
changed their party identification in 1976 remain in the analysis) reveals similar results.

[85] Philpot, *Race, Republicans, and the Return of the Party of Lincoln.*

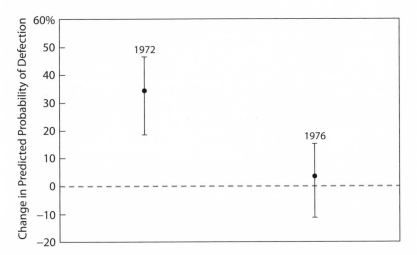

Figure 5.3: Effect of Racial Cross-pressures on Predicted Probability of Defection, 1972 and 1976

Note: Figure indicates that the effect of being cross-pressured on the issue of busing is statistically significant in 1972, but not 1976. Shown is the difference in the predicted probability of defection for cross-pressured Democrats compared to consistent Democrats, holding constant other variables in the model. A Wald test rejects the null hypothesis of equal coefficients across elections. Data source is the American National Election Study 1972–1976 panel.

the NES cumulative file, we estimate the relative effects of racial and moral cross-pressures across election years.

Why would the original southern strategy need to change? Perhaps because of its success. The GOP's emphasis on racial conservatism appealed to many white Democrats, but gradually some of those racially conservative Democrats realigned to the Republican Party.[86] While scholars disagree over the exact causes of the transformation of the once solidly Democratic South to the current stronghold of the GOP, the result was that by the end of the 1980s, Republican presidential candidates could reliably count on substantial support among southern voters.[87] As the party coalitions changed, so too did the potential cleavages available to Republican candidates.

[86] Just over 20 percent of Democratic respondents who defected and voted for Nixon in 1972 changed their party identification in the 1976 wave of the panel study.

[87] Arguments about the reasons for the change in Democratic Party identification across the South range from in-migration of Republican Party industrialists, cohort replacements with younger more conservative voters, the efforts of religious groups across the South, ideological decisions among voters to align themselves with the Republican

Explicitly emphasizing racial issues during campaigns also increasingly risked violating the American norm of equality, and was earning the Republican Party the reputation of racial insensitivity. Many scholars and journalists have argued that Ronald Reagan strategically moved away from explicit racial appeals and instead implicitly primed negative racial predispositions among white voters by emphasizing issues like welfare and crime.[88] In *The Race Card*, Tali Mendelberg argues that "racial appeals did not disappear; they were transformed, often consciously and strategically."[89] In a much-quoted interview about the use of racial campaign appeals, Reagan's political advisor Lee Atwater, explained the evolution of the Republican southern strategy,

> As to the whole Southern strategy that Harry Dent and others put together in 1968, opposition to the Voting Rights Act would have been a central part of keeping the South. Now [a candidate] doesn't have to do that. All you have to do to keep the South is for Reagan to run in place on the issues he's campaigned on since 1964 . . . and that's fiscal conservatism, balancing the budget, cut taxes, you know, the whole cluster. . . . You start out in 1954 by saying "nigger, nigger, nigger." By 1968 you can't say "nigger"—that hurts you. Backfires. So you say stuff like forced busing, states' rights and all that stuff. You're getting so abstract now [that] you're talking about cutting taxes, and all these things you're talking about are totally economic things and a byproduct of them is [that] blacks get hurt worse than whites. And subconsciously maybe that is part of it. I'm not saying that. But I'm saying that if it is getting that abstract, and that coded, that we are doing away with the racial problem one way or the other. You follow me—because obviously sitting around saying, "we want to cut this," is much more abstract than even the busing thing, and a hell of a lot more abstract than "nigger, nigger."[90]

Certainly by the 1990s, following reactions to the infamous "Willie Horton" ad during the 1988 presidential election, many Republicans worried about a backlash among new groups of swing voters they were hoping to court, especially women.[91] The national Republican Party, for instance, quickly distanced itself from former KKK member David Duke when he ran for governor on the Republican ticket, and

---

Party, an extension of elite conflict among some voters, etc. For extensive reviews, see Green et al., *Partisan Hearts and Minds*.

[88] Mendelberg, *The Race Card*, chapter 3; Black and Black, *The Rise of the Southern Republicans*; Aistrup, *The Southern Strategy Revisited*; James Glaser, *Race, Campaign Politics, and the Realignment in the South*, 69–70.

[89] Mendelberg, *The Race Card*, 67.

[90] Lamis, *Southern Politics in the 1990s*, 8.

[91] Hutchings et al., "The Compassion Strategy: Race and the Gender Gap in Campaign 2000."

Republican Senator Trent Lott was forced to step down as majority leader after saying that the country would have been better off had Strom Thurmond won the 1948 election.[92] In 2005 Republican National Committee chairman Ken Mehlman apologized to the NAACP for the GOP's southern strategy saying, "Some Republicans gave up on winning the African American vote, looking the other way or trying to benefit politically from racial polarization. I am here today as the Republican chairman to tell you we were wrong."[93]

To be sure, many white Americans continue to hold conservative racial policy preferences. The 2004 NES indicates that most white Democrats support the Republican Party position on affirmative action.[94] Likewise, state-level ballot initiatives banning affirmative action in employment, education, and public-contracting decisions have easily won electoral support. But with the realignment of many racially conservative Democrats to the Republican Party, and with the increased potential for a backlash, Republicans have turned their attention to other potentially persuadable voters. Discussing the 1984 Reagan electoral strategy, Atwater explained that "we must remember the fundamentals of Southern politics with an electorate divided into three groups: country clubbers (Republican), populists ('usually Democratic: will swing to the GOP under the right circumstances'), and blacks (Democratic). . . . We must assemble coalitions in every Southern state largely based on the country clubbers and the populists."[95] In his memoirs, Richard Nixon explained that "the Republican counterstrategy was clear. . . . We should aim our strategy primarily at disaffected Democrats, and blue-collar workers, and at working-class white ethnics. We should set out to capture the vote of the forty-seven-year-old Dayton housewife."[96]

GOP strategists decided that cultural issues could potentially bridge the country clubbers and populists. The abortion debate, the quickly rising divorce rate, and other societal problems brought attention to issues that continue to split Democrats in the contemporary American electorate. Attempting to reach socially conservative Democrats,

[92] Thomas B. Edsall, "Lott Decried for Part of Salute to Thurmond: GOP Senate Leader Hails Colleague's Run as Segregationist," *Washington Post*, 7 December 2002, A6.

[93] Mike Allen, "RNC Chief to Say It Was 'Wrong' to Exploit Racial Conflict for Votes," *Washington Post*, 14 July 2005, A4.

[94] On the other hand, racial policies do not seem to be a great concern to white Democrats today—not a single Democrat volunteered a racial issue as a reason for disliking John Kerry or the Democrats in 2004.

[95] Brady, *Bad Boy*, 117–18.

[96] Nixon, *RN: The Memoirs of Richard Nixon*, 491. This strategy could be traced to Scammon and Wattenberg's, *The Real Majority*.

Republican candidates began to emphasize social issues like school prayer, flag burning, pornography, and gay rights. The motivation behind a campaign emphasis on such issues was confirmed by Chris Henick, the RNC's southern political director during the late 1980s, who explained that linking Dukakis and the Democrats to "opposition to certain anti-pornography laws and to prayer in the schools provide ideal 'wedge issues' to encourage moderate-to-conservative Democrats to abandon their party."[97] In his 1988 nomination speech, George H. W. Bush ran through a litany of wedge issues that might divide the traditional Democratic coalition:

> Should public school teachers be required to lead our children in the pledge of allegiance? My opponent says no—and I say yes. Should society be allowed to impose the death penalty on those who commit crimes of extraordinary cruelty and violence? My opponent says no—but I say yes. And should our children have the right to say a voluntary prayer, or even observe a moment of silence in the schools? My opponent says no—but I say yes. And should, should free men and women have the right to own a gun to protect their home? My opponent says no—but I say yes. And is it right to believe in the sanctity of life and protect the lives of innocent children? My opponent says no—but I say yes.[98]

A content analysis of campaign news coverage by the *New York Times*, shown in figure 5.4, indicates the increasing focus on moral issues in presidential elections as news coverage of racial issues declined.[99] Beginning in 1984 the percentage of articles discussing morality outnumbered the percentage of articles addressing race—and the focus on moral issues continued through the 2004 presidential contest.

Perhaps ironically, cultural issues are now the primary issues on which Republican candidates attempt to appeal to minority voters. For example, in the 2000 election, candidate George W. Bush emphasized

---

[97] Thomas Edsall, "Why Bush Accentuates the Negative: Beyond Beating Dukakis, the GOP Aims at Permanent Political Change," *Washington Post*, 2 October 1988, C1. Certainly there are still campaign appearances of racially charged political messages, such as the classic Willie Horton ad.

[98] The full transcript of the speech is available online through the American Presidency Project (www.presidency.ucsb.edu).

[99] More detailed information about the data coding can be found in Sigelman and Buell, "Avoidance or Engagement?" This estimate likely underestimates news coverage of racial issues in 1976 because coding was limited to the general-election campaign. During the primary season, George Wallace's candidacy as a Democratic hopeful helped to focus attention on the busing issue in particular. For instance, Nixon made more than eleven television statements about the busing issue between January and September alone (compiled from www.presidency.ucsb.edu). After Wallace was shot in May 1972, the focus on the busing issue declined somewhat.

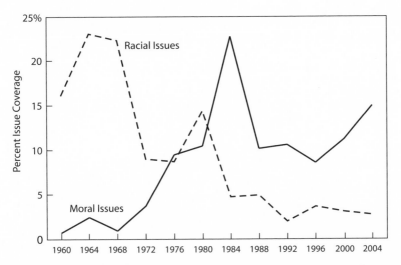

Figure 5.4: Racial and Moral Issues as Percentage of Campaign News Coverage
Note: Figure shows the percent of *New York Times* general election campaign coverage devoted to racial and moral issues, 1960–2004. Data provided by Lee Sigelman and Emmett Buell.

policies like faith-based initiatives and school vouchers when he spoke to African American audiences. At a conference held by the National Urban League during the 2004 presidential contest, President Bush encouraged the predominantly black audience to consider voting Republican: "If you believe the institutions of marriage and family are worth defending and need defending today, [then] take a look at my agenda." Following a round of applause, President Bush continued, "If you believe in building a culture of life in America, take a look at my agenda."[100]

The Effects of Racial and Moral Cross-pressures over Time

To examine the role of racial and moral cross-pressures over time, we rely on the closed-ended policy questions in the NES cumulative file. We again estimate the substantive effect of racial and moral cross-pressures on the probability that a Democrat voted for the Republican presidential candidate in each of the last eleven presidential campaigns,

---

[100] The White House, 23 July 2004. President emphasizes minority entrepreneurship at Urban League. Remarks by the president to the 2004 National Urban League Conference. Washington, D.C.: Retrieved 10 November 2005.

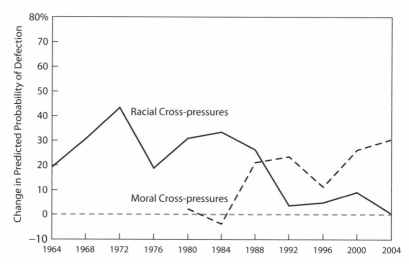

Figure 5.5: Effect of Racial and Moral Cross-pressures on the Predicted Probability of Defection, 1964–2004

Note: Figure indicates that the impact of racial cross-pressures has declined in recent years, while the impact of moral cross-pressures has increased. Reported is the change in the predicted probability of defection between highly cross-pressured white Democrats and congruent Democrats, holding constant all other variables in the model. Data source is the American National Election Study cumulative file.

reported in figure 5.5.[101] These results follow the general pattern that we would expect given the strategic campaign decisions we have discussed throughout this chapter. Those who are highly cross-pressured on racial issues were much more likely to defect in the 1960s–1980s, compared to those not cross-pressured, while racial policy incongruence has little impact in recent years. In contrast, Democrats highly cross-pressured on social issues, like abortion, were more likely to defect in recent years compared to the 1980s (when questions were first asked). It was with the 1992 presidential election that the effect of moral cross-pressures exceeded the effect of racial cross-pressures, perhaps reflecting the prominence of moral criticisms of then-candidate Bill Clinton.

There is little doubt that race was central to the early transformation of the South, but the importance of race in American attitudes and be-

---

[101] See appendix 1 for issues included by year, and appendix 3 for full results. Reported are the changes in the predicted probability of moving from 0 to 75 percent (95th percentile) on the policy incongruence scale, holding other variables at their global means or modes from the earliest survey year. The results are substantively similar, albeit muted, if we also control for retrospective evaluations of the national economy, ideology, attitudes toward Vietnam and strength of partisanship.

havior in the later part of the twentieth century has been a topic of considerable debate. Some scholars have argued that racial issues no longer explain voting behavior by the 1970s, while others contend it remains an important predictor of vote choice.[102] Alan Abramowitz concludes, for instance, that "attitudes toward racial issues had a negligible impact on voting decisions" by the late 1980s.[103] Our findings suggest that the extent to which voters weighed racial policies in their vote decisions has depended on the particular campaign context. When presidential candidates took divergent positions on questions of race and were willing to emphasize those differences in their campaigns, voters' racial attitudes played a stronger role in their decision-making processes. In recent elections, Republican candidates have been more likely to focus their strategic efforts on winning over culturally conservative Democrats, and we see those efforts reflected in the behavior of Democrats who face inconsistent policy positions on social and moral issues.

Conclusion: Civil Rights and the Reciprocal Campaign

To win a presidential election, candidates must build a coalition between their base supporters and persuadable voters. Throughout this book, we have argued that candidates look for wedge issues that will divide the potential winning coalition of the opposition party and will appeal to groups of swing voters. The Republican southern strategy is a classic example. We have made the case that Richard Nixon strategically emphasized conservative racial policies in his 1968 and 1972 presidential campaigns because he perceived the persuadable voters to be racially conservative Democrats, especially in the South. In contrast, Nixon in 1960 and Ford in 1976 viewed other groups as swing voters and adjusted their issue agendas accordingly.

While our focus on the Republican southern strategy offers a clear example of our expectations about the interaction of candidate strategy and voter decision making, it is worth considering whether this is an especially unique case. It is important to delineate where and how racial issues might be distinct from other divisive issues that might be used as a campaign wedge issue.

At the most general level, racial policy attitudes, more than other policy attitudes, run wide and deep in the public consciousness—there has not been a more difficult or sustained policy question since the founding of the country than that concerning issues of race. Unlike

---

[102] For example, see Valentino and Sears, "Old Times There Are Not Forgotten: Race and Partisan Realignment in the Contemporary South." For arguments that race was less important see Shafer and Johnston, *The End of Southern Exceptionalism*.

[103] See Abramowitz, "Issue Evolution Reconsidered," 21.

many other political issues, questions about race also touch a number of different policy areas. In both direct and indirect ways, questions about race remain central to policy areas as far-reaching as schooling, welfare, taxes, crime, and income redistribution. Other wedge issues— whether stem cell research, minimum wage, or gay marriage—may not have consequences for as many different areas of public policy, nor have they affected as many people.

The racial issues considered in this chapter also presented a rather unique strategic opportunity for Republican candidates in the mid-twentieth century because the issues so deeply divided the Democrats but were ones for which there was generally consensus (or indifference) among their own supporters. Once Republicans abandoned their attempts to appeal to black voters, they ran little risk of alienating white Republicans by taking racially conservative stands—especially as their conservative policies were typically accompanied by rhetorical commitments to basic principles of equality. Even the early social wedge issues emphasized by the candidates—school prayer, the Pledge of Allegiance, and so on—enjoyed wide support among all segments of the electorate except for die-hard liberals who were highly unlikely ever to support a Republican candidate anyway.

These types of wedge issues sharply contrast with policies that divide both the opposition coalition *and* one's own supporters. Some divisive issues—like abortion, stem cell research, and school vouchers— might allow candidates to lure policy-conflicted out-partisans but may simultaneously turn off members of their own party. For issues that cut both ways, candidates take a much greater risk in making it part of their national presidential campaign dialogue. Yet today's increasingly competitive electoral environment, in which presidential candidates win or lose based on razor-thin margins in a handful of states, encourages candidates to look for every strategic opportunity. More importantly, as we discuss in the next chapter, the contemporary information environment enables candidates to use more divisive issues than was ever possible in previous eras.

Six

Candidate Strategy in the 2004 Campaign

IN HIS NOMINATION ACCEPTANCE SPEECH at the 1988 Republican National Convention in New Orleans, President George H. W. Bush made his now famous pledge:

> I'm the one who will not raise taxes. My opponent now says he'll raise them as a last resort, or a third resort. But when a politician talks like that, you know that's one resort he'll be checking into. My opponent, my opponent won't rule out raising taxes. But I will. The Congress will push me to raise taxes and I'll say no. And they'll push, and I'll say no, and they'll push again, and I'll say, to them, "*Read my lips: no new taxes.*" (italics added)[1]

Bush would later find it impossible to make good on that promise. Facing an economic recession, a congressional mandate to reduce the deficit, and a Democratic Congress that opposed cuts to entitlement programs, Bush had little room to maneuver. In a press release in June 1990, Bush explained, "It is clear to me that both the size of the deficit problem and the need for a package that can be enacted require all of the following: entitlement and mandatory program reform, tax revenue increases, growth incentives, discretionary spending reductions, orderly reductions in defense expenditures, and budget process reform." Bush broke his campaign promise.

Many argued that Bush's reversal on taxes contributed to his electoral defeat in 1992. Pat Buchanan threw his hat into the Republican primary, explaining, "We Republicans can no longer say it is all the liberals' fault. It was not some liberal Democrat who said 'Read my lips: no new taxes,' then broke his word to cut a seedy backroom budget deal with the big spenders on Capitol Hill."[2] Democratic television ads replayed a clip of Bush's pledge, labeling him untrustworthy and unprincipled. Although a number of other prominent Republicans agreed that a tax increase was necessary, Bush was criticized because

---

[1] In an initial draft of the nomination speech, Bush's economic advisor, Richard Darman, crossed out the phrase calling it "stupid and dangerous." Darman, *Who's in Control*? Full text of speech is available through American Presidency Project at www .presidency.ucsb.edu.

[2] Robin Toner, "Buchanan, Urging New Nationalism, Joins '92 Race," *New York Times*, 11 December 1991, B12.

he reneged on a campaign promise. Republican pollster Richard Wirthlin called Bush's pledge "the six most destructive words in the history of presidential politics."[3] Political consultant Ed Rollins called it "the most serious violation of any political pledge anybody has ever made."[4]

As Bush's experience so clearly illustrates, there are appreciable risks associated with staking out a position on a political issue. Once in office, the policy stance can tie the hands of an elected official, limiting policy-making options. Candidates who later change their position are labeled "flip-floppers" or "wafflers." Concerned about such negative consequences, it is understandable why politicians work aggressively to carry out their campaign agendas after winning office. In general, scholars find a strong relationship between campaign policy promises and government policy agendas after an election.[5]

But it is also risky to take a stand on a policy issue because of the potential for alienating voters who disagree. Richard Nixon, for instance, recognized that opposing civil rights policies might win votes among white southerners, but that it would also cost votes among blacks. Candidates must consider both the gains and losses that come with staking a position on a divisive policy issue. For these reasons, it has long been thought that rational candidates will avoid taking stances on policy issues in a political campaign.[6]

Yet, despite the incentives to avoid controversial issues, presidential candidates *do* make policy promises. Candidates routinely outline their policy agendas in their nomination acceptance speeches, detail their positions on campaign Web sites, and highlight issue priorities in their campaign communications, stump speeches, and media appearances. In every campaign, candidates make choices about which issues to discuss and which to avoid. But political scientists do not have a clear understanding of why candidates emphasize some issues while ignoring or downplaying others. There is broad recognition that candidates try to frame salient issues in a way that advantages their candidacy, but it is less clear why candidates choose particular policy agendas and priorities.[7] Charles Franklin laments that "the political nature of elections lies in the choices candidates make about strategy. . . . As we have become adept at studying voters, it is ironic that we have virtu-

[3] Colin MacKenzie, "How Bush Blew It," *The Globe and Mail*, 4 November 1992, A1.

[4] Germond, *Mad as Hell*, 35.

[5] Pomper, *Elections in America*; Jeff Fishel, *Presidents & Promises*.

[6] Page, *Choices and Echoes in Presidential Elections*.

[7] There is a growing body of research in political science recognizing that candidates try to frame, prime, or otherwise set the campaign agenda to control the context in which voters make a decision, but it is largely silent about divisive issues. For overview, see Druckman et al., "Candidate Strategies to Prime Issues and Image."

ally ignored the study of candidates. Yet it is in candidate behavior that politics intrudes into voting behavior. Without the candidates, there is only the psychology of vote choice and none of the politics."[8] To be sure, there exist a number of rich, descriptive accounts of individual campaigns, but what is lacking is an underlying theory of candidate strategy about issue agendas. And the limited existing research is largely silent about why a candidate might emphasize positional issues in particular.

In this chapter, we look more closely at the implications of our arguments for candidate behavior in contemporary presidential campaigns. In particular, we focus on the link between the information environment and campaign strategy. While the Republican southern strategy offered an illustration of the long-standing incentive to use wedge issues, in this chapter we turn to an examination of why and how contemporary candidates narrowly target a wide range of wedge issues. Certainly, candidates today are taking stances on more issues and more divisive issues than ever before. Figure 6.1 traces over time the average number of unique issue positions taken in party platforms and candidate speeches.[9] More striking is the fact that presidential candidates in 2004 took positions on more than *seventy-five* different political issues in their direct-mail communications. Just the sheer number of different issues discussed raises questions about the reasons for such diverse and fragmented issue agendas and about the implications for issue dialogue in the campaign. By examining the volume, content, and targeting of television and direct mail advertising in the 2004 presidential campaign, we are able to evaluate the candidates' issue strategies. Our findings suggest that information and communication technologies have changed not only how candidates communicate with voters, but also who they communicate with and what they are willing to say, with potentially troublesome implications for political inequality.

Conventional Wisdom about Candidates' Issue Strategies

Why and how do candidates choose particular campaign issues? To some extent, the issue content of a political campaign is constrained by conditions outside the candidates' control. When an issue of overarching national interest is in the limelight, like an economic or foreign-

---

[8] Franklin, "Eschewing Obfuscation," 1201.

[9] Party platforms are especially informative because they are typically not consumed by (or intended for) the general public, but they provide the candidate with credibility on the issues emphasized in the campaign. Selection of speeches and coding described in appendix 2.

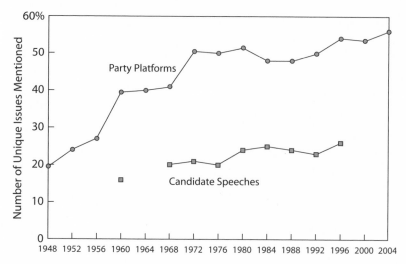

Figure 6.1: Growth in the Policy Position Taking of Presidential Candidates, 1948–2004

Note: Figure shows an increase in the unique number of policy positions taken by presidential candidates. Data sources are the U.S. Party Platforms and the Annenberg/Pew Archive of Presidential Campaign Discourse.

policy crisis, candidates cannot ignore it. Journalists will cover it, debate moderators will press candidates to discuss it, and voters will expect to hear how the candidates will handle it. Candidates are also compelled to address any issues Americans consider to be among the most pressing problems of the day, issues like health care, education, and other valence issues—policies that everyone considers important and laudable, even if they disagree on the means for improvement.[10] It is hard to imagine that a credible presidential candidate could campaign without addressing the issues the public identifies as the "most important problems" facing the country.[11] But beyond the issues that candidates *must* discuss, there are those that they *choose* to emphasize. In addition to responding to the exogenous environment, candidates try to control the issue context of the campaign. Among the topics candidates put on the agenda are "positional" issues—those about which

[10] To be sure, even a consensual issue can be used as a wedge issue if there is considerable disagreement about one side's performance on the issue or if there is disagreement about how to best achieve the goal. For instance, vouchers versus school funding in promoting education.

[11] Since the 1950s, the Gallup election-year polls find that economics, foreign conflicts, health care, and education are consistently volunteered as the most important issues facing the nation.

people take different sides—minimum wage, school prayer, and stem cell research.[12] But why would rational candidates take stands on such divisive political issues?

The conventional wisdom has been that rational office-seeking candidates will avoid controversial issues or will at least be ambiguous on such issues to avoid offending someone who might disagree. Yet this expectation does not seem to hold up to the empirical reality of contemporary presidential campaigns. More recently, political observers and scholars have suggested that candidates might be willing to take positions on controversial issues as a way of appealing to their core partisan supporters. From this perspective, candidates must invigorate their base with policy promises in order to generate financial contributions, sustain volunteer efforts, and motivate citizens to turn out. For instance, Jacob Hacker and Paul Pierson argue that Republican politicians have recently moved away from the center because they are kowtowing to party activists: "What is the great force that pulls Republican politicians to the right? In a word, the 'base.' . . . The base has always had power, but never the kind of power it has today. With money more important in campaigns than ever, the base has money. With the political and organizational resources of ordinary voters in decline, the base is mobilized and well organized."[13] The underlying assumption of this line of reasoning is often that candidates will generally ignore nonbase voters either because they are unlikely to vote or they can be swayed with nonideological campaign appeals.[14]

In contrast, we suggest that the use of these issues logically follows from the preferences and behaviors of the voters—specifically the cross-pressured partisans who might be receptive to campaign appeals. To reiterate our now familiar empirical and theoretical conclusions thus far, a candidate can win over a persuadable voter by increasing the salience of a cross-cutting issue that provides an advantage over the opponent. In order to make the wedge issue salient, the candidate must stake out a position on the issue that is clearly distinguishable from the positions of the opposition party. And the relative distinctiveness of the two candidates is often clearest on divisive positional issues. The particular policy disagreements that have the potential to be exploited will depend on the broader political environment as well as the characteristics of the opposing candidates, but we expect that vote-seeking candidates will look for strategic opportunities to emphasize wedge issues.

---

[12] See Stokes, "Spatial Models of Party Competition."

[13] Hacker and Pierson, *Off Center*, 9.

[14] Bartels, "Partisanship and Voting Behavior."

Our expectation that candidates develop their campaign strategy with an eye toward Independents and policy-conflicted partisans fits nicely with some existing political science research about legislative voting behavior. In a study about U.S. Senators, for example, Gerald Wright found that senators' policy votes more closely reflected the preferences of Independents than the full electorate or even partisan identifiers.[15] He concluded that "senators balance their appeals between their own party's activists and the ideological leanings of the Independents of their states. In this view, the opposition party adherents—at least those that are ideologically in tune with the out-party—are not heeded."[16] Another study concluded that Republican senators lost control of the chamber following the 1986 midterm elections because their policy voting primarily reflected the preferences of their base supporters and was not sufficiently responsive to the policy concerns of Independents and dissident Democrats who had helped elect Ronald Reagan in the previous presidential election.[17] Our analysis builds on this research by linking the incentives of presidential candidates to their campaign agendas.

Information Technology and the Microtargeting of Wedge Issues

Presidential candidates have always had incentives to use wedge issues, but today's information environment has enabled greater use of divisive political issues in presidential campaigns. A candidate's willingness to use a wedge strategy is influenced by the information available about the electorate and the tactics available to disseminate campaign messages. As illustrated by Bush's campaign promise on taxes, taking a stand on an issue—even one that enjoys widespread support—carries political risk. The more information candidates have about the preferences of individual voters, the better they can calculate the costs and benefits of emphasizing a particular position. Critically, politicians today have more detailed information about citizen preferences than ever before. As Matthew Dowd, Ron Fournier, and Douglas Sosnick recently observed in *Applebee's America*, "If you're a voter living in one of the 16 states that determined the 2004 election, the Bush

---

[15] Wright, "Policy Voting in the U.S. Senate."

[16] Ibid., 483.

[17] Hurley, "Partisan Representation, Realignment, and the Senate in the 1980s."

team had your name on a spreadsheet with your hobbies and habits, vices and virtues, favorite foods, sports, and vacation venues, and many other facts of your life."[18]

This information is combined with communication technologies that allow candidates to microtarget campaign messages; that is, candidates can send a tailored message to a narrow subgroup of the electorate on the basis of information about that subgroup. Microtargeting allows candidates to surgically deliver different messages to different constituencies, thus expanding the arsenal of potential wedge issues that can be used in the campaign. With direct mail, email, telephone calls, text messaging, Web advertising, and the like, candidates can narrowcast issue messages to some voters even if others in their coalition might disagree or consider the issue less important. Microtargeting enables candidates to use double-edged issues. Thus, the campaign tactics that contemporary candidates rely on to communicate with voters ultimately shape the substance of the messages that are communicated. So whatever the impact of microtargeted messages on the voters, this tactic has the potential to influence campaign dynamics by changing the behavior of candidates.

Certainly, there are numerous examples of candidates emphasizing wedge issues even before contemporary communication technologies. In the 1948 presidential election, Harry Truman complained that the Republican strategy was intended to "divide the farmer and the industrial worker—to get them squabbling with each other—so that big business can grasp the balance of power, and take the country over lock, stock and barrel."[19] In previous political eras, however, wedge strategies were more often used when the cleavages within a party coalition were readily apparent and when the issue not only divided the opposition but also created consensus among the candidates' own supporters. When campaign messages are communicated to a broader audience, candidates have to carefully consider the consequences of taking a stand on a divisive issue. In the 1976 campaign, for instance, President Ford's strategists acknowledged the difficulty of narrowly targeting strategically important voters. In recommending that the president tailor his campaign activity to different groups, President Ford was advised that "actions to get target constituency groups . . . should be rifle shots aimed at the specific group involved. These efforts should not be undertaken with the objective of getting national press

---

[18] Sosnik et al., *Applebee's America*, 13.
[19] Truman Library documents. 18 September 1948, Dexter, Iowa.

coverage (although we must keep in mind that this will happen if any mistakes are made)."[20]

Because of the link between the information environment and the use of wedge issues, our expectations are consistent with candidate polarization trends over time. One of the key puzzles in political science stems from the empirical reality that candidates' campaign agendas are increasingly divergent from academic predictions that candidates will moderate their policies to appeal to the pivotal voter in the electorate. Considerable research has documented the fact that political elites have grown more polarized across policy issues in recent decades, with candidates taking decidedly distinctive policy positions. Morris Fiorina poses the question, "Whatever happened to the median voter? Rather than attempt to move her 'off the fence' or 'swing' her from one party to another, today's campaigners seem to be ignoring her."[21] Previous research has offered a number of different explanations for the recent increase in political polarization, including the realignment of the South, partisan gerrymandering, the greater numbers and influence of interest groups, and growing income inequalities in the electorate.[22] We leave to other scholars the important (and difficult) task of sorting through and testing all the proposed catalysts of party polarization. We simply add another potential explanation to the list: information about individual voters.

With the explosion of information about individual voters political communication has become more diverse, fragmented and complex. This changing context influences not only how candidates communicate with citizens, but also who they are contacting and what they are willing to say. Our information-centric perspective on the relationship between candidates and voters in presidential campaigns recognizes that just as changing the information available about the candidates can change the behavior of the voters, so too can changes in the amount, type, or accessibility of information about the voters shape the behavior of the candidates. The information environment helps determine a candidate's ability and willingness to use a wedge strategy. Candidates should be less willing to stake a position on an issue if they are uncertain about the preferences of voters or if the issue message will be disseminated to voters who disagree with the position. In a

[20] Campaign Strategy Plan, August 1976; folder "Presidential Campaign—Campaign Strategy Program (1)-(3)," box 1, Dorothy E. Downton Files, Gerald R. Ford Library, 70–71.

[21] Fiorina, "Whatever Happened to the Median Voter," 3.

[22] For an excellent review of this literature and its implications, see Layman et al., "Party Polarization in American Politics."

game theoretic model, Ed Glaeser, Giacomo Ponzetto, and Jesse Shapiro show that the ability to microtarget messages produces more extreme party platforms.[23]

We are by no means the first to call attention to the importance of information technology for campaign politics. Political scholars have long recognized that information and communication technologies fundamentally affect how candidates run campaigns. Communication scholars David Swanson and Paolo Mancini observe that

> electronic wizardry elongates the campaign day by affording opportunities for candidates, freed from the six o'clock imperative, to make news anytime; it elongates the campaign season and proliferates its cycles by enhancing chances for candidates to build name recognition, establish a voter support base, and raise funds at a campaigner's pace, not in conformity with short- or long-term media scheduling.[24]

Scholars have also documented how Web sites, online fund-raising, and email communication have become integral to political campaigns.[25] As one report lamented following the 2000 presidential election,

> Eighty years ago, radio allowed people to hear candidates by their firesides for the first time. Thirty years later, television added pictures, which transformed even party conventions into events arranged for people to absorb in their living rooms. Videotapes, computers, and direct mail added to the precision. This year, the Internet, with its personal "cookie" technology, joined automated celebrity phone calls, push-poll proselytizing, issue Web sites, and political e-mails to drive politics even further into a personalized, invisible space."[26]

Often, however, these new technologies are viewed as a supplemental communication tool for conducting "politics as usual"— presumed to change the style of political campaigns, but not the basic structure of political interaction.[27] As one study summarized, the Internet is "nothing more than a new medium in which old patterns of political behavior and information flows are played out anew."[28] In contrast, we argue that information and communication technologies have changed not just how candidates communicate with voters, but also the substance of their communication.

---

[23] Glaeser et al., "Strategic Extremism."

[24] Swanson and Mancini, *Politics, Media and Modern Democracy*, 38.

[25] For instance, Bimber and Davis, *Campaigning Online*.

[26] Bill Kovach and Tom Rosenstiel, "Campaign Lite," *Washington Monthly*, 13. January/February 2001, 31.

[27] Margolis and Resnick, *Politics as Usual*.

[28] Xenos and Foot, "Political as Usual, or Politics Unusual," 3.

History offers us several examples of this link between the information environment and campaign strategy. For instance, the first mass political party, the Jacksonian Democrats in 1828, could be built from a "patchwork of conflicting interest groups, classes, and factions" because of changes in transportation and communication technologies that allowed Jackson to communicate with and mobilize a far-flung population.[29] Likewise, the introduction of radio broadcasting in presidential campaigns changed the style and substance of candidate speeches. In discussing the introduction of radio in the 1924 presidential election, journalist Don Moore observed, "While before candidates spoke mainly to the party faithful, they now had to tailor their speeches more for the undecided, and even the opposition. . . . Because radio audiences did not feel as if they had to show signs of support for the speaker, the audience became not only bigger, but more heterogeneous. Undecided and opposing voters, who might not be comfortable attending a rally, could easily tune in at home."[30] Whereas the introduction of previous communication technologies, especially television, was used to expand and broaden the audience receiving a campaign message, technologies today are used to more narrowly communicate individualized messages to smaller and more segmented audiences.

In many ways, microtargeting revives the campaign strategy of the late nineteenth century, where whistle-stop campaigns and segmented news markets allowed candidates to communicate different messages to different voters. Based on information about various constituencies from local party leaders, candidates would modify their stump speeches in order to maximize their appeal to whatever group they were currently addressing. In the 1948 presidential campaign, for instance, Harry Truman criticized the Taft-Hartley Act, calling it "a termite, undermining and eating away your legal protection to organize and bargain collectively," when speaking to a group made up largely of union members in Scranton, Pennsylvania. In contrast, his stump-speech outline for Queens, New York, was marked with the note (in all capital letters), "DO NOT MENTION LABOR OR TAFT-HARTLEY ACT." Meanwhile, in Dexter, Iowa, Truman declared, "The Democratic Party is fighting the farmer's battle."[31]

---

[29] Aldrich, *Why Parties*, 106; Remini, *The Life of Andrew Jackson*, 72–73.

[30] Don Moore, "The 1924 Radio Election," *Monitoring Times Magazine*, July 1992.

[31] Truman Library documents, Scranton, Pennsylvania speech dated 23 October 1948; Queens New York notes, dated 29 October 1948; Dexter, Iowa speech 18 September 1948.

Evolution of Microtargeting

Before we analyze the candidates' strategies on wedge issues in the 2004 presidential election, we first provide a brief history of the campaign tactic of microtargeting. To be sure, the notion that candidates should target specific messages to individual voters is as old as American political campaigns. A Whig-committee campaign memo in 1840 advised that it was the duty of a party subcommittee to "keep a constant watch on the doubtful voters, and have them talked to by those in whom they have the most confidence, and also to place in their hands such documents as will enlighten and influence them."[32]

More recently, advisors to President Ford recommended targeting Hispanic voters with special messages by creating "a direct mail program to be developed to special interest groups that are predominantly Spanish-oriented with specific issues (expressed in layman's language) that would appeal to the particular special interest group (e.g.—day care centers for working mothers to residents residing in low-income housing developments)."[33] Although microtargeting as a tactic is not new, changes in the information environment and lessons from commercial marketing, grassroots mobilization, and direct-mail fundraising have made contemporary microtargeting more precise, efficient, and individualized. As we discuss in the conclusion, it remains unclear whether these messages are also more effective. But whatever the influence on voter behavior, we argue that these campaign tactics have had a profound influence on candidate behavior.

In the commercial world, companies began using microtargeted direct marketing in the 1980s as the mass media fragmented and diversified. The proliferation of cable channels, radio, the Internet, and other communication alternatives made it more difficult to reach and influence consumers with television advertising. With the emergence of database-management and data-mining capabilities, advertisers were better able to identify the likes and dislikes of potential customers and could then tailor ads to the individual consumer. Thus, the credit-card offers, catalogs, and other junk mail that clog our mailboxes every day

---

[32] Quoted in Wielhouwer, "In Search of Lincoln's Perfect List," 632–33.

[33] The memo goes on to ask, "Does any of the Ford family speak Spanish? Maybe Jack or Susan should learn. Does the Mexican Ambassador to the United States have a daughter that Jack can date?" Campaign Strategy Plan, August 1976; folder "Presidential Campaign—Campaign Strategy Program (1)-(3)," box 1, Dorothy E. Downton Files, Gerald R. Ford Library, Tab I, Strategy Details.

have been personalized, based on our purchasing and lifestyle habits to maximize the likelihood that they catch our attention and interest.

Political candidates observed similar inefficiencies in reaching their intended audiences. As suffrage in the United States expanded and overall voter turnout declined, candidates and parties realized that they needed to more efficiently and strategically use their resources. Candidates have long concentrated resources in those states thought to be most critical to an election outcome. In the first presidential campaign to use television advertising, Dwight Eisenhower purchased spot buys in thirty-nine states, but saturated the airwaves (four to five spots heard by voters each day) in eleven states.[34] Later, candidates used precinct voting history and census information about the income or racial composition of a neighborhood for *geotargeting*, the targeting of efforts to specific precincts and geographic areas in a state that might have a cluster of supporters. For instance, Democratic candidates would concentrate their canvassing in urban precincts where mobilization efforts would be more likely to increase the number of votes for the Democratic candidate. Focusing campaign efforts in a limited number of neighborhoods was more efficient than blanketing an entire state, but it still wasted resources on opposition supporters living in the canvassed neighborhoods and missed potential supporters in other areas. Talking about his experience campaigning for governor of Massachusetts, Michael Dukakis quipped that if he walked up a flight of stairs, he was going to knock on every door—he wasn't going to skip over an apartment just because a Republican lived there.[35]

Generally, these geotargeting appeals were more frequently GOTV (get-out-the-vote) messages or broad-based persuasive appeals. Even a demographically homogeneous neighborhood does not guarantee homogeneity in political preferences. Political polling was used to collect information about the preferences of the voters, but given the cost of polling, sample sizes typically allowed for only crude breakdowns by demographic or geographic characteristics. It was risky to talk about divisive issues in geotargeted communications. A campaign strategist for George H. W. Bush explained the geotargeting strategy in the 1988 presidential campaign, "There are some areas where we can play hardball. . . . Abortion and gun control and going heavy on crime plays in most of the South and most of the West. Where it gets

---

[34] O'Shaughnessy, *The Phenomenon of Political Marketing*, 48; also interesting is that the content of the ads was determined from George Gallup's polling about the issue of importance to the public.

[35] Remarks made at Conference on Swing Voters in American Politics, Northeastern University, 10 June 2006.

trickier is when we try to go after groups like ethnic Catholics in the North, where the roots to the national Democratic Party are stronger and there are neighborhoods where you mix ethnics with yuppies and every kind of group, so you have to be much more careful."[36] Rather than targeting just state by state, or even neighborhood by neighborhood, candidates today can target household by household. Candidates now know which households to target in a neighborhood and which ones to skip, and candidates can surgically locate the one sympathetic supporter in an otherwise unsympathetic neighborhood.

When available, presidential candidates have always used information about individual voters, but historically such information was available for only a limited subset of voters, such as contributors or volunteers. Using target lists donated, bought, or rented from like-minded candidates or causes, direct-mail fund-raising has been a hallmark of political campaigns since the 1980s. Direct-mail fund-raising was pioneered by Richard Viguerie, the self-proclaimed "funding father" of the conservative movement. In 1965 Viguerie hand-copied the list of twelve thousand individuals who contributed fifty dollars or more to Barry Goldwater's 1964 presidential campaign. In the forty-plus years since, Viguerie estimates he has mailed out more than 2 billion letters, raising billions of dollars for conservative causes and helping to raise awareness of front-burner conservative issues.[37] A candidate's Rolodex of potential contributors remains one of the most critical elements of a political campaign. Robin Parker, former Democratic Senatorial Campaign Committee political director, explained that the very first question asked of a Senate candidate was "who has your lists?"[38] She recalled that these limited target lists were often kept on index cards in shoe boxes before the advent of electronic databases. Today, candidates have information not just about contributors but about *every* voter.

Political parties have created enormous databases that include information about nearly every one of the roughly 168 million registered voters in the United States. With the growth in computing power and information technology, parties and candidates now collect, store, and analyze an overwhelming range of information about individual voters.[39] These databases start with voter registration files. Voters' registra-

[36] Thomas B. Edsall, "GOP May Find 'Wedge' Issues No Longer Cutting as Deep," *Washington Post*, 30 August 1988, A1.

[37] Bill Berkowitz, "Personal profile; Viguerie, Richard: Still Thundering After All These Years," www.MediaTransparency.org, 19 February 2005. Accessed 29 April 2007.

[38] Interview with Robin Parker conducted by Sunshine Hillygus on 21 November 2005.

[39] In 2004 the Democrats' database, Demzilla, included an estimated 166 million registered voters and the Republicans' database, *Voter Vault*, contained 168 million registered voters.

tion records—including name, home address, voting history, and in many states, party affiliation, phone number, date of birth, and other information—are available to political parties and candidates (twenty-two states have no restrictions on who can access these files).[40] The statewide database of 15 million voters in California is available for just thirty-five dollars, for example.[41] Several states have put individual voter records online, giving free and open public access. A quick last-name search on the North Carolina State Board of Elections Web site, for instance, pulled up the name, home address, race, gender, party affiliation, polling place, and vote history since 1992 of a colleague at Duke University.

Candidates have been using voter registration rolls, where available, for many years. But until recently there was incredible variability across states in regard to the information collected and the accessibility of that information.[42] A few states created electronic files as early as the 1980s, but more often the data were available only as hard copy from the county registrar or municipal jurisdictions, and often included the names of voters long since moved or dead. To build a state-wide voter list in Michigan, for instance, candidates had to contact and acquire the voter list from 1,800 different jurisdictions. One consultant noted that these voter registration lists were "barely an improvement over the phone book."[43] States slowly began moving toward computerized registration files following the 1993 National Voter Registration Act. Often called "motor voter," this legislation required states to allow residents to register to vote when they applied for a driver's license. In many cases this new law called attention to the poor quality of the registration record systems kept in most states and sparked movement

---

[40] Web sites like www.spiesonline.com recommend voter registration files as "especially helpful in locating someone" because "information included with the voter registration information might include an unlisted phone number, birth date or a social security number, in addition to the address information." There are slight variations across states in terms of who is given access to the electronic databases (all states give access to parties), with some states selling the data for a small administrative fee and others requiring that access to the data be limited to scholarly research. In practice, private companies specializing in database building have not had problems gathering the data. As www.spiesonline.com advises "if you say you need the information for research purposes . . . people will be more cooperative about giving you this kind of information by mail."

[41] The exact regulations on use, content, and cost vary across states. For an overview, see Alexander and Mills, "Voter Privacy in the Digital Age."

[42] Simultaneously, some political consultants were compiling lists of individuals who had contributed to a political candidate or a related cause. These lists were not of general voters, but were viewed as critical for tapping additional contributions.

[43] Malchow, *The New Political Targeting*, 4.

toward electronic files. An additional push in the quality and accessibility of voter information came with the 2002 Help America Vote Act, which mandated states to develop a single, uniform, centralized, interactive voter registration database that would be updated regularly. The majority of states now have easily accessible electronic information on every registered voter.

Although databases start with voter registration files, statistical and computing power have made it possible to match consumer data to individual voter records. Data-management companies such as Equifax, Axciom, Experian, HomeData, D&B, Advo, and ChoicePoint compile individual-level information from myriad sources, both public records and material purchased from other companies. Such databases include names, addresses, address histories, driving record, criminal records, consumer purchases, and a variety of other personal information that allows campaigns access to more information about individual voters than ever before. Increases in computing power and data-storage capabilities, coupled with consumers' desires for conveniences and discounts, led to a data revolution starting in the 1990s. As explained in a recent account,

> Nearly every time a person takes out a loan, uses a credit card, makes an Internet transaction, books a flight, or conducts any of hundreds of other business transactions, he or she leaves a data trail. The average consumer travels through life trailed by thousands of clues to future buying and voting habits, a veritable gold mine for any organization with the money and motivation to solve the mysteries of his or her political attitudes.[44]

As new information technologies were developing, it became apparent that traditional television campaigning was less effective. In the 1998 congressional races, after years of pouring money into television ads that were increasingly expensive yet less effective, labor unions recommitted money to "ground war" activities—telephone calls, direct mail, and personal canvassing. The decision rested in large part on internal studies of the 1997 New Jersey gubernatorial race that found an 8 percentage-point increase in support for the labor-backed gubernatorial candidate among those contacted compared to those not contacted.[45] Such an influence far exceeded any estimates of television advertising effects. Democrats ended up gaining seats in the House in the 1998 election, the first time since 1934 that a president's party had gained seats in a midterm election. In the 2000 presidential and congressional elections,

[44] Sosnick et al., *Applebee's America*, 37.
[45] Thomas B. Edsall, "Grass-Roots Organizing Tops TV Ads in AFL-CIO Political Agenda," *Washington Post*, 20 May 1998, A3.

Democratic candidates once again performed better on Election Day than predicted by preelection polls, which political observers attributed to superior grassroots campaigning.[46]

In response, Republicans developed a plan to improve their own ground-war efforts, borrowing tactics from the commercial world. Bolstered by academic studies suggesting that nonpartisan GOTV efforts were effective at increasing turnout, as well as changes in campaign finance laws that cracked down on television advertising but left ground-war activities unregulated and undisclosed to the Federal Election Commission (FEC), political will and technological capabilities fully came together for the 2004 presidential campaign. A recent study reports that Kerry campaign staff and volunteers knocked on 8 million doors and made 23.5 million phone calls, while the Bush campaign estimated that their party faithful knocked on 9.1 million doors and made 27.2 million phone calls.[47] Importantly, while limited information available about voters once encouraged campaigns to concentrate on GOTV and other mobilization efforts, the expansion of information about voters now allows grassroots efforts to use persuasive appeals.

How has this information influenced campaign strategy and candidates' issue agendas? With great precision, contemporary candidates are now able to predict the probability that an individual is going to vote, the probability that she is going to vote for a particular candidate, as well as her issue priorities. Ken Mehlman explained, "Basically, what it is, is spending a lot more time IDing people, spending a lot more time figuring out what issues people care about and contacting them on the basis of those issues."[48] Thus, a letter or email highlighting a candidate's position on the second amendment will be sent to a registered Independent who owns a gun, while a message focused on gay marriage will be sent to a registered Republican who is a member of an evangelical church but has voted sporadically in recent elections. As one political consultant explained, "You don't have to shotgun anymore. You can now bullet."[49]

Alex Gage, Republican consultant and head of TargetPoint consulting, explained step by step how the Republican National Committee translated voter information into campaign strategy.[50] First, they

---

[46] Shaw, "Door-to-Door with the GOP."

[47] Bergan et al., "Grassroots Mobilization and Voter Turnout in 2004."

[48] James O'Toole "RNC, Expecting Tough Elections, Mobilizes Troops," *Pittsburgh Post-Gazette*, 7 August, 2005.

[49] Dana Milbank, "Virtual Politics: Candidates' Consultants Create the Customized Campaign," *New Republic*, 5 July 1999, 23.

[50] Interview with Alex Gage conducted by Quin Monson and David Magleby; Alexandria, Va.; 15 December 2004. Steps were also discussed in Magleby et al., *Dancing without Partners*.

obtained the voter registration file from the state with whatever information was included. Second, they appended to the voter file any proprietary data available from the RNC, including previous contributions or membership in like-minded organizations. Third, they merged in consumer data, including magazine subscriptions, mortgage information, credit-card purchases, gun ownership, and the like. Fourth, from this master list, they conducted a survey of roughly 5,500 respondents in the state, asking a variety of questions about political attitudes and behavior including the particular issues that angered or excited the respondents. Based on the survey data, the RNC conducted extensive data-mining studies in order to find out which characteristics predicted a Republican vote. Voters were then segmented into about thirty different groups based on the type of issues that were likely to drive them to vote for Bush, groups like "tax and terrorism moderates" or "religious weak Republicans." The full database of registered voters was then assigned to one of the segments "based on the lifestyle and political habits he or she shared with those surveyed and already placed in groups."[51]

Bush strategist Sara Taylor further explained that individuals in each of these segments were evaluated and ranked based both on their probability of voting and their probability of voting for Bush. The campaign then made strategic decisions about where campaign resources should be spent and what messages should be sent to different individuals. This information was then used to microtarget messages through direct mail, email, telephone calls, and personal visits. Sara Taylor summed it up: "We could identify exactly who should be mailed, on what issues, and who should be ignored completely."[52]

These campaign tactics have created incentives for candidates to make explicitly ideological and issue-based appeals to narrower portions of the public. As one consultant explained, "In previous campaigns Republicans would call potential voters with a tape-recorded message from Ronald Reagan or a similar personage on the generic importance of voting. In 2004, a voter concerned about abortion would hear 'if you don't come out and vote, the number of abortions next year is going to go up.' "[53] This campaign tactic is used to communicate with both base supporters and persuadable voters, but we suggest that microtargeting is particularly significant because it enables the use of wedge issues to appeal to persuadable partisans.

---

[51] Sosnick et al., *Applebee's America*, 36.

[52] Interview with Sara Taylor conducted by Sunshine Hillygus on 21 November 2005.

[53] Republican consultant Alex Gage, as quoted in Thomas B. Edsall and James V. Grimaldi, "On Nov. 2, GOP Got More Bang for Its Billion, Analysis Shows," *Washington Post*, 30 December 2004, A1.

Evaluating Campaign Strategies in 2004

Our analysis will evaluate candidate strategy by comparing the volume and content of messages across mode, source, and recipients. The alternative explanations for candidates' use of divisive issues—a partisan base versus persuadable voter appeal—have very different observable implications for the patterns of issue content in targeted messages. If candidates are primarily concerned with mobilizing a partisan base, we expect candidate efforts to be focused on targeting campaign communications to partisan identifiers. Candidates should emphasize their shared party affiliation to these core supporters and should use wedge issues to raise funds or recruit volunteers. In contrast, if candidates are primarily concerned with persuading "swing voters," we should find that candidates focus on persuasive rather than mobilization appeals. Further, we expect candidates to target campaign communications to Independents and cross-pressured partisans and to use wedge issues in their appeals to persuadable voters rather than core supporters. It is of course a simplification to suppose that any candidate will use a pure strategy of either type, but we can observe which group received more resources and attention, on balance, in direct mail from the 2004 presidential campaign.

Our analysis of campaign strategy primarily looks at direct mail sponsored by either the candidate's campaign or the political parties (interest group mailings are excluded). There are several reasons to focus attention on direct mail instead of just television advertising. First, both Republicans and Democrats spent unprecedented amounts on the ground-war activities in the 2004 campaign.[54] Second, campaign strategy, especially on wedge issues, should be more apparent in the candidates' "ground war" communications since they are narrowly targeted. In contrast, television commercials will be viewed by partisans and Independents alike, making it difficult to sort out the intended target audience. To be sure, candidates try to target television advertising where possible—in 1984, for instance, Ronald Reagan advertised on *60 Minutes* (a "prestige" market), local news, *Hill Street Blues* (a "high-income male" market), *Love Boat* (an "older women with high participation rate" market)—but these audiences are still sufficiently heterogeneous to demand broader themes compared to the narrow message possible with direct mail.[55] Finally, there already exist several rich studies of television advertising strategy. Two of the most comprehensive studies come from the last two election cycles—Daron Shaw's, *The Race*

---

[54] Magleby et al., *Dancing Without Partners.*
[55] O'Shaughnessy, *The Phenomenon of Political Marketing,* 60.

to 270 and *The 2000 Presidential Election and the Foundations of Party Politics* by Richard Johnston, Michael Hagen, and Kathleen Hall Jamieson. These works offer compelling evidence that candidates strategically targeted their television advertising to the most competitive states and media markets. While we offer a cursory analysis of the 2004 candidate strategy through television advertising, we focus our attention on the microtargeted messages sent through direct mail.

In the analysis and discussion that follows, we have omitted campaign communications from interest groups so that we are able to more cleanly outline and test candidates' motivations. Throughout the book, our focus has been on the relationship between voters and candidates, but this unfortunately minimizes the role and influence of other political actors on campaign dynamics. Interest groups undoubtedly shape campaign discourse, both directly through television advertising or communications with their members and indirectly by pressuring candidates to take positions on their preferred policies. Almost by definition, interest groups will focus their efforts on narrow policy objectives. Thus, the NRA sends gun owners direct mail about the candidates' positions on gun control policy, and the Sierra Club sends its members messages about environmental policy. It is likely the case, then, that we actually underestimate the extent to which divisive issues were prevalent in the 2004 presidential election.

In focusing on direct mail, we also overlook other means of microtargeting issue messages, since candidates often use telephone calls, personal visits, Web advertising, text messaging, and the like to communicate with narrow audiences. Candidates have long used targeted messages in advertising on African American and Hispanic radio stations, for instance.[56] Because radio audiences do not usually overlap, candidates can send issue messages that will generally not be received by other groups. Like direct mail, radio targeting is also difficult to track. As one *New York Times* journalist reported, "Candidates keep careful track of their opponents' television advertisements, but just as low-flying planes avoid radar, radio commercials are often able to escape detection."[57] In 1988 Michael Dukakis used radio advertisements to send explicitly contradictory messages on gun control. In television advertisements playing in Texas, the Dukakis message asserted, "[O]ne candidate for President has voted for Federal gun control. Only one. George Bush." At the same time, radio advertisements playing to predominantly black listening audiences proclaimed, "[I]n George Bush's

---

[56] Glaser, *Race, Campaign Politics, and the Realignment in the South.*
[57] Elizabeth Kolbert, "Fueled by Words Alone, Radio Ads Are Nastier," *New York Times,* 5 October 1992, A17.

Washington, they just say 'no' to gun control."[58] Private meetings and rallies closed to the press also provide a venue for tailored appeals. For example, in an invitation-only "Family, Faith and Freedom Rally" with Christian evangelicals at the 2004 Republican National Convention, speakers used apocalyptic language to rally the participants on issues like gay marriage, abortion, activist judges, and policy in Israel. According to one account, "The rally struck a very different tone from the speakers behind the lectern inside the Republican convention, where talk of national unity and cultural inclusiveness has been the rule."[59] Although these examples highlight other ways in which candidates are able to microtarget messages, the ability to collect direct mail from a random sample of respondents allows us to concretely evaluate candidate strategies.

Geographical Targeting

We first turn to a cursory comparison of campaign strategy pursued through television advertising compared to direct mail in the 2004 presidential campaign. The first point worth making is that the presidential candidates in 2004 prioritized their direct mail to battleground states, as they did with their other resources and efforts. Reported in table 6.1 are the average campaign efforts in battleground versus non-battleground states. Candidates' strategies for both direct-mail and television advertising highlight the prioritization that candidates gave to some geographic localities over others. Daron Shaw calculates that candidates spent an average of $8.7 million (14.8 gross point ratings) in the sixteen states that were labeled "battleground" by either of the candidates.[60] Although reported at the state level, candidates' television-advertising strategy is actually conducted at the media-market level.[61] Since Bill Clinton, candidates have ranked media markets ac-

[58] Michael Oreskes, "Thrust of TV Campaign Ads Can Vary with the Territory," *New York Times*, 1 November 1988, A1.

[59] David Kirkpatrick, "The Republicans: The Convention in New York—the Religion Issue," *New York Times*, 1 September 2004, P1.

[60] Based on Shaw, *The Race to 270*, the battleground states include seven states that were considered battleground by both candidates: Florida, Iowa, New Hampshire, New Mexico, Ohio, Pennsylvania, Wisconsin, and another nine states thought to be a battleground state by at least one of the candidates: Maine, Michigan, Minnesota, Oregon, Washington, Missouri, Nevada, West Virginia, Colorado.

[61] Not included in these estimates are cable buys—which reach across state boundaries. Although the Kerry campaign did not make any cable buys, the Bush campaign made the first significant advertising buy on national cable stations. These buys included stations such as Fox News, Fox Sports Net (during NASCAR programs), the golf channel, and conservative comic Dennis Miller's show on CNBC.

cording to their "cost per persuadable vote" in an effort to more efficiently spend advertising dollars.[62] The decision rule of thumb for the Clinton campaign was to "buy ads in markets that had a low price per swing voter. In markets where the price was too high . . . President Clinton would travel there to exploit the power of the bully pulpit."[63] In his recent account of candidates' Electoral College strategies, Daron Shaw notes that George Bush used this same strategy, although campaign advisors would sometimes amend it in order to ensure that top-priority states were not missed. Within media markets, television advertising then tends to be concentrated on programs that are more likely to reach a target demographic. For instance, careful analysis of television-viewing data found, somewhat ironically, that *Will and Grace* was a favorite program of young Republican women, so the campaign aired campaign spots on this gay-friendly program at the same time as they campaigned against gay marriage in direct-mail communications.

Looking at direct mail, we find similar gaps in the amount of campaign material received by individuals living in competitive and non-competitive states—respondents in battleground states received an average of 7.1 pieces of direct mail compared to less than 3 pieces for participants living in safe states. Direct-mail spending is difficult to calculate, but consultants from both sides agree that spending on "ground war" activities had dramatically increased from previous elections. Republican officials estimated that they spent $125 million on "ground war" activities, including a $3.25 million contract with the firm TargetPoint Consulting.[64]

For direct mail, however, candidates take it one step further. Rather than simply targeting individuals living in competitive states, candidates target only those likely to vote. In the CCS data, we find that inactive voters in safe states received less than one direct mail piece on average, compared to more than seven direct-mail pieces received by active voters in battleground states. We see a similar gap in self-reported party contact in the 2004 NES, shown in figure 6.2. Just 14 percent of those not registered to vote reported being contacted by the political parties compared to 68 percent of those registered to vote and living in a battleground state. We can also clearly see this link between information and campaign strategy by looking at errors in the information that candidates have about individual voters. Individuals regis-

[62] For more detailed discussion, see Shaw, *The Race to 270*, or Sosnick et al., *Applebee's America*.

[63] Sosnick et al., *Applebee's America*, 25.

[64] Thomas B. Edsall and James V. Grimaldi, "On Nov. 2, GOP Got More Bang for Its Billion, Analysis Shows," *Washington Post*, 30 December 2004, A1.

TABLE 6.1
Campaign Communication by State Competitiveness

	Direct Mail Received	Advertising Dollars (Millions)	Candidate Visits
Battleground States	7.2	8.7	11.8
Nonbattleground States	2.9	0.0	1.2

Note: Table shows campaign efforts were concentrated in battleground states. Advertising spending and candidate visits estimated with data provided by Daron Shaw. Mail estimates calculated using 2004 Campaign Communication Study.

tered to vote outside the country in which they live (students, individuals who recently moved, snowbirds, etc.) were nearly as unlikely to be contacted as those not registered at all, presumably because candidates lacked the correct contact information. Only 23 percent of these individuals reported being contacted during the campaign. Although nearly 70 percent of these voters indicated that they voted in the election, they were virtually ignored by the political parties.

Campaign Dialogue on Issues

We turn next to the issue content of direct mail in the 2004 presidential election. Coupled with information about the voters, we have argued that direct mail enables candidates to emphasize more issues and more divisive issues than other forms of political communication. The implication is that candidates often will be talking past each other in the ground-war campaign, even as they might be engaging on broader issues in their television advertising. For instance, recent research has found more than two-thirds of issue attention in presidential campaigns is devoted to the same issues.[65] As previously noted, we identified more than seventy-five issues discussed in the direct mail, and have reported the most prominent issues in table 6.2.

The first two columns present the percentage of unique direct-mail pieces containing messages related to a particular policy area. There are several notable findings presented in this table. First, we see that,

[65] Kaplan et al., "Dialogue in American Political Campaigns?"; Sigelman and Buell, "Avoidance or Engagement?" Using the Kaplan et al. measure we estimate an issue convergence score of 48.3 (out of 100); the Sigelman and Buell campaign convergence score is 62 (out of 100). For comparison, estimates from the 2000 presidential campaign found campaign coverage scores of 71 using *New York Times* campaign coverage data and 68 using television advertising.

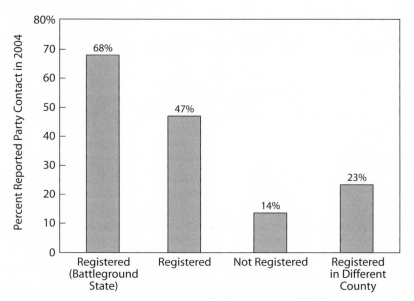

Figure 6.2: Voter Information and Party Contact in 2004
Note: Figure shows party contact is related to registration status and information. Data source is the 2004 American National Election Study.

even in direct mail, the key issues of the campaign—war, the economy,
health care, and education—were also featured prominently in the
mailings from both candidates.[66] Thus, although candidates were indeed discussing more issues through direct mail compared to other
forms of campaign communication, in many ways, the mailings were
also used to reinforce more general campaign themes. There are, however, notable gaps in issue attention between the Bush and Kerry campaigns, and many of the discrepancies are consistent with the theory
of issue ownership. The pro-Bush mail was more likely to emphasize
the war on terrorism, while the pro-Kerry mail was more likely to emphasize health care and education. Even more notable in terms of our
expectations about wedge issues is the gap in campaign attention on
the most divisive political issues. The pro-Kerry mail included mention
of the environment, stem cell research, minimum wage, social security,
the national debt, and outsourcing, while the pro-Bush mail was much

[66] The Wisconsin Advertising project reports that 60 percent of Bush ads mentioned
terrorism or domestic security compared to 37 percent of Kerry ads, while more than 50
percent of Kerry ads were about jobs compared to 23 percent of Bush ads.

TABLE 6.2
Issue Dialogue in 2004 Presidential Campaign Mail

	Percentage of Mail Pieces Mentioning Each Issue		Percentage of Individuals Receiving Mail from Both Candidates
	Pro-Kerry Mail	Pro-Bush Mail	
Social Issues			
Environment	10	2	2
Abortion	2	10	2
Gay Issues	1	9	1
Stem Cell Research	9	1	0
Gun Policy	1	5	0
Economic Issues			
Taxes	24	29	31
Health Care	42	13	30
Education	27	11	25
Prescription Drugs	30	8	24
Jobs	33	13	23
Social Security	16	7	14
Outsourcing/Trade	14	1	9
National Debt	14	1	0
Minimum Wage	9	0	0
Tort Reform	0	5	0
Corporate Reform	5	0	0
Foreign Policy			
Terrorism	13	21	30
Iraq	23	10	28
Defense	9	10	19

Note: Reported in first columns are the percentage of mail pieces mentioning each issue. In last column is the percentage of individuals receiving mail from both candidates calculated for those who received the issue message from either side. Table shows that even when the candidates talked about the same issues, it was rarely to the same individuals. Data source is the 2004 Campaign Communication Study.

more likely to mention abortion, gay marriage, and tort reform. So, although the campaigns talked about *a few* of the same major issues of the day, the candidates emphasized different wedge policies.

The power of the CCS data is that we know who actually received the direct mail, so we can assess whether individuals actually received the same issue messages from one or both candidates. Reported in the final column of table 6.2 is the percentage of respondents who received an issue message from both candidates out of those respondents receiving a piece of mail with the particular issue from either candidate. For example, 31 percent of respondents who received an issue message

TABLE 6.3
Wedge-issue Content of Direct Mail and Television Advertising

	Direct Mail		Television Advertising	
	Percent General Wedge Issue	Percent Moral Wedge Issue	Percent General Wedge Issue	Percent Moral Wedge Issue
Candidate Funded	30	9	0	0
Party Funded	23	7	3	3
Both	25	8	1	1

Note: Table indicates that divisive issues were more prominent in direct mail than television advertising. Direct mail estimates calculated using Campaign Communication Study; television ad estimates provided by Joel Rivlin of Wisconsin Advertising Project based on data from the Campaign Media Analysis Group.

about taxes received a message from both the Republican and Democratic candidates. What is striking about this comparison is that even though the candidates talked about some of the same issues, *they typically talked about them to different individuals.*

Given the wide range of different issues not covered in table 6.2 above, we created a *general wedge issues* category that includes all policies on which the candidates took opposing positions about the policy goal (in contrast to opposing positions about the means of accomplishing a shared goal), like abortion, immigration, minimum wage, school prayer, and so on. Capturing three of the most prominent wedge issues of the campaign—abortion, stem cell research, and gay marriage—is our *moral wedge issues* measure. A full description of our classification is reported in appendix 2.

Comparing the content of television advertising and direct mail allows us to identify message variation based on the message audience. As reported in table 6.3, direct mail was significantly more likely than television advertising to reference a candidate's position on issues like abortion, stem cell research, and gay marriage. Indeed, there was not a single reference to a wedge issue in any candidate-sponsored ad airing in the 2004 presidential election. There were just a few party-sponsored ads including a reference to one of the wedge issues. Interestingly, the only pro-Bush television advertisements to mention abortion were Spanish-language ads televised on Spanish-language television, itself a rather narrow audience.

This comparison suggests candidates focused on consensual policy issues when communicating with a broad-based audience in television ads, but were willing to make wedge appeals in narrowly targeted campaign messages. If candidates had been purely policy motivated, there would have been less reason to communicate different messages to different audiences, but the evidence suggests that candidates did just this in the 2004 campaign. Clearly, television advertising offers only a limited picture of candidates' overall campaign policy agendas.

To be sure, candidates continue to spend vast amounts on television advertising—and considerably more than they spend on direct mail and other forms of political communication. And campaigns still do more "macrotargeting" than "microtargeting." Our key point is simply that these two forms of communication produce very different campaign dialogue, and to the extent that microtargeting continues to grow, scholars must be aware of the potential consequences for campaign dialogue.

Content of Direct Mail

To evaluate whether candidates' campaign agendas were primarily used to mobilize the base or win over the persuadable voters, we turn to a more detailed analysis of the focus and content of direct mail. Table 6.4 summarizes direct-mail communication, separated by candidate and party sponsorship.

As shown in the first column, almost none of the direct mail could be classified as pure GOTV appeals. Just 5 percent of direct mail funded by the candidates or parties was limited to simply urging the recipient to vote without also suggesting which candidate they should support. Despite the fact that political parties have generally opposed campaign finance restrictions because of the alleged impact on GOTV or party-building efforts, these data make clear that mobilization appeals are almost always accompanied by persuasive appeals.[67] It seems clear that there is a blurry line between mobilization and persuasive appeals. Political science research on campaign effects is generally divided between those studying mobilization effects on the one hand and those studying persuasion effects on the other, but the findings here suggest that this may well be a false dichotomy. Candidates rarely, if ever, send out campaign messages that tell people to vote without explicitly telling them who to vote for and why they should vote that way. These findings highlight the disconnect between much of the existing academic research about the campaign "ground war" efforts and actual campaign behavior. Most of the existing research focuses on the mobilizing effect of nonpartisan GOTV campaign messages, but it appears that such messages were rare in the heat of the 2004 presidential contest.[68]

---

[67] We cannot say, however, whether the direct mail contained *any* mobilization message, in part because it is difficult to define what exactly that would mean.

[68] Gerber et al., "The Effects of Canvassing, Telephone Calls, and Direct Mail on Voter Turnout."

TABLE 6.4
Campaign Appeals in 2004 Presidential Direct Mail

	Percent Pure Mobilization Appeal	Percent Volunteer Appeal	Percent Fund-raising Appeal	Percent Both Party Labels	Percent Own Party Label	Percent Issue Appeal
Candidate Funded	0	14	9	0	9	70
Party Funded	5	4	10	11	50	69
Both	5	5	10	10	48	70

Note: Table indicates that direct mail in the 2004 election emphasized issue appeals more than turnout reminders, fund-raising or volunteer requests, or partisan appeals. Data source is the 2004 Campaign Communication Study.

Although it is difficult (perhaps even impossible) to distinguish mobilization versus persuasive appeals, we are able to identify whether pieces of direct mail included explicit appeals for money or time. Despite the fact that this is one of the key explanations for why candidates have been polarized in recent years, comparatively few of the 2004 direct-mail campaign pieces included appeals for resources or for volunteer efforts. At least in direct-mail communication, our findings suggest that candidates were primarily concerned with raising money or soliciting volunteers, as we might expect if the party-activist hypothesis was correct. The lack of fund-raising and volunteer appeals is especially notable because for many decades political direct mail was primarily a tool for political fund-raising. Today, however, candidates have information about nearly every voter, not just the activists, so direct mail is more commonly used as an alternate form of political communication and advertising.

Perhaps more telling of candidate strategy is the fact that just 9 percent of candidate-sponsored direct-mail pieces mentioned the candidate's political party, and just half of the pieces sponsored specifically by the political party did so. Despite some expectations that candidates would try to activate the partisan base by reinforcing and highlighting partisan attachments, the majority of mail advertising did not mention a candidate's party affiliation. Although candidates may very well have been trying to activate their partisan base by motivating them with an issue appeal, they were not simply reminding their supporters of their partisan identities. Yet the vast majority (70 percent) of direct-mail pieces included issue-based appeals. Looking at the overlap of partisan and issue content highlights even further that partisan activation did not appear to be the foremost motivation of the direct mail. We find that mail omitting the party affiliation of the favored candidate included an average of 5.2 issue positions compared to just 2.4 positions in the mail that included the candidate's party affiliation. Moreover, mail without party labels was twice as likely to mention a wedge issue (34 percent versus 16 percent) and three times as likely to mention a moral issue (4 percent versus 12 percent).[69] If candidates were following a coalitional strategy in which they were using issues to appeal across party lines to those who might be amenable on the issue, we would expect just this pattern—candidates downplaying their party attachments and highlighting issues in an effort to make the

[69] In contrast, 88 percent of party fund-raising appeals included an explicit party label.

issue salient in the minds of persuadable voters. As one Bush advisor explained, core supporters were not ignored; they just received fewer "touches" than swing voters.[70]

Recipients of Direct Mail

Examining who actually receives direct-mail advertising also helps clarify what strategies candidates were pursuing. We again focus not only on the amount of mail received, but also on the content. Table 6.5 reports the percentage of mail pieces received containing divisive issue appeals received by Democrats, Republicans, and Independents.[71] We look not only at the "moral wedge issues" and "general wedge issues" classifications previously used, but also at a category we call "targeted issues." This final category is an even more encompassing classification including any policy area of concern to a particular voting constituency—these include all moral and general wedge issues as well as issue topics such as senior health care, agricultural issues, and local issues. The specific issues included are listed in appendix 2. As reported in table 6.5, we see that political Independents received more mail on average and were more likely to receive advertising with targeted, wedge, and moral issue appeals. This finding is notable because the expectation of a base mobilization strategy would be that partisans should have been *more* likely than Independents to receive direct mail about divisive issues. And it stands in contrast to research concluding that core party supporters are more likely to be targeted with campaign information.[72] This table also highlights that candidates are often going after the same voters, even if they are targeting them with different messages. At the same time that candidates try to peel away voters from the opposition coalition, they are also attempting to hold on to their own cross-pressured partisans.

Unfortunately, the CCS survey does not include questions about an individual's policy preferences, so we are unable to precisely identify cross-pressured partisans as we have in previous chapters. Although it is a less ideal measure, the American National Election Study asks

[70] Interview with Mark McKinnon conducted by Sunshine Hillygus on 17 November 2005.

[71] Estimates for active voters in battleground states. With a one-way ANOVA, we can reject the null hypothesis that the mean number of mail pieces received is equal.

[72] Holbrook and McClurg, "Presidential Campaigns and the Mobilization of Core Supporters."

TABLE 6.5
Direct Mail Received by Partisan Identification

	All Presidential Mail	Party & Candidate Mail	Percent Received Moral Appeal	Percent Received Wedge Appeal	Percent Received Targeted Appeal
Democrat	6.4	3.2	19	29	36
Independent	8.5	5.5	24	32	41
Republican	6.5	4.6	18	31	39

Note: Table indicates that Independents received more mail on average than partisans, and mail received was more likely to contain divisive issue content. Data source is the 2004 Campaign Communication Study.

respondents if they were contacted by each of the political parties. Using our earlier measure of cross-pressured partisans, we found that 53 percent of cross-pressured partisans reported being contacted by the opposing party in the 2004 presidential election, compared to just 29 percent of consistent partisans.[73] This gap in contact rates suggests that candidates are concentrating their efforts on the individuals who are most likely to be responsive.

Although we cannot precisely distinguish between the persuadable partisans and the consistent core supporters in the CCS survey, we can use strength of party identification as a proxy. Although a blunt classification, particularly given our findings in chapter 2 showing that cross-pressures exist even among strong partisans, this proxy allows us to compare the content of direct mail received by core supporters (strong partisans) to that received by persuadable voters (weak partisans and Independents). Are we more likely to find wedge appeals used in mail received by the partisan base or in the mail received by persuadable voters? Figure 6.3 reports the percentage of pro-Kerry and pro-Bush mail containing wedge, moral, or targeted appeals received by strong Democrats, weak/leaning Democrats, Independents, weak/leaning Republicans, and strong Republicans.

Despite the conventional wisdom that the 2004 presidential candidates used divisive issues to mobilize and motivate their base, we find compelling evidence that mail sent to persuadable voters was more likely to contain wedge issues than that received by the partisan base. Wedge, moral, or targeted appeals were actually *less* prevalent in the direct mail received by a candidate's own strong partisans. Looking at each type of wedge appeal, we find a nonmonotonic relationship over the partisan scale, with a candidate's own base supporters and his opponent's base supporters receiving the lowest percentage of direct-mail advertising with divisive content. Persuadable voters—Independents and weak partisans—received the highest percentage of divisive-issue content. For instance, roughly 8 percent of pro-Bush direct-mail pieces received by strong Republicans included messages about abortion, homosexuality, or stem cell research, compared to 11 percent of pro-Bush ads received by Independents, and 16 percent of those received by weak Democrats. Similarly, 40 percent of pro-Kerry ads received by

---

[73] We find similar results looking at those cross-pressured on specific policy issues. For instance, 58 percent of those with social-security cross-pressures were contacted compared to 48 percent among those consistent on the issue; 54 percent of those cross-pressured on abortion were contacted versus 48 percent of those consistent on abortion; and 53 percent of those cross-pressured on gay marriage reported being contacted compared to 48 percent of those consistent on the issue.

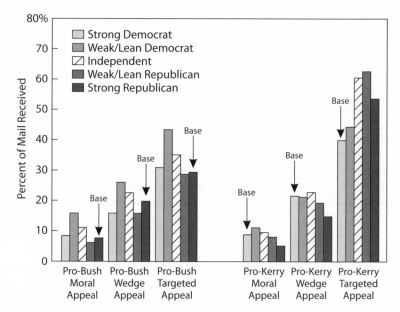

Figure 6.3: Targeted Issues as a Percentage of Mail Received
Note: Graph indicates that direct-mail advertising sent to weak partisans and Independents was more likely to contain divisive issue content than direct-mail advertising sent to a candidate's own strong partisans. Data source is the 2004 Campaign Communication Survey.

strong Democrats included targeted issues, compared to 44 percent of pro-Kerry ads received by weak Democrats, 61 percent received by Independents, and 63 percent received by weak Republicans. Put simply, if a candidate sent a message to someone from the other side in the 2004 election, the campaign appeal was quite likely to give the recipient an explicit policy reason to abandon her affiliated party.

Figure 6.3 does hint at an interesting difference between the two political parties. It appears that both campaigns were more likely to use wedge appeals to target wavering Democrats than wavering Republicans. In other words, the Bush campaign appeared more likely to engage in an offensive strategy—looking to pick off Democrats who agreed with the president on some divisive issues—while the Kerry campaign appeared to be more defensive in their strategy—attempting to hang on to wavering Democrats. It appears that Kerry was using divisive issues to "microshield" his own cross-pressured partisans. This pattern may also be consistent with common interpretations in the media and among pundits that the Republicans did a better job of taking advantage of the information databases to target campaign messages. According to one journalistic account, "Both parties engaged in this microtargeting. . . . But strategists on both sides agreed that the depth of the Republican files grew far greater, included more information, and were put to smarter use in the field, thus increasing the data's predictive power."[74]

Overall, our analysis here suggests that candidates do not use wedge issues solely, or even primarily, to motivate their base. Media accounts following the 2004 presidential election seemed to have interpreted the candidates' focus on divisive issues as evidence that candidates were engaging in a base mobilization strategy, but this interpretation appears incomplete. Consultants and party leaders, in contrast, were more likely to acknowledge that the campaigns were also focused on winning Independents and opposing partisans. Bush's campaign manager, Ken Mehlman, explained, "The press, unfortunately for them, believes that it's zero-sum, that it's either a base or a swing strategy. And the fact is, we appeal to both."

Why did the media get it wrong? In part, it may be an issue of semantics. When Republican advisors talked about "expanding the base," they were indicating that they were appealing to Independents and Democrats who agreed with Bush on a particular policy dimension. Brent Seaborn, vice president of TargetPoint Consulting, explained:

> We wanted to most effectively allocate the resources we have. Some of those resources need to go to mobilization, some of them need to go to persuasion. That was all built around this idea that Rove always talked about mobilizing and expanding the base. Most people tended to focus on that mobilizing the base as [sic] what the campaign was supposed to be about. But there was also this very heavy element on expanding the base and finding what these people had in common with the president already and treating them as if they were in the base. Traditionally we would ignore these people because they don't have an R next to their name. But being able to say, "These people might have a D or an I next to their name, but there are three issues that [they] are right with the president on." This wasn't about going out and persuading people, "You don't agree with the president on any issues, but you should vote for him anyway."[75]

More importantly, the persuadable voters were not viewed as a homogeneous group of unsophisticated, ideologically moderate, political Independents who would make up their minds based on candidate personality and charisma. Instead, candidates looked for persuadable voters who might be receptive on an issue about which they disagreed

[74] Hamburger and Wallsten, *One Party Country*, 150.
[75] Interview of Brent Seaborn conducted by David Magleby and Quin Monson; Alexandria, Va., 15 December 2004.

with their own party's nominee. Bush strategist Matthew Dowd explained that the campaign made the assumption that "voters are smart. They're not dumb. They can't be spun. We can't put up a television spot to convince them of something that they don't believe. . . . We assumed voters were able to take information, factor it in, factor it out, and come to the conclusion in a very smart, intelligent way."[76]

In today's political context in which the elections are razor close and the political parties are more evenly divided than ever before, candidates look for every possible angle that might make a difference in the election outcome. The candidates did not try to change the policy preferences of voters; rather, they tried to raise the salience of a policy preference that was consistent with the preferences of their partisan base. Consultant Hal Malchow explained, "Once I can get them on that one issue, then I can get them to take action and get them to be involved politically and ideologically. . . . You don't have to change 50 percent of Americans, you don't have to change 30 percent. You move 2 percent or 3 percent in New Mexico or Missouri or Wisconsin on one issue, then you've done a whole lot."[77] With detailed information about the preferences of the electorate, candidates look for any possible issue—no matter how small or inconsequential to others in the electorate—that could be exploited for electoral gain.

Implications of Campaign Strategy for Political Inequality

What are the implications of this persuadable-voter strategy? On the one hand, some might view these findings in a positive light. After all, candidates are not simply catering to their base supporters and ignoring the general electorate as some have decried. It has been argued that a base mobilization strategy has either contributed to or resulted from the polarization in the electorate and holds detrimental consequences for American democracy. Political reporter Thomas Edsall argues that a "collapse of the middle" has allowed President Bush to "discard centrist strategies" and to promote "polarizing policies designed explicitly to appeal to the conservative Republican core."[78] The tactic of microtargeting has been credited with engaging people because it connects with them on their interests. Political scientist David Dulio argues that microtargeting should be good for democracy because it at least "fo-

[76] Jamieson, *Electing the President 2004*, 26.

[77] Jon Gertner, "The Very, Very Personal Is the Political," *New York Times Magazine*, 15 February 2004, 43.

[78] Edsall, *Building Red America*.

cuses attention on the issues that are important to voters . . . [and] strengthens debate between two candidates."[79] Consultant Alex Gage similarly concluded that "from an institutional standpoint we think it's beneficial. It's going to the voter, and indeed talking to them about what is important to them."[80]

Our analysis provides evidence that candidates focus on swing voters, but the findings are hardly reassuring from a normative standpoint. In today's hyperinformation environment, the campaign tactics for winning over persuadable voters have changed, with potentially negative consequences. In the conclusion of this book, we consider in more detail the potential implications of microtargeting for democratic accountability and governance. For now, we point out the clearly observable implications that these campaign tactics have for political inequality.

As candidates become more efficient in targeting their resources, some people in the electorate are increasingly marginalized and ignored. Republican consultant David Hill explained, "There is a practical reason that we don't focus on those unlikely to vote. . . . [It] comes down to a budgeting issue."[81] With the explosion in the amount, type, and quality of information about individual voters, candidates can more efficiently allocate their political and financial resources, exacerbating political inequalities in party contact. More than ever before, presidential candidates can now ignore large portions of the public—nonvoters, those committed to the opposition, and those living in uncompetitive states. The preferences of these individuals are not unknown, rather they are deliberately disregarded.

Scholars have long been concerned about inequalities in party contact, primarily because it is thought to be an important determinant of political participation, and participation, in turn, is consequential for the policies that our representatives pursue.[82] Sidney Verba, Kay Schlozman, and Henry Brady argue that "[d]emocracy rests on the notion of the equal worth of each citizen. The needs and preferences of no individual should rank higher than those of any other. This principle undergirds the concept of one person one vote as well as its corollary, equality of political voice among individuals."[83] Our work extends this important political inequality literature by suggesting that microtar-

---

[79] Dulio, *For Better or Worse*, 182–83.

[80] Interview with Alex Gage conducted by Quin Monson and David Magleby on 16 December 2004.

[81] Conversation between David Hill and Sunshine Hillygus on 10 June 2006.

[82] Rosenstone and Hansen, *Mobilization, Participation and Democracy in America*; Verba et al., *Voice and Equality.*

[83] Verba et al., *Voice and Equality,* 10.

geting influences the policy promises that candidates make *even before they are elected*. In today's information environment, candidates are surgically targeting issue appeals to persuadable voters, while ignoring those individuals inconsequential to a winning coalition. In a recent study, Markus Prior attributed changes in the composition of the electorate over time to changes in voluntary media consumption—in today's media environment those not interested in politics can avoid it altogether.[84] To this explanation, we would add that the candidates' decision to ignore these citizens also shapes their involvement in the political process. Candidates today more precisely target their campaign efforts to those individuals likely to vote thereby reinforcing and exacerbating the participation gap between those politically unengaged and those politically engaged. There is a perverse trend that increasing information about the American public makes it less likely that our political system offers equal representation for all citizens. As it becomes easier to differentiate the less politically motivated from the engaged citizens in the electorate, it becomes less likely that the views of the former are reflected in election outcomes.

Conclusion

In this chapter, we examined the implications of our arguments for candidate strategy and behavior. Because persuadable voters can be won over if a policy cross-pressure is activated, candidates have an incentive to prime wedge issues in their campaign appeals. Given the complexity and diversity of voter belief systems—and a data-rich information environment that has informed the candidates of those belief systems—candidates attempt to microtarget different campaign messages to different persuadable voters. One consequence of this campaign strategy is that candidates are taking positions on more issues, and more divisive issues, than ever before.

Although our data help explain how the information environment today provides the conditions for divergent policy platforms, we must acknowledge the limits of our analysis. There are a great number of issues—many of which may be the most important to voter decision making—on which the candidates still have an incentive to take a centrist opinion. On the issues that most voters believe are pressing—typically consensual issues like education and health care—candidates will likely take widely supported policy positions. Nearly every candidate

---

[84] Prior, *Post–Broadcast Democracy.*

promises to be the "education" president. For example, referring to George W. Bush's campaign strategy in 2000, Mark McKinnon, director of media for the Bush campaign, explained their strategy on important consensual domestic issues,

> [W]hen you looked at the issue matrix on this election, all the issues that people typically care about were Democratic issues: education, Social Security, health care. So, we knew that while we probably couldn't win on those issues, we had to at least keep them close. Fortunately, we had a candidate who had been talking about those issues, not just in this campaign, but for years as governor in Texas. So there was a platform there, and a history. Our strategy was to stay close on those issues. Those were the issues Bob Dole had been wiped out on by 20 or more points.[85]

Of course, even while emphasizing the importance of these consensual issues, Bush focused on specific aspects of these policies that were consistent with traditional conservative values like limited federal government, local control, and market-based reforms. This highlights the fact that candidate strategy is not just about selecting issues, it also involves strategic calculations about how issues should be framed and discussed. Similarly, even when taking a position on a divisive wedge issue, candidates routinely use code words and symbols to soften the message or to present the message in a way that indirectly "speaks" to the targeted audience. For example, rather than saying he thinks homosexuality is immoral, President Bush's direct mail emphasized his support for traditional families.

The bigger question left unanswered is the impact of these wedge-issue appeals on the voters. Did microtargeting bring 4 million lost evangelicals to the polls in 2004? Does a single campaign mailer about gay marriage have an impact above and beyond the dozens of other mailers, phone calls, and front-door visits that bombard residents of battleground states? The issue landscape of a political campaign is quite complex, and we have shown only that voters respond to the broader issue agenda of which the candidate has only limited control. The media, for instance, might focus on issues that the candidate hopes to avoid. In a fragmented information environment, each voter has considerable control over the issues about which she becomes informed. Moreover, with both candidates targeting persuadable voters with wedge issues, there are more voters who receive messages from both sides, albeit often on different issues. In the CCS study, for in-

---

[85] Mark McKinnon quoted in Jamieson and Waldman, Electing the President, 2000, 145–46.

stance, 38 percent of respondents received both pro-Bush mail and pro-Kerry mail. Which message is more likely to resonate? Can we predict the decision of the elderly pro-life Democrat who receives a message on social security from the Democrat and a message on abortion from the Republican? Recent research has begun to tackle these questions, and early evidence suggests that the candidate who sends more direct mail is afforded a small, but predictable, electoral advantage.[86]

The 2006 congressional elections perhaps highlight the limits of microtargeting. Despite increased reliance on microtargeting of wedge issues, most accounts suggest that Republicans were handily defeated because of issues epiphenomenal to the "ground war" campaign. One of the lessons from the 2006 congressional elections seems to be that the electorate is tired of polarization. One journalist explained that the 2006 election "represented a striking repudiation of both the performance and the political strategy of the Bush administration and the Republican Party. Voters punished a Republican Party that subordinated . . . the politics of national unity to the politics of polarization."[87] Pundits have predicted that the 2008 presidential candidates will have to moderate, cater to the ideological middle of the American public, and avoid divisive wedge issues. The candidates have already focused early rhetoric on themes of national unity rather than appearing to contribute to the partisan divide. Presidential candidate Bill Richardson explained his bipartisan appeal and effort, "Our next President must be able to bring a country together that is divided and partisan. . . . I just got re-elected with 69 percent of the vote—in a red state—and I got 40 percent of the Republican vote. I can bring people together to solve problems."[88] Yet, it is hard to imagine that the candidates will ignore their capability to microtarget wedge issues, particularly once the election strategies are in place and careful analysis of voter preferences has been made. And even if candidate sound bites and television advertising might focus on a message of national unity, we expect to find that the ground war will still attempt to exploit cleavages in the electorate as each candidate tries to capture crucial persuadable voters.

[86] Hillygus and Monson, "Campaign Microtargeting and Presidential Voting in 2004."

[87] Al From, "Democrats Must Adopt A Centrist Course," *San Diego Union-Tribune*, 19 November 2006, G1.

[88] Bill Richardson, "On the Issues: Partisanship," Bill Richardson for President. http://richardsonforpresident.com. Accessed 11 March 2007.

Seven

Conclusions:
Consequences for Democratic Governance

ELECTIONS ARE THE PRIMARY mechanism by which citizens in a democracy express their wants and desires to their elected officials, and it is through political campaigns that this interaction is managed. Campaigns oblige politicians to define their policy priorities, inform the electorate of the policy alternatives offered by opposing candidates, and provide a forum for policy debate, discussion, and change. We have argued that information about the voters shapes campaign messages and candidate strategies. And information from the campaign influences voter decision making. The dynamics we observe in a presidential campaign, in other words, reflect a reciprocal flow of information and influence between voters and candidates, with this relationship governed by the amount, type, and quality of information each has about the other. This broad perspective of presidential campaigns provides insights into why candidates emphasize some issues instead of others, why some voters are more likely than others to be responsive to those appeals, and ultimately, why we observe the dynamics that we do.

Building on a diverse body of research in political psychology, political communication, voting behavior, and campaign strategy, we have offered three key theoretical propositions in this book:

1. Individual-level responsiveness to presidential campaigns depends on the strength and consistency of voters' predispositions and on the issue context of the campaign dialogue. Voters facing competing considerations, especially between policy preferences and party identification, are more likely than other voters to rely on campaign information when making up their minds.

2. In an attempt to build a winning coalition between their base supporters and persuadable voters, candidates, motivated by electoral concerns, will target cross-pressured partisans and Independents. The candidates will highlight issues on which these voters disagree with the position taken by the opposing party candidate. In other words, candidates deliberately use wedge issues as part of an electoral strategy.

3. New information and communication technologies have enabled candidates to microtarget different policy messages to different voters, thereby increasing the prevalence and precision of wedge campaign messages.

Throughout this book, we have evaluated our theoretical expectations with a variety of methodological approaches. We have relied on both original and secondary data sources, and have used both quantitative and qualitative methods of analysis. We have covered a lot of ground and presented a number of empirical findings:

1. Partisans are likely to disagree with their preferred political party on policy issues more often than is generally believed. This finding is robust across different policy measures, surveys, and even among the most sophisticated partisans. In addition, contemporary partisans are more likely to hold policy disagreements on cultural, rather than economic, issues.

2. Persuadable voters are not a homogenous group of unsophisticated and indifferent policy moderates, as has often been believed. Rather, persuadable voters hold diverse policy preferences, making it less clear which candidate offers a better match.

3. When exposed to campaign information, persuadable partisans are more likely to be undecided about their presidential vote choice, more likely to change their mind over the course of the campaign, and more likely to defect at the ballot box.

4. Because the campaign helps determine which issue preferences receive greater weight in the vote decision, the content of campaign dialogue shapes who supports which candidate and why. Partisans who disagree with their party on an important policy issue are more likely to defect if that issue is the focus of campaign dialogue.

5. Contrary to expectations that candidates will avoid divisive policy positions or target policy messages to core partisans alone, candidates deliberately attempt to prime wedge issues in order to win over persuadable voters.

6. Candidates are more likely to use divisive wedge issues when they have more information about the preferences of the voters and when they are able to narrowly target their campaign messages.

Taking into account the incentives, interests, and behaviors of both candidates and voters offers a more comprehensive understanding of the role of campaigns in American democracy, and this broader perspective leads to new insights about the dynamics we observe in contemporary campaigns. Perhaps most fundamentally, these arguments have direct implications for how we understand the relationships between citizens and their representatives, as well as the nature of democratic governance more generally. The question of whether political candidates are responsive to citizens' preferences is at the very heart of how democracy functions, and it is in the context of political campaigns that we can find the answer.

Much of the theoretical and empirical work in political science tends to view the relationship between the governed and governors as domi-

nated either by a "top-down" or "bottom-up" flow of influence. According to the top-down perspective, mass-elite linkages are characterized by elites leading (some would say manipulating) a passive
citizenry. In contrast, the bottom-up perspective holds that candidates
simply represent the preferences of the public, with the electorate holding accountable any politician who deviates from the public's preferences. In other words, the basic question is whether political candidates *reflect* public opinion or *shape* public opinion. Our findings
suggest that the flow of information and influence is neither purely a
top-down nor bottom-up process. Rather, campaigns reflect a reciprocal relationship between candidates and voters.

Candidates do not manipulate voters to change their policy attitudes
or to vote against their preferences. Rather, campaigns help voters
translate their predispositions into their candidate selection by increasing the salience of one consideration over another. To be sure, some
might view priming effects as a form of manipulation. Yet responsiveness to campaigns still fundamentally depends on the voters' own
preferences. Further, unresponsive voters are not simply those blindly
following their partisan loyalties. Policy-congruent partisans are quick
to support their party's nominee, but our findings suggest that they
would also reconsider that support if the party or candidate were to
change policy positions. Socially conservative Republicans were
among President Bush's core supporters in 2004, for example, but we
would expect them to become persuadable voters if Republicans nominated a pro-choice candidate and Democrats nominated a pro-life one,
and the issue of abortion was a salient issue in the campaign. In this
respect, then, all voters are potentially persuadable. This conclusion
mirrors that of H. Daudt's classic study of floating voters:

> Is it perhaps so that everyone is a potential floater? . . . Saying that all enfran-
> chised persons are potential floaters is not the same as saying whether per-
> sons actually float and, if so, how many of them. This will depend on the
> political problems, the ways the political parties propose dealing with them
> and the voters' reactions to these proposals. Consistent voting behavior on
> the part of persons or groupings may, then, imply that they are satisfied with
> the way in which their party approaches the political problems.[1]

Our conclusions also differ from those who propose a bottom-up process. According to this perspective, the flow of influence is reversed,
with political candidates responsive to voter preferences. Politicians
are "like antelope in an open field, they cock their ears and focus their
full attention on the slightest sign of danger."[2] President Bill Clinton,

---

[1] Daudt, *Floating Voters and the Floating Vote,* 160–61.
[2] Stimson et al., "Dynamic Representation," 559.

for instance, has been described as "a weathervane, constantly shifting to and fro in response to the fickle wind of opinion polls."[3] Although this perspective paints a more optimistic picture of electoral accountability, our findings suggest that candidates are not in fact equally responsive to all citizens. Indeed, instead of moving to the center of the ideological spectrum across policy areas, we find that candidates build electoral coalitions by surgically targeting narrow constituencies of interests. From a pluralistic perspective, a candidate attempting to reach out to a diversity of voting blocs should be applauded because of the potential for increased responsiveness.[4] Yet many of the classic criticisms of pluralism also apply within the electoral context. Just as interest group politics raises concerns about the scope and bias associated with the interests that are represented during policy making, so does a campaign dominated by pluralistic strategies. We consider some of the most troubling potential consequences.

Implications of the Microtargeted Wedge Strategy

The full impact of this changing information environment on candidate and voter behavior is not yet known, but there are at least three potentially grim prospects for the impact of a microtargeted campaign on American democracy: (1) political inequality; (2) superficial politics; and (3) a crisis in governance.

Political Inequality

We have argued that one consequence of increased efficiency in campaign targeting is that candidates are less likely to mobilize individuals who are unlikely to vote. This has clear implications for government policy, as a long and rich literature about the participation gaps in American politics documents. All voters are not equal in the eyes of presidential candidates.

Candidates are particularly responsive to those voters who are strategically valuable in building a successful, short-term electoral coalition. Candidates are simultaneously (and intentionally) ignoring the preferences of those who are not critical to their coalition's electoral success. As candidates increasingly rely on sophisticated technology to narrowcast their campaign messages to strategically chosen voters living in strategically chosen states, the issues of interest to these voters outweigh all others.

[3] Berinsky, *Silent Voices*, 1.
[4] Robert Dahl, *Who Governs?*

When campaigns attempt to reach out to the full electorate, a candidate must harmonize and synthesize interests, incorporating them into a policy message that resonates with the general interest of the nation. The extent to which contemporary microtargeted campaigns give priority to the needs and desires of only the electoral expedient citizens affects the degree to which the electoral process fails to live up to the democratic ideal. As Steven Schier has argued, "The narrow strategic focus of activation makes majority rule at best an incidental byproduct of this system. Candidates seek to win elections by targeting a small group of swing voters in search of a plurality of those who vote, not a majority of all citizens. Groups have little incentive to command majority opinion if they can prevail without it—and they often can."[5] These microtargeted campaign strategies exacerbate inequalities in the American political system, contributing to a system of democracy "of and by" a myriad of narrowly focused groups of swing voters, not democracy "of and by" the people.

Superficial Politics?

Indeed, even when candidates are attentive to a particular group of voters, candidates will emphasize wedge issues because they help create a strategic advantage, not because they are necessarily the most important issues to the targeted voters. Such voters are not so much being manipulated as induced (some might say bribed) with promises to enact a preferred policy. What might be a rational behavior on the part of the individual voter is perhaps not the best policy for the collective. In 1996, for instance, Bill Clinton was often derided for emphasizing "bite-sized, or 'small-bore' initiatives . . . too puny for presidential action."[6] With detailed information about individual voters, candidates are able to activate narrow policy interests that might be considered superficial, or at least less significant, than those issues of concern to the broader public.

The 2004 presidential election highlights the potential disconnect between the priorities of the public and campaign messages. According to the 2004 National Annenberg Election study, the typical respondent consistently reported that the issues of unemployment, the War in Iraq, terrorism, and health care were at the top of their "most important problem" list.[7] Among Democrats, Republicans, and Independents,

[5] Schier, *By Invitation Only*, 36.

[6] Sosnik et al., *Applebee's America*, 23.

[7] National Annenberg Election Survey, press release 28 October 2004, "Terrorism Seen as Most Important Problem for Bush Backers; Kerry's Worry Most about Economy, Annenberg Data Show."

these same four issues were consistently mentioned as the policy areas that citizens believed were the most important. In fact, only 3 percent of Democrats and 5 percent of Independents reported that a "lack of moral/family values" was among the most important issues during the 2004 presidential elections. Yet, we found that 19 percent of direct-mail issue appeals targeted to Democratic voters focused on moral issues, and 24 percent of direct-mail issue appeals targeted to Independents emphasized moral wedge issues. Clearly, the policies emphasized in the 2004 ground-war campaign did not reflect the issue priorities that the general American public believed to be most important. Instead, the targeted messages emphasized wedge issues that candidates believed offered them a unique advantage relative to their opponent. To the extent that candidates emphasize these narrower policy interests during their campaign, the energy and resources remaining that may be devoted to other policy areas are limited. And once elected, the winning candidate has the difficult task of turning fragmented campaign promises into governing priorities.

A Crisis in Governance?

Following the 2004 election, President Bush proclaimed that "the people made it clear what they wanted. . . . Let me put it to you this way: I earned capital in the campaign, political capital, and now I intend to spend it."[8] Such political rhetoric notwithstanding, if different individuals intend their vote to send different policy messages, interpreting election outcomes as an indicator of what "the public wants" misses the fact that election outcomes represent a cacophony of divergent policy goals. Quite simply, interpreting the meaning of an election is difficult when there is a fragmented and narrowly tailored campaign dialogue (not to say anything of narrow electoral margins).

Popular elections are often believed to provide presidents with the political leverage to forge policy changes. Under the model of responsible party government, political parties should present distinct policy alternatives, so that a vote cast for one candidate over the other provides a clear signal of the voters' preferred policy direction. In 1952, for instance, Republican General Dwight D. Eisenhower campaigned on one key promise—to end the war in Korea, giving him an unambiguous popular mandate when he won. When candidates present a clear and limited set of policy alternatives, communicated to the entire elec-

---

[8] Richard Stevenson, "Confident Bush Outlines Ambitious Plan for 2nd Term," *New York Times*, 5 November 2004, A1.

torate, the winning candidate has a greater claim that his policy priorities reflect the will of the people.[9] Yet in contemporary presidential campaigns, a fragmented and diverse policy agenda undermines the potential for an election outcome to indicate public support for any one policy.

It is difficult to construct a sustainable notion of electoral accountability without a shared public discourse on the candidates' policy positions and future agendas. Democratic accountability rests on some minimal conditions that voters at least know their own policy preferences and the policy positions of candidates. Although political scientists have long argued that individual citizens do not always live up to this standard, scholars have often taken comfort in the finding that politicians are responsive to collective public opinion, which is thought to be more informed, stable, and rational.[10] At its extreme, a fragmented campaign dialogue undercuts the very notion that a collective public opinion even exists. Peter Swire, the Clinton administration's chief counselor for privacy, explained,

> In the nightmare, every voter will get a tailored message based on detailed information about the voter. . . . [This] means that the public debates lack content and the real election happens in the privacy of these mailings. The candidate knows everything about the voter, but the media and the public know nothing about what the candidate really believes. It is, in effect, a nearly perfect perversion of the political process.[11]

How do we maintain electoral accountability if democratic deliberation occurs alone rather than as a public collective?

In 2004 journalists and pundits concluded that the public supported Bush because of his conservative stance on moral issues like gay marriage and abortion. The *London Times*, for instance, reported that "Americans voted in record numbers for a Republican president primarily because they identified with his moral agenda."[12] In fact, what "the people" said they wanted was not very clear at all because campaign dialogue was reflective of individual, rather than aggregate, preferences. Empirical analyses of voter behavior in the 2004 election have found that the public did not offer Bush a "moral mandate"—the

---

[9] There is a long-standing debate in political science about presidential mandates. See Conley, *Presidential Mandates*; Grossback et al., *Mandate Politics*.

[10] Page and Shapiro, *The Rational Public*.

[11] Jon Gertner, "The Very, Very Personal Is the Political," *New York Times Magazine*, 15 February 2004, 43.

[12] James Harding, "Electorate Puts Moral Concerns Ahead of Policy," *Financial Times* (London), 5 November 2004, A8.

average voter cast her ballot on the basis of economic considerations, party identification, the War in Iraq, and concerns over terrorism.[13] Of course, the story of the average voter does not fully capture the more complex and nuanced relationship between voters and candidates in the 2004 election.

As the broader campaign was being waged primarily on issues of the economy and war, millions of Christian social conservatives were told that moral issues were at stake in the election. The Republican National Committee, for instance, mailed voters in Arkansas and West Virginia flyers that printed the word *allowed* over a picture of a same-sex couple and *banned* over an image of the Bible. Simultaneously, the Bush campaign targeted elderly investors, military families, small-business owners, and so on. For the state of Michigan alone, the Republican Party created a 157-page report separating likely voters in this battleground state into dozens of separate "microtargeting segments"—ranging from "tax-and-terrorism moderates" to "traditional-marriage Democrats" to "terrorism and health care Democrats." Once voters were identified in these specific groups, they were targeted with messages that directly corresponded to the issues that predisposed them to support President Bush.[14] Different segments of the population were each told that some issue they cared about was a top priority of President Bush. This type of segmentation means that any interpretation of what the election was "about" was incomplete because there was a multiplicity of policy agendas presented to the public and a multiplicity of different agendas supported by voters.

When an election is finally over and the ballots are counted, the winning candidate must decide which policies to pursue. Yet, candidates' campaign agendas are largely divorced from strategic decisions regarding how candidates might successfully govern if they are elected. Communications scholar Nicholas O'Shaughnessy argues that "coalitions of support are created with much greater ease than in former times, for the thrust of the new technology is towards segmentation and its results. . . . [G]roups can now be solicited as individuals on their key interests and enthusiasms; but the loyalties of such coalitions are also more fickle since they no longer depend on organic linkages to political parties."[15] Inevitably, each of the targeted segments expect the candidate to fulfill the promises made to them during the campaign.

---

[13] Hillygus and Shields, "Moral Issues and Voter Decision Making in the 2004 Presidential Election."

[14] Sosnik et al., *Applebee's America*, 34–35.

[15] O'Shaughnessy, *The Phenomenon of Political Marketing*, 13.

Following the 2004 campaign, Rev. D. James Kennedy, a broadcast evangelist, declared, "[N]ow that values voters have delivered for George Bush, he must deliver for voters. The defense of innocent unborn human life, the protection of marriage, and the nomination and confirmation of judges who will interpret the Constitution, not make law from the bench, must be first priorities come January."[16]

In many ways, the microrecruiting of various voting coalitions raises problems similar to the concerns raised by John Mueller and his "coalition of minorities" theory of presidential leadership.[17] Mueller argued that it was inevitable for presidential popularity to decline over the course of an administration, as any presidential decision would antagonize at least some group of supporters. Voters supporting different policy interests might come together temporarily for electoral purposes, but their solidarity is severely tested when it comes to policy making. Once the pressure of governing becomes real, these loose electoral coalitions are likely to break, often leaving the governing party without substantial leverage to accomplish its goals. While Mueller has noted that the negative trend in presidential popularity affects nearly all presidents, contemporary campaign strategies may exacerbate this pattern.

The Terri Schiavo incident, for example, clearly laid bare the governance fractures within the Republican Party's 2004 electoral coalition. Terri Schiavo, a Florida woman in a persistent vegetative state for fifteen years, ended up at the center of a legal battle over euthanasia. Schiavo's husband battled with her parents over the right to make life-terminating decisions, and the courts ultimately sided with him. In March 2005 the Republican majority in Congress, with President Bush's approval, returned from legislative recess to pass a special bill—after midnight on a Sunday night—to prevent doctors from removing Schiavo's feeding tube. The courts ultimately rejected the bill, but the move angered many of Bush's supporters. A *Wall Street Journal*/NBC News poll found that 48 percent of Republicans surveyed thought that reinserting Schiavo's tube was the "wrong thing to do" compared to 39 percent who said it was the "right thing to do."

Conservative commentator and former Republican Congressman Robert Barr criticized the federal government intervention, "To simply say that the 'culture of life,' or whatever you call it means that we don't have to pay attention to the principles of federalism or separation of

---

[16] Larry Eichel, " 'Values Voters' Seek Their Reward in Policy," *Philadelphia Inquirer*, 7 November 2004.

[17] Mueller, "Presidential Popularity from Truman to Johnson."

powers is certainly not a conservative viewpoint."[18] While the issue of euthanasia was an important concern to some Christian conservatives, others in the Republican electoral coalition were frustrated to see government attention distracted from problems like the War in Iraq, terrorism, tax reform, or deficit reduction. Also revealing is the timing of the Schiavo incident, which came just after a failed attempt to reform social security—a campaign promise to investment-minded Republicans that also found mixed support among the larger Republican coalition.

The political fallout that President Bush and congressional Republicans endured so quickly after claiming mandates from the voting public shows just how difficult it can be to maintain electoral coalitions once governing begins.[19] Although Christian evangelicals were supportive of Bush and the Republican Party during the Schiavo hearings, they would later become frustrated by Bush's lack of action on moral issues as his attention turned to other priorities. According to one report, "In the last several weeks, Dr. James C. Dobson, founder of Focus on the Family and one of the most influential Christian conservatives, has publicly accused Republican leaders of betraying the social conservatives who helped elect them in 2004. He has also warned in private meetings with about a dozen of the top Republicans in Washington that he may turn critic this fall unless the party delivers on conservative goals."[20]

Even with a GOP-controlled Congress, President Bush found it difficult to fulfill his myriad campaign promises. The 109th Congress was often described as one of the least productive in decades, resurrecting Harry Truman's taunt of a "do-nothing" Congress. The list of campaign promises failing or receiving scant attention during this administration—ranging from a constitutional amendment to ban gay marriage to social security reform—is substantial. But given Bush's campaign strategy, perhaps such dissatisfaction should not be surprising. Thomas Mann and Norman Ornstein have lamented, "Campaigning has become increasingly antithetical to governing. Candidates decreasingly use campaigns to build public support for governing decisions or to forge public consensus before making policy.... Candidates often frame campaign themes and take positions in ways that frustrate rather than facilitate the task of governing after the election."[21] The strategic decisions that help candidates create winning electoral coalitions do not always translate into successful governing coalitions.

[18] "Political Fallout over Schiavo," CBS News online, 23 March 2005.

[19] Shailagh Murray and Mike Allen, "Schiavo Tests Priorities of GOP," *Washington Post*, 26 March 2005, A1.

[20] David Kirkpatrick, "Conservative Christians Warn Republicans Against Inaction," *New York Times*, 15 May 2006, A1.

[21] Ornstein and Mann, *The Permanent Campaign and Its Future*, 225.

We have painted a bleak future and potentially grim pitfalls for presidential campaigns in a hyperinformation environment. We emphasize these negative consequences in part because so many scholars and political observers have tended to highlight the positive benefits of information technology for democracy. Scholars have argued that information and communication technologies can be used to improve democratic deliberation by creating online forums, by enhancing citizen engagement, and by overcoming political and social inequalities.[22] To be sure, a few scholars have offered a more pessimistic view, suggesting that the contemporary information environment has exacerbated gaps in political interest, political knowledge, and political participation. Our analysis shows that technology also carries potential negative consequences for democracy by virtue of the impact on political candidates—particularly in the role technology plays in gathering and communicating information. Of course, these troublesome predictions reach beyond the bounds of our empirical evidence, so we leave it to the reader to evaluate the extent to which technology represents promise or cause for concern.

Beyond U.S. Presidential Campaigns?

Throughout the book we have focused on presidential elections, making it unclear whether the relationships between information, candidate strategies, and voter decision making generalize to lower-level races, such as Senate or gubernatorial elections, or if our arguments extend to the electoral systems in other countries. It is possible that American presidential campaigns offer conditions that might be uniquely suited to wedge strategies. The two-party system means that the parties will always be heterogeneous coalitions, and the prominence of the contest means that voters are more likely to be informed about the policy positions of the candidates and that cross-pressured voters are still likely to show up on Election Day.

In lower-level races, a sufficiently homogeneous district, or perhaps an election in which turnout is dominated by core supporters, candidates can and do avoid a wedge-issue strategy. Indeed, candidates in uncompetitive races may be able to largely avoid controversial issues altogether, instead focusing on personal appeals and name recognition. In these electoral contexts, we might also be more likely to find that potential wedge issues are neutralized by the position taking of the selected candidates. In 2006, for instance, in some congressional districts

---

[22] Dahl, *Democracy and Its Critics*; Barber, *Strong Democracy*.

in which abortion had the potential to be used as a wedge issue by Republican candidates, the Democrats put forward a pro-life candidate—which effectively neutralized abortion as a potential wedge issue. In lower-level races, candidates and parties are at greater liberty to "take off the table" those issues that have the greatest potential for dividing their coalition of supporters. This would be more difficult in a presidential election in which the constituency is more diverse and there are stronger pressures to adhere to the party platform.

Even still, there are a number of lower-level races in which we have observed wedge-issue campaigns. Competitive congressional races, for instance, are often characterized by explicit attempts to appeal to persuadable voters on the basis of wedge issues. In her run against Republican incumbent Senator Jim Talent, Democratic candidate Claire McCaskill emphasized her support for stem cell research in an attempt to reach out to Republican voters who did not share President Bush's opposition to such research. McCaskill's message received considerable assistance once a ballot measure about embryonic stem cell research became a focal point of the campaign. According to one journalist account of the campaign, Democrats emphasized stem cell research

> to exploit a division between conservatives who oppose the science and other Republicans more open to it. . . . With the Talent-McCaskill race too close to call, the initiative has thrust Mr. Talent into a treacherous Republican crosscurrent. On one side are Christian conservatives. . . . On the other are business-minded Republicans . . . saying the science holds promise not only for patients, but also for the economic health of the state.[23]

Eventually, McCaskill, and the ballot measure, received the support of a slim majority of Missouri voters.

As the Senate race in Missouri suggests, the recent growth in the use of state ballot initiatives illustrates an attempt on the part of other political actors besides candidates to prime divisive issues. A recent study reiterated our warning that "wedge initiatives" have potential negative consequences for democratic governance because they are typically motivated by campaign politics rather than policy making. According to Thad Kousser and Mathew McCubbins, "Political parties, individuals and interest groups are all scouring the policy space to find niche issues for the purpose of affecting elections or rewarding or punishing candidates and parties."[24] According to their report, in

[23] Sheryl Gay Stolberg, "Democrats Hope to Divide G.O.P. over Stem Cells," *New York Times*, 24 April 2006.

[24] Kousser and McCubbins, "Social Choice, Crypto-Initiatives, and Policymaking by Direct Democracy."

the 2004 election alone, there were 162 ballot initiatives in thirty-four states. These initiatives highlight the deepest cleavages in the party coalitions. Republican groups have used gay marriage and immigration issues to reach cross-pressured Democrats, while Democratic groups have organized initiatives based on minimum wage and environmental protection in an effort to reach cross-pressured Republicans. These ballot initiatives are often organized and funded by out-of-state groups interested in using controversial issues to win both national and local electoral office. They are anything but the idealized picture of a grassroots effort of concerned citizens trying to influence public policy.

Similar to lower-level races, it is also unclear if the incentives for using wedge issues remain in the comparative context. Certainly, campaign strategies will reflect the institutional features of a political system, including the basic institutional structure of government, electoral laws, procedures governing elections, and nature of political actors. We might expect, then, that campaigns in proportional electoral systems, by lowering the hurdles to office, would be see fewer divisive issues used in the campaign. The coalition building that we observe within the campaign process in the United States might instead occur after elections among party leaders and elected representatives in other political systems.

On the other hand, recent research has highlighted that many countries have "Americanized" their electoral campaigns. Campaigns are increasingly characterized by everything from an expanded use of consultants and negative advertising to targeted campaign appeals. Evaluations of political marketing in Western democracies, and in the British Labor party in particular, suggest that microtargeting of wedge issues may be on the rise. According to Darren Lillenker,

> Over the past four decades, parties across Europe have brought in consultants to support their campaigning, conducted research to aid the design of communication and used techniques associated with branding when constructing symbolic representations of their party. Leaders' style and image, key messages, party motifs, as well as the various modes of advertising, are all part of sophisticated marketing strategies more associated with producers of fast moving consumer goods than with political parties.[25]

Obviously, the extent to which the trends we have identified in American presidential elections occur in other electoral and institutional contexts is an important topic for future research. Somewhat more apparent in other polished systems is the more fundamental relationship between the information environment and campaign strategies.

[25] Lillenker, "The Impact of Political Marketing on Internal Party Democracy," 570.

Australia serves as a prime example. It maintains a proportional electoral system requiring compulsory voting of all eligible citizens. Despite these institutional differences, a cursory examination of recent campaign strategies reveals a similar relationship between the information available about individual voters and the use of microtargeted wedge campaign strategies as we have identified in our earlier analysis.

Stemming from the legal requirements for mandatory voter turnout, the Australian Election Commission (AEC) possesses an incredible amount of information about the voting public. The AEC maintains and regularly updates a centralized database, including a registrant's full name and address, telephone number, date of birth, sex, occupation (optional), mobile number (optional), and date of naturalization. With information from the central registration system as the base, the major political parties in Australia maintain internal databases that match this registration data with other important facts about the voters, including information gathered following contact with politicians, letters to the editor, party donation history, and so on.[26] The Coalition's *Feedback* database, for instance, includes fields for three hundred different issue interests and preferences.[27] The local-party office staff is trained to log all constituency correspondence into the database, although members in safe seats or in their last term appear less motivated to make comprehensive entries. The parties use these data to attract potential supporters; for instance, the local representative will send a welcome letter to individuals moving into the area. The information is also used to tailor campaign messages.[28]

Using this information, these targeted campaign messages can contain divisive content. The 2001 federal election, for instance, is often cited as a classic example of dog-whistle politics. The Australian economy was in crisis in 2001—several corporations had collapsed, unemployment had dramatically increased, and the Australian dollar plunged to all-time lows—but the campaign communication of the Labor Party focused on issues of border security, immigration, and terrorism. Labor Party advertisements showed a picture of a clenched-fisted John Howard proclaiming, "We decide who comes into this country." As one political commentator wrote, "Howard's brand of wedge politics very much follows the tactics used by the US Republi-

[26] The ALP's database is called *Electrac*; the Coalition's is called *Feedback*. These systems date to the 1990s, but did not become fully operational until 1996.

[27] Privacy laws prevent community and public organizations from handing out lists of members.

[28] Onselen and Errington, "Electoral Databases."

cans. . . . 'Politically correct,' 'free speech,' 'family values' and 'values neutral' are key phrases that have made their way across the Pacific."[29]

While certainly not definitive, the Australian case is suggestive of the link between the information that candidates have about persuadable voters and their willingness to take a position on a divisive issue in the political campaign.

Voter Response to Microtargeted Messages

Another critical topic for future research is to isolate and understand more completely the influence of wedge campaign messages on voters in the context of a complex campaign environment. What is the impact of microtargeted campaign messages above and beyond the dozens of other mailers, phone calls, and personal visits that bombard residents of battleground states? We have argued that microtargeting is consequential even if it has little impact on the voters because it shapes the specific policy promises candidates make and determines a candidate's perceived constituency. Yet the prominence of this strategy will undoubtedly depend on its influence. Is the targeted mail piece more persuasive because it is individualized on an issue the recipient cares about? Or is a mailing more easily discarded as a piece of junk mail?

We might actually expect that microtargeted messages are in fact *more* persuasive than other campaign communications. An individualized and personalized message should be more compelling than the broad-based appeal in a television ad. Further, compared to television advertising, targeted communications receive less scrutiny from the media and opposition camps so they are not only more likely to contain divisive issues, they should also be more likely to contain sensational and inflammatory content. Mike Russell, a spokesman for Swift Vets and POWs for Truth, explained: "If direct mail were food, it would be hot salsa."[30] In 2004, for instance, the Bush campaign was exceptionally careful in campaign commercials to avoid the appearance that they were exploiting 9/11 for political gain. These concerns, however, did not carry over into the messages communicated through direct mail— one mailing in particular contained several images of the destroyed World Trade Center with the caption "How can John Kerry lead America in a time of War?" Of course, Republicans were not the only ones willing to use direct mail to send provocative campaign mes-

---

[29] Iain Lygo, "Racism Rather than Relief in Australia," *Z Magazine*, 25 May 2004.

[30] Glen Justice, "In Final Days, Attacks Are in the Mail and Below the Radar," *New York Times Magazine*, 31 October 2004, 30.

sages. From the other side of the aisle, Democrats also sent campaign messages and images through direct mail they would not likely want to convey to wider audiences. For example, one Democratic mailing contained an image of a 1960s white fire fighter blasting an African American with a fire hose, with the caption "This is what they used to do to keep us from voting. Don't let them do it again."

The extent to which direct mail is a persuasive form of campaign communication is an especially important question for future research because it will help us predict the broader impact of these campaign tactics on election outcomes.

Final Words: Speculations about Future Campaign Technology

We cannot overstate the economic and social impact of new information and communication technologies. A recent study concluded, "As canals and railroads were the infrastructure for the emerging industrial economy in the 19th century, information might be thought of as the infrastructure for the new 'knowledge economy.' "[31] And we expect changes in the information environment also have important implications for electoral politics—a political campaign takes place within a specific social and technological context, and this environment shapes the dynamics of the campaign. At different stages in history, the introduction of radio, TV, and other technologies has had a profound influence on the relationship between citizens, government, and the campaigns. Candidates continually look for strategies to gain the slightest edge over their competition, and technological innovations are one way that candidates look for an electoral advantage. It is, of course, difficult to predict exactly what or how new technologies will be used. Regardless, one prediction seems clear—as technological advances continue to change the political landscape at an exponential pace, we expect to see candidates attempting to find and use even more detailed information about individual voters. A recent white paper from one microtargeting firm proposed mining online resumes (there are more than 50 million online) to collect information about where and what someone studied in college. With the emergence of online communities through MySpace, Facebook, and other Web sites, candidates may be able to penetrate social networks to quickly and efficiently target like-

[31] Hillygus et al., *The Hard Count*, 76.

minded individuals through trusted personal connections rather than broad, impersonal appeals. Given the link between driver's-license databases and voter registration lists, it may not be too much of a stretch to imagine that voter databases could eventually include photographs of individual voters. Candidates could then send extremely personalized campaign messages that contain not only the issues an individual cares about but also the individual's own image. Already, we see direct mailings that are personalized by the race of the recipient—with African Americans receiving direct mail showcasing African Americans, and Hispanics receiving mailings with images of Hispanics. In Steven Spielberg's science-fiction blockbuster *Minority Report*, the future—the year 2054—is characterized by individualized advertising based on "Big Brother"–like surveillance. In the political world, that imagined future is perhaps closer than many realize.

At the same time, there is the potential for new technological innovations to limit the effectiveness of microtargeting. New technologies may make it more difficult for candidates to get away with sending blatantly conflicting messages to different voters. It seems possible that as the public (and other candidates) become increasingly aware of the discrepancies in campaign messages between different communication modes, the incentive to use targeted messages could be reduced. With video-sharing Web sites like YouTube, microtargeted stump speeches can be uploaded and shared with a broader audience, bringing the "under-the-radar" messages of the grand war into the public sphere. In the 2006 Virginia election, for example, Senator George Allen was videotaped calling an Indian American a "macaca." Although Senator Allen apologized, hundreds of thousands of viewers watched the clip on YouTube, and Senator Allen's lead in the polls began a steady decline and he was ultimately defeated. Of course, accountability via the Internet assumes that audiences are interested in what candidates are saying to different groups and that candidates can be linked to specific messages. It is already common practice for divisive campaign messages to originate with the party rather than the candidate, making it easier for candidates to distance themselves from anything controversial. But the Internet allows for an unprecedented level of anonymous, unregulated political mudslinging and rumor spreading. Early in the 2008 Democratic presidential primary season, for instance, an unauthorized amateur "1984" video attacking Hillary Clinton as Orwellian and promoting Barack Obama was anonymously posted on YouTube. It received nearly 4 million hits in five months. Revealing his identity on the *Huffington Post* blog two weeks later, the ad's author observed,

"This ad was not the first citizen ad, and it will not be the last. The game has changed."[32]

Whatever the future holds for new information technologies, it seems apparent that the electorate of tomorrow will face an increasingly fragmented and diverse information environment. With hypermedia campaigns, it is ever more difficult for voters to "tame the information tide."[33] This is especially the case for Independents and cross-pressured partisans who are targeted from both sides of the partisan aisle. Targeted communications contribute to a swirl, some might say tornado, of information in contemporary political campaigns. In this context, the full landscape of policy differences between the candidates can be obscured and it becomes more difficult for voters to remove the "chaff" from the "wheat."

In this age of narrowcasted campaigns and segmented issue messages, it perhaps becomes increasingly important for the mainstream media to monitor the exchange of information between citizens and their representatives. So fundamental is the media's role in ensuring democratic accountability—by informing the electorate of the policy debates, distilling complicated events and policies into comprehensible narratives, and reporting on the behaviors and misbehaviors of political leaders—that Thomas Jefferson once remarked, "Were it left to me to decide whether we should have government without newspapers, or newspapers without a government, I should not hesitate a moment to prefer the latter."[34] The media often obsess over candidates' spending on television commercials, setting up elaborate "campaign ad watches" to ensure the veracity of television campaign commercials, but our analysis makes clear that these communication venues provide only a limited perspective of the candidates' campaign agendas. The targeted ground-war communication may be more difficult to track, but is more divisive and less connected to the broader issue dialogue of the campaign. The media have an obligation to bring candidates' rhetoric and promises to the broader public discussion and to expose any inconsistencies between candidates' broadcast policy goals and their narrowcast promises on wedge issues. While the news media often scrutinize the candidates' campaign tactics and motivations, they must also consider the overlap between campaign tactics and the policy substance of the campaign.

---

[32] Phil de Vellis, "I Made the Vote Different ad," *Huffington Post Blog*, posted 21 March 2007.

[33] Graber, *Processing the News*.

[34] Kurland and Lerner, *The Founders' Constitution*.

Presidential campaigns remain the fundamental link between citizens and their government in an electoral democracy. Understanding how voters make up their minds in an election and why candidates offer the policy alternatives they do is critical if we are to successfully evaluate the state of American democracy. We hope to have offered a slice of insight by identifying the incentives behind candidates' campaign promises and policy position taking and by offering a general perspective of who in the electorate responds to information presented during the campaign. Although American democracy is far from flawless, and new information technologies certainly have the potential to exacerbate the faults, we nonetheless conclude with the observation that the balance of power in American democracy is still held by its citizens. And our analysis suggests that these citizens have the capacity and motivation to deliberate about their vote decision. Although the fragmentation of campaign dialogue has potentially negative implications for political inequality and governance, we remain reassured that candidates are ultimately constrained by voters, even if not by all voters. It is still in the interaction of citizens and government during an American presidential campaign that we find the basic structure, however imperfect, of a democratic process.

Appendixes

To ease the interpretation of the analyses presented in the book, we have presented the results in a way that required little detailed knowledge of statistics, data collection, or data analysis. In these appendixes, we present more detailed discussion for the interested reader.

Appendix 1 ────────────────────

Question Wording and Coding

2004 Blair Center Survey

The 2004 Blair Center Survey and the 2000 Knowledge Networks Election Study were conducted by the survey firm Knowledge Networks. Knowledge Networks conducts their surveys online, but remains a probability-based sample because panel members are recruited using random digit dialing sampling methods and then provided with an Internet connection if they do not have one. All telephone numbers have an equal probability of selection, and the sampling is done without replacement. In exchange for the Internet connection, Knowledge Network panelists are asked to complete surveys three to four times per month. Participants are sent an email informing them that their next survey is ready to be taken and individuals then complete the survey at their own convenience.

The 2004 Blair Center Survey was a national postelection survey. The sample plan consisted of 2,800 interviews from three strata: 1,150 from southern states, 1,150 from other states, and 500 from the general adult population. The overall survey completion rate was 68.1 percent. Poststratification weights that adjust for nonresponse and the survey sampling design were provided by Knowledge Networks.

When classifying individuals as incongruent or congruent, we created a conservative measure. If the question-response format included a middle, neutral, or don't-know category, individuals selecting these responses were coded as being congruent with their political party, even if they might consider their moderate position incongruent with their party's more extreme position. Thus, to be classified as a cross-pressured partisan, an individual must not only disagree with the position taken by her own party but also agree with the position of the opposition party. For the 2004 measure from the Blair Center Survey, we also included only those issues that respondents indicated were "extremely" or "very" important to them personally. The 2004 cross-pressures measure was constructed from the following ten policy questions.

Social Security: "Some people have proposed allowing individuals to invest portions of their social security taxes in the stock market, which might allow them to make more money for their retirement, but would involve greater risk than the current government-run system. Do you favor or oppose allowing individuals to invest a portion of their social security taxes in the stock market? [completely favor, somewhat favor, neither favor nor oppose, somewhat oppose, completely oppose]"

Income Equality: "Do you favor or oppose the federal government in Washington trying to reduce the income differences between the richest and poorest Americans? [completely favor, somewhat favor, neither favor nor oppose, somewhat oppose, completely oppose]"

Taxes: "Which of the following do you think should be emphasized more in an economic recovery plan: an increase in minimum wage or tax cuts for businesses? Where would you place yourself on the scale below? [7-point scale with minimum wage increase more important on one end, tax cuts more important on the other]"

Health Care: "In thinking about health care reform, which of the following do you think should be emphasized more in a reform plan: expanding coverage for low-income adults through federal and state health care programs or aiding small businesses in offering health care to their employees? Where would you place yourself on the scale below? [7-point scale with more important to expand coverage through government programs on one end, more important to aid small businesses in offering coverage on the other end]"

Gay Marriage: "Would you favor or oppose an amendment to the U.S. Constitution that would define marriage as being between a man and a woman, thus barring marriages between gay or lesbian couples? [completely favor, somewhat favor, neither favor nor oppose, somewhat oppose, completely oppose]"

Stem Cell Research: "On the whole, do you favor or oppose the use of stem cells taken from human embryos in medical research? [completely favor, somewhat favor, neither favor nor oppose, somewhat oppose, completely oppose]"

Gun Control: "Do you favor or oppose the registration and licensing of all new handguns sold in America? [completely favor, somewhat favor, neither favor nor oppose, somewhat oppose, completely oppose]"

Affirmative Action: "Some people say that affirmative action programs are still needed to counteract the effects of discrimination against minorities, and are a good idea as long as there are no rigid quotas. Other people say that affirmative action programs have gone too far in favoring minorities, and should be ended because they unfairly discriminate against whites. Still others have opinions somewhere in between these two. Where would you place yourself on the scale below? [7-point scale with affirmative action is necessary on one end, affirmative action should be ended on other]"

Environment: "Do you favor or oppose relaxing some environmental standards to increase oil and gas production in the United States? [completely favor, somewhat favor, neither favor nor oppose, somewhat oppose, completely oppose]"

Abortion: "Which of the following opinions comes closer to your view about abortion? [It should never be permitted; it should only be permitted when the woman's life is in danger; it should only be permitted if the woman's health or life is in danger; by law, a woman should always be able to obtain an abortion as a matter of personal choice]"

Policy Importance Measure: "Regardless of where you stand on the following political issues, please indicate how important each issue or policy is to you personally (abortion policy; gay marriage policy; gun control policy; health care policy; stem cell research policy; education policy; social security policy; environmental policy; welfare policy; military issues like global terrorism; employment issues like job security; business issues like regulation; legal issues like tort reform; racial issues like affirmative action; policies about prescription drugs; policies about school prayer) [extremely important, very important, moderately important, slightly important, not at all important]"

Open-ended Question: "We find that many people disagree with their political party on a variety of different political issues. You said that you consider yourself to be a (Democrat or Republican). Can you think of any political issues about which you disagree with the (Democratic or Republican) Party?" The coding of open-ended questions started with the fifty issue categories used by the American National Election Studies in classifying the open-ended likes/dislikes responses. Additional categories were added as needed.

As measures of campaign exposure in the 2004 presidential election, we used the number of presidential visits to the state in which a respondent lived, whether or not the state was defined as a battleground state by the presidential campaigns (using data provided by Daron Shaw) and measures of political attention and political awareness from 2004 Blair Center Survey. The measure of political attention was based on the question, "Some people seem to follow what's going on in government and public affairs most of the time, whether there's an election going on or not. Others aren't that interested. Would you say you follow what's going on in government and public affairs . . . [most of the time, some of the time, only now and then, never]?" To measure political awareness we created an additive scale of the number of eight political issues—abortion, gay marriage, gun control, stem cell research, environment, welfare, business regulation, and affirmative action—for which the respondent was able to correctly identify the Republican Party as more conservative than the Democratic Party. Respondents correct on seven or more issues were coded as politically aware, while those who were correct on less than seven issues were coded as unaware.

As a control variable, we coded a respondent's general level of political knowledge as the number of correct answers from the following questions. "Who is the current attorney general of the United States? [Donald Rumsfeld, John Ashcroft, Condoleezza Rice, or Colin Powell]"; "What is the term of office of a U.S. senator? [two years, four years, six years, eight years]"; "Who is responsible for nominating judges to federal courts? [the president, Congress, the Supreme Court]"

2000 Knowledge Networks Election Study

The 2000 Knowledge Networks Election Study was created from repeated interviews of 28,000 panelists. Over the course of the campaign, seventy-five randomly assigned surveys (with widely varying sample sizes) were sampled from the Knowledge Networks panel. The political questionnaires varied from a single vote choice question added to the end of a market survey to a 10–15 minute survey about political attitudes, behaviors, and experiences. Following the election, a post-election survey of 12,000 respondents was conducted.

The resulting data set is a two-way unbalanced panel in that the number of observations are not the same for every respondent and the intervals between observations are not equal. The modal number of interviews per respondent was three and the average was five. Given that the intermittent missing values are random (i.e., individuals have missing observations because they were not part of the random sample selected for a given survey), it is reasonable to assume that the analysis should give the relevant inferences. Data were weighted to independent population estimates based on the 2000 Current Population Survey. These weights take into account age, gender, race, region of residence, and MSA.

Because of the structure of the data, the number of issue questions asked of each respondent varied. Among partisans in the postelection sample, more than one third were previously asked no issue questions and 50 percent were asked three or more issue questions. Analysis is restricted to the subset of respondents who answered at least three policy issues. In the event that respondents were asked more than one question in the same policy domain, a combined measure of the policy attitude was created. A respondent was not coded as cross-pressured on the issue if they gave conflicting responses to multiple questions in the same policy domain. The following policy questions were used to create the 2000 cross-pressures measure.

Gun Control: "Do you support or oppose making it illegal to buy or sell handguns anywhere in the United States? [support strongly, support somewhat, oppose somewhat, oppose strongly]"; "How well does the phrase 'an NRA supporter' describe you? [very well, somewhat well, not very well, not well at all]"

Gay Rights: "Do you support or oppose making gay and lesbian marriages legal? [support strongly, support somewhat, oppose somewhat, oppose strongly]"; "Do you think marriages between homosexuals should or should not be legal, with the same rights as traditional marriages? [not legal, legal, don't know]"

School Prayer: "Do you support or oppose allowing public schools to start each day with a prayer in the classrooms? [support strongly, support somewhat, oppose somewhat, oppose strongly]"; "Would you favor or oppose an amendment to the U.S. Constitution that would permit prayers to be said in public schools? [favor, oppose, don't know]"

Assistance to Minorities: "How much do you agree that the government in Washington should make every effort to improve the social and economic position of minority groups? [7-point scale with agree strongly on one end, disagree strongly on the other]"

Abortion: "Do you agree or disagree that it should be legal for a woman to have an abortion? [agree strongly, agree somewhat, disagree somewhat, oppose strongly]"; "How well does the phrase "pro-life" describe you? [very well, somewhat well, not very well, not well at all]"; "Under what circumstances should abortion be legal? [always; only in cases of rape, incest, or to save mother's life; never]"

Environmental Protection: "How urgent do you think the problem of pollution and environmental damage is? [5-point scale with not very urgent on one end, extremely urgent one the other]"; "How well does the phrase 'an environmentalist' describe you?" [very well, somewhat well, not very well, not well at all]"; "How about government spending on the environment? [spending too much, about right, spending too little]"

Tax Cut Priority: "As you may know, the federal government is currently running a budget surplus, meaning it is taking in more money than it spends. Which is the most important thing to do with the surplus? [tax cuts, reduce debt, increase spending on important programs and services]"

Privatization of Social Security: "Some people have suggested allowing individuals to invest portions of their social security taxes on their own, which might result in more money for their retirement but would also involve greater risk. What do you think of this idea? [good idea, bad idea]"; "Of the following two statements by candidates about social security, which do you agree with more? Candidate A: People should be allowed to invest some of their social security money in the stock market. It's their money, so they should be allowed to invest it themselves; Candidate B: Investing social security money in the stock market is too risky. Some people would end up getting much less than what they get now with Social Security. [candidate A, candidate B, don't know]"

Defense Spending: "How about government spending on defense? [spending too much, about right, spending too little]"

Political awareness is an indicator variable constructed from two different measures. For roughly 2,700 respondents, an individual's awareness was estimated based on whether she could correctly identified the party of the incumbent candidate in the Senate race in her state (or whether the race was an open seat). For those respondents not asked this question, an individual was coded as aware if she had a college degree.

Design and Questions for Survey Experiment

The survey experiment was fielded in November 2006 as part of the 2006 Cooperative Congressional Election Study (CCES). The CCES was a collaborative survey project conducted by Polimetrix, an online survey company. The CCES was coordinated through the MIT Political Science Department and Polimetrix by Stephen Ansolabehere, Doug Rivers, and Lynn Vavreck. Research teams at more than thirty universities participated, each designing a 1,000-person survey for a total of 30,000 cases in the common content survey. The common content always preceded each university's module. The common content questionnaire was developed by Stephen Ansolabehere, Robert Erikson, Elisabeth Gerber, Donald Kinder, Wendy Rahn, Jeremy Pope, and John Sides. Our sample of 1,000 respondents was randomly assigned to three different treatments. All respondents received the information presented to the control group, but those assigned to an experimental vignette received an additional screen of information. All respondents were then asked a series of survey questions about their attitudes and behaviors.

Control Group: "We are interested in people's opinions about potential candidates for the 2008 presidential election. Currently, neither party has a clear front-runner for the nomination. Some party leaders have suggested it would be best to choose a new face—someone with less political baggage than the high-profile politicians. Among the names being discussed are Senators Tim Johnson and Larry Craig. Senator Johnson is a mainstream Democrat and a popular two-term senator from the Midwest. Senator Craig is a mainstream Republican recently elected to his third term as senator of a large midwestern state. Both candidates are thought to have strong records on national security and economic policies."

Stem Cell Vignette: "Political analysts predict that one of the key issues of the campaign will be stem cell research. According to a leading analyst, 'By 2008, many Americans will agree on the direction the country should take on foreign policy, so attention will likely shift to focus on the growing debate over stem cell research.' Senator Johnson supports federal funding for stem cell research while Senator Craig opposes it. Given the distance between these candidates on this issue, the future of stem cell research policy could be one of the biggest issues at stake in the 2008 presidential election."

Social Security Vignette: "Political analysts predict that one of the key issues of the campaign will be social security reform. According to a leading analyst, 'By 2008, many Americans will agree on the direction the country should take on foreign policy, so attention will likely shift to focus on the growing debate over social security privatization.' Senator Craig supports a proposal that has been made that would allow people to put a portion of their social security payroll taxes into personal retirement accounts that would be invested in stocks and bonds. Senator Johnson opposes this proposal. Given the distance between these candidates on this issue, the future of social security policy could be one of the biggest issues at stake in the 2008 presidential election."

Stem Cell Research: "Do you favor or oppose the use of stem cells taken from human embryos in medical research? [completely favor, somewhat favor, neither favor nor oppose, somewhat oppose, completely oppose]"

Social Security: "A proposal had been made that would allow individuals to invest portions of their social security taxes in the stock market. Some say that this proposal would allow individuals to make more money for their retirement, while others say the proposal involves too much risk. Do you favor or oppose the proposal? [completely favor, somewhat favor, neither favor nor oppose, somewhat oppose, completely oppose]"

Questions Included in Cross-pressure Measures from the American National Election Studies Cumulative File

Detailed information about question wording and methodology of the American National Election Study can be found on their website at www.electionstudies.org.

The following issues were used in creation of the general cross pressures measures for the temporal analysis in chapter 3.

1972: civil rights; segregation; busing; aid to blacks; health insurance; guaranteed jobs

1976: civil rights; segregation; busing; aid to blacks; health insurance; guaranteed jobs

1980: civil rights; busing; aid to blacks; guaranteed jobs; abortion; defense spending

1984: civil rights; busing; aid to blacks; guaranteed jobs; abortion; defense spending; assistance for blacks; food stamps

1988: civil rights; aid to blacks; guaranteed jobs; abortion; defense spending; assistance for blacks; food stamps; homeless; discrimination against homosexuals

1992: civil rights; aid to blacks; guaranteed jobs; abortion; defense spending; assistance for blacks; food stamps; homeless; discrimination against homosexuals; affirmative action; homosexuals in the military

1996: aid to blacks; guaranteed jobs; abortion; defense spending; food stamps; homeless; discrimination against homosexuals; affirmative action; homosexuals in the military

2000: aid to blacks; guaranteed jobs; abortion; defense spending; assistance for blacks; food stamps; discrimination against homosexuals; affirmative action; homosexuals in the military

2004: aid to blacks; guaranteed jobs; abortion; defense spending; assistance for blacks; food stamps; discrimination against homosexuals; affirmative action; homosexuals in the military

The following issues were used in creating the racial cross-pressures measure for the temporal analysis in chapter 5.

1964–1968: civil rights; segregation

1972–1980: civil rights; segregation; busing; aid to blacks

1984: civil rights; busing; aid to blacks; government assistance for blacks

1988: civil rights; aid to blacks; government assistance for blacks; discrimination makes it difficult for blacks; blacks should have special favors; blacks should try harder; blacks have gotten less than they deserve

1992: civil rights; aid to blacks; government assistance for blacks; affirmative action; discrimination makes it difficult for blacks; blacks should have special favors; blacks should try harder; blacks have gotten less than they deserve

1996: aid to blacks; affirmative action

2000: civil rights; integration; aid to blacks; government assistance for blacks; affirmative action; discrimination makes it difficult for blacks; blacks should have special favors; blacks should try harder; blacks have gotten less than they deserve

2004: aid to blacks; affirmative action; discrimination makes it difficult for blacks; blacks should have special favors; blacks should try harder; blacks have gotten less than they deserve

The following issues were used in creation of the moral cross-pressures measure for the temporal analysis in chapter 5.

1980–1984: abortion

1988: abortion; moral views should change with society; traditional family ties should be emphasized more; new lifestyles contribute to the breakdown of society; tolerate new moral standards; protect homosexuals from discrimination; spending for AIDS

1992: abortion; homosexuals in the military; moral views should change with society; traditional family ties should be emphasized more; new lifestyles contribute to the breakdown of society; tolerate new moral standards; protect homosexuals from discrimination; spending for AIDS; homosexual adoptions

1996: abortion; homosexuals in the military; moral views should change with society; traditional family ties should be emphasized more; new lifestyles contribute to the breakdown of society; tolerate new moral standards; protect homosexuals from discrimination; spending for AIDS

2000: abortion; homosexuals in the military; moral views should change with society; traditional family ties should be emphasized more; new lifestyles contribute to the breakdown of society; tolerate new moral standards; protect homosexuals from discrimination; spending for AIDS; homosexual adoptions

2004: abortion; homosexuals in the military; moral views should change with society; traditional family ties should be emphasized more; new lifestyles contribute to the breakdown of society; tolerate new moral standards; protect homosexuals from discrimination; homosexual adoptions

Appendix 2 _____

Content Analysis Coding

Candidate Speeches

Coding of candidate speeches relied on the Annenberg/Pew Archive of Presidential Campaign Discourse, which contains the transcripts of speeches from September 1 through Election Day for the two major party nominees 1952 through 1996, with the exception of Barry Goldwater.

In calculating the speeches related to racial policies from 1960 through 1976, as reported in chapter 5, the following subject categories were used: affirmative action; African Americans; *Brown v. Board of Education*; busing; civil rights; bigotry; criminal justice, African Americans; desegregation; discrimination; ethnic/racial discrimination; equal opportunity; ethnic/racial education; employment discrimination; employment quotas; employment, minorities; equal opportunity; housing discrimination; integration; discrimination military personnel; minorities, business; minorities, employment; minorities, unemployment; minorities, prejudice; ethnic/racial quotas; race relations.

To code the total number of issues addressed by presidential candidates across this time, reported in chapter 6, a sample of thirty speeches (fifteen from each candidate), excluding nomination speeches, was randomly selected from the Annenberg/Pew Archive of Presidential Discourse for each election year. Research assistants then calculated the number of issues in the speech sample using the issue categories from the Campaign Communication Study, adding additional categories as necessary.

2004 Presidential Direct Mail

The data for the 2004 presidential direct mail came from the Campaign Communication Study conducted by the Center for the Study of Elections and Democracy (CSED) at Brigham Young University. The field work for the Campaign Communication Study was conducted by the Social and Economic Sciences Research Center (SESRC) at Washington State University, and followed the method for mail and mixed mode surveys in Don Dillman's book, *Mail and Internet Surveys: The Tailored*

Design Method. The sample was obtained from the "Datamart" national database of registered voters maintained by the Democratic National Committee. Because the survey design required some telephone contact, the population was defined as registered voters living in households with telephones. The sample design was intended to maximize the participation of respondents most likely to receive campaign communications. To this end the sample was stratified by past turnout behavior and by expected state competitiveness, with oversamples in Ohio and Florida. The national sample response rate for the post election telephone survey was 50 percent while the response rate for the questionnaire/log booklet portion of the survey was 37 percent.

The SESRC was responsible for recording data from the questionnaire/log booklet as well as the initial coding of the 2,466 unique federal mail pieces (coding an identification number, a brief description, the candidate/party/group that sponsored the piece, and the key electoral contest). A research team at the CSED then conducted a much more comprehensive coding of the federal mail pieces using a detailed coding instrument (with 100 to 350 coded items depending on the length and complexity of the mail piece). Any remaining errors in the final classification of issues are the responsibility of the authors.

The issue classifications began with approximately ninety issue categories, based on the coding instrument used in coding television advertising by the Wisconsin Advertising Project (www.polisci.wisc .edu/tvadvertising/Index.htm). Issues that did not fit into one of the categories were then either combined with existing categories or an additional category was created, resulting in a total of just over one hundred final issue categories. In the tables presented in chapter 6, we categorize the divisive issues into moral issues, wedge issues, and targeted issues. Moral issues included abortion, gay marriage (as well as other homosexual issues), and stem cell research. Wedge issues included minimum wage, unions, poverty, welfare, abortion, gay marriage, gay issues, tobacco, affirmative action, race relations, gambling, assisted suicide, euthanasia, gun control, racial profiling, stem cell research, civil liberties/privacy, civil rights, voting rights, family laws, parental leave policies, pledge of allegiance, flag burning, boy scouts, separation of church and state, vouchers, judicial nominations, environment, Kyoto protocol, immigration, union benefits, work safety, pensions, overtime, tort reform, and the United Nations. Targeted issues included all of the wedge issues as well as farming, agriculture, veteran's issues, local issues, social security, Medicare, prescription drugs, health for seniors, Florida ballot reform, and references about policies toward Israel, Cuba, Africa, China, Latin America, Europe, or Asia.

Appendix 3 _____

Statistical Results

To EVALUATE THE INFLUENCE of the presidential campaign on voter decision making, we compare the effect of cross-pressures across levels of campaign exposure or in different campaign contexts. Because the dependent variable is a binary outcome (1 = voted for opposing party candidate, 0 = voted for own party candidate), we have estimated the effects in separate models. We do not estimate an interaction between cross-pressures and campaign exposure because it is not possible in nonlinear models (e.g., logit model) to evaluate an interaction effect simply by looking at the sign, magnitude, or statistical significance of the coefficient on the interaction term. For instance, see discussion in Ai and Norton, "Interaction Terms in Logit and Probit Models." For easier interpretation of the results, we have estimated the substantive effects across all relevant models for the same respondent type (based on global means and modes) using Clarify software to calculate the 90 percent confidence bounds around those estimates. We also calculate the Wald chi-squared statistic to determine if the difference in estimated coefficients across the low-exposure and high-exposure groups is statistically significant (assuming residual variation is the same across groups).

TABLE A1
Model Results Used to Calculate Substantive Effects Reported in Figure 4.2

	Non-battle	Battle	No Visits	Many Visits	Less Attentive	Most Attentive	Less Aware	Most Aware	Non-battle (Most Attentive)	Battle (Most Attentive)
Constant	**-2.64**	**-4.57**	**-3.52**	**-4.06**	**-2.24**	**-3.27**	**-2.13**	**-4.32**	-3.5	-1.1
	(.58)	(1.08)	(1.13)	(.91)	(.91)	(.97)	(.84)	(.88)	(1.16)	(1.73)
Strength of Partisanship	**-1.78**	**-2.15**	**-1.85**	**-2.40**	**-1.61**	**-2.03**	**-1.25**	**-2.27**	**-2.3**	**-3.5**
	(-.29)	(.52)	(.52)	(.57)	(.54)	(.48)	(.45)	(.40)	(.498)	(1.06)
Age	0.09	0.05	0.18	0.06	-0.08	0.03	-0.11	**0.21**	**0.3**	**-0.5**
	(0.08)	(0.11)	(.14)	(.10)	(.14)	(.12)	(.12)	(.09)	(.154)	(0.272)
Minority	0.09	-0.86	0.09	0.02	-0.30	-0.29	-0.30	0.42	0.2	-0.9
	(.29)	(.69)	(.67)	(.59)	(.51)	(.61)	(.44)	(.44)	(.539)	(0.961)
Female	0.12	-0.80	0.36	**-1.08**	0.20	-0.50	-0.10	0.14	-0.3	**-2.2**
	(.26)	(.42)	(.44)	(.39)	(.42)	(.48)	(.38)	(.33)	(.475)	(0.996)
Education	0.03	**0.66**	0.20	0.49	-0.08	0.30	0.19	0.22	0.1	0.6
	(.13)	(.20)	(.21)	(.18)	(.24)	(.20)	(.18)	(.18)	(.246)	(0.417)
Political Knowledge	-0.09	-0.07	-0.20	0.06	0.26	-0.35	0.06	-0.06	-0.4	-0.7
	(.12)	(.23)	(.18)	(.21)	(.22)	(.23)	(.19)	(.20)	(.246)	(0.423)
Cross-pressures Scale	**3.44**	**5.49**	**3.68**	**4.96**	2.19	**7.21**	1.56	**5.61**	**6.4**	**12.3**
	(.72)	(1.09)	(1.32)	(.98)	(1.32)	(1.29)	(1.20)	(.86)	(1.29)	(3.19)
Wald Chi-square Statistic		2.45		0.61		7.38		7.53	2.95	
Cross-pressured Dummy	**0.83**	**2.31**	0.82	**2.00**	0.30	**2.77**	0.21	**1.78**		
	(.25)	(.57)	(.44)	(.49)	(.44)	(.56)	(.36)	(.35)		
Wald Chi-square Statistic		5.75		3.26		11.98		9.88		
N	1325	570	516	600	381	758	444	1108	545	213
LR Chi-square	74.22	81.82	31.90	57.89	15.09	39.09	15.60	93.30	65.92	51.10
Pseudo R-square	0.14	0.29	0.16	0.28	0.08	0.31	0.03	0.28	0.31	0.50

Note: Bolded coefficients are statistically significant at p<.05. Reported are logit results of model predicting a vote for the opposing party candidate. Sample limited to self-identified partisans only (leaners not included). Included in the table are the coefficients, standard errors, and Wald chi-square statistic for both the cross-pressures scale measure (percent of important cross-pressured issues) and the cross-pressured dummy variable (1 = greater than mean, the estimate used to calculate total effects on 2004 election outcome). Control variables and model fit statistics are reported for model with cross-pressures scale. Data source is the 2004 Blair Center Election Survey.

TABLE A2
Model Results Used to Calculate Substantive Effects Reported in Figure 4.3

	Non-battle	Battle	No Visits	Many Visits	Less Aware	Most Aware	Less Attentive	Most Attentive	Non-battle (Undecided)	Battle (Undecided)
Constant	-1.22	-2.45	-1.09	-1.88	-2.05	-2.90	-1.08	-2.46	-1.59	-0.28
	(.35)	(.55)	(.46)	(.40)	(.22)	(.50)	(.53)	(.67)	(.69)	(1.25)
Strength of Partisanship	-1.79	-1.74	-1.57	-1.80	-1.86	-1.08	-1.51	0.05	-1.22	-2.37
	(.17)	(.27)	(.21)	(.20)	(.17)	(.32)	(.32)	(.15)	(.41)	(.81)
Age	-0.02	0.05	0.02	0.00	0.04	-0.04	0.05	-0.10	0.05	-0.15
	(.04)	(.06)	(.06)	(.05)	(.04)	(.09)	(.07)	(.08)	(.08)	(.16)
Minority	-0.34	-0.57	-0.26	-0.34	-0.64	0.41	-0.54	0.09		
	(.18)	(.45)	(.24)	(.23)	(.21)	(.37)	(.31)	(.32)		
Female	0.05	-0.17	-0.04	-0.04	0.05	-0.15	0.01	0.33	0.23	-1.37
	(.14)	(.21)	(.18)	(.16)	(.14)	(.29)	(.22)	(.24)	(.27)	(.52)
Education	-0.30	-0.11	-0.32	-0.19			-0.37	-1.75	-0.11	-0.28
	(.08)	(.13)	(.11)	(.09)			(.13)	(.25)	(.16)	(.31)
Cross-pressures Scale	2.51	3.28	1.37	3.02	1.74	3.62	1.75	3.26	1.95	4.14
	(.28)	(.43)	(.28)	(.31)	(.23)	(.56)	(.40)	(.47)	(.55)	(1.06)
Wald Chi-square Statistic	2.27			15.77		9.73		6.02	3.35	
N	2553	1176	1520	2016	2444	746	791	1280	344	145
LR Chi-square	292.6	137.19	116	246.78	244.56	76.72	66.38	127.44	27.22	39.19
Pseudo R-square	0.17	0.18	0.12	0.18	0.14	0.18	0.10	0.19	0.07	0.27

Note: Bolded coefficients are statistically significant at $p < .05$. Reported are logit results of model predicting a vote for the opposing party candidates. Sample limited to self-identified partisans only (Independent leaners not included). Data source is the 2000 Knowledge Networks Election Study.

TABLE A3

Model Results Used to Calculate Substantive Effects Reported in Figures 4.5 and 4.6.

	Conventions		Debates	
	Transition	Defection	Transition	Defection
Constant	0.21	−1.18	−0.69	−2.09
	(.27)	(.67)	(.35)	(.93)
Strength of Partisanship	−0.68	−1.03	−0.64	−0.85
	(.06)	(.31)	(.09)	(.42)
Age	−0.02	−0.19	−0.16	−0.19
	(.04)	(.09)	(.05)	(.12)
Minority	−0.12	−0.79	0.08	−0.05
	(.17)	(.45)	(.26)	(.65)
Female	0.20	0.07	0.12	0.40
	(.11)	(.27)	(.16)	(.42)
Education	−0.16	−0.40	−0.05	−0.28
	0.07	0.16	0.09	0.22
Previous Volatility			1.40	2.89
			(.27)	(.67)
Cross-pressured Dummy	0.83	1.16	0.99	0.87
	(.16)	(.27)	(.24)	(.41)
N	1918	1313	1663	777
LR Chi-square	172.36	55.07	104.80	32.37
Pseudo R-square	0.08	0.11	0.09	0.13

Note: Bolded coefficients are statistically significant at $p < .05$. Reported are logit results of model predicting any change in vote choice (transition) or a change to support the opposing party candidate (defection) from before to after the event. Sample restricted to respondents interviewed before the event and with 10 days after the event; transition model includes partisans and Independents and defection model limited to partisans who did not already support the opposing party candidate. Previous volatility is an indicator if the individual had previously changed vote choice prior to pre-event interview. Data source is the 2000 Knowledge Networks Election Study.

TABLE A4

Model Results Used to Calculate Substantive Effects Reported in Figure 5.1

	All White Democrats		Southern White Democrats	
	1960	*1968*	*1960*	*1968*
Constant	**−2.13**	−1.38	−0.99	−1.27
	(.64)	(.78)	(.86)	(.159)
Strength of Partisanship	**−1.33**	**−1.40**		
	(.28)	(.32)		
Age	0.02	0.01	0.00	−0.02
	(−.01)	(.01)	(.01)	(.02)
Female	0.33	0.04	0.23	0.70
	(.27)	(.30)	(.42)	(.69)
Education	0.08	0.13	0.05	0.24
	(.16)	(.18)	(.21)	(.33)
Cross-pressured, Racial Issue	0.66	**2.70**	0.42	2.27
	(.52)	(.83)	(.57)	(1.27)
N	390	321	117	58
LR Chi-square	31.20	39.90	1.3	7.3
Pseudo R-square	0.08	0.11	0.01	0.11

Note: Bolded coefficients are statistically significant at p<.05. Reported are logit results of model predicting defection. Sample restricted to white Democrats (including Independent leaners). Cross-pressures measure is an indicator if the individual volunteered a racial policy dislike about the Democratic candidate or party or a racial policy like about the Republican candidate or party. Data source is the American National Election Study cumulative file.

TABLE A5
Model Results Used to Calculate Substantive Effects Reported in Figure 5.3

	1972	1976
Constant	**−2.67**	**−3.24**
	(1.01)	(1.15)
Strength of Partisanship	**−0.84**	**−0.85**
	(.31)	(.36)
Age	**0.03**	0.01
	(.01)	(.01)
Female	−0.24	**0.63**
	(.26)	(.32)
Education	0.00	0.11
	(.01)	(.08)
Political Knowledge	0.05	0.14
	(.16)	(.18)
Cross-pressured, Busing	**1.80**	0.32
	(.57)	(.55)
N	280	269
LR Chi-square	42.89	15.33
Pseudo R-square	0.11	0.05

Note: Bolded coefficients are statistically significant at $p<.05$. Reported are logit results of model predicting defection. Sample restricted to white Democrats (including leaners) who had the same opinion on busing in both 1972 and 1976. Cross-pressures measure is an indicator of whether the individual was opposed to busing to achieve integration. Data source is the American National Election 1972–1976 panel.

TABLE A6

Model Results Used to Calculate Substantive Effects Reported in Figure 5.5

	1964	1968	1972	1976	1980	1984	1988	1992	1996	2000	2004
Constant	-4.74	-0.48	-0.99	-2.62	-1.97	-3.31	-2.38	-8.07	-6.68	0.54	-5.42
	(.771)	(.705)	(.623)	(.843)	(1.08)	(1.43)	(1.17)	(1.62)	(1.72)	(1.9)	(1.91)
Strength of Partisanship	**-1.39**	**-1.35**	**-1.09**	**-0.75**	**-1.86**	**-1.08**	**-2.22**	**-2.08**	**-1.42**	**-1.33**	**-1.34**
	(.319)	(.248)	(.236)	(.317)	(.408)	(.484)	(.584)	(.634)	(.659)	(.601)	(.635)
Age	0.01	0.00	**0.02**	-0.01	0.00	0.01	-0.02	0.00	0.01	-0.03	-0.01
	(.009)	(.007)	(.007)	(.008)	(.009)	(.013)	(.011)	(.013)	(.013)	(.016)	(.013)
Female	0.11	-0.21	-0.04	0.38	0.24	0.37	0.41	0.84	-0.22	0.20	0.99
	(.278)	(.22)	(.197)	(.258)	(.311)	(.402)	(.401)	(.484)	(.451)	(.495)	(.569)
Education	**0.53**	-0.09	-0.18	0.26	0.04	-0.11	-0.13	**0.60**	0.49	-0.50	0.08
	(.164)	(.14)	(.123)	(.163)	(.197)	(.269)	(.235)	(.284)	(.288)	(.344)	(.347)
Political Knowledge		-0.02	-0.15	0.09	-0.15	0.38	0.19	0.34	0.22	-0.22	**0.82**
		(.11)	(.11)	(.144)	(.19)	(.266)	(.211)	(.262)	(.252)	(.232)	(.259)
Cross-pressures Scale, Racial	**0.03**	**0.02**	**0.03**	**0.02**	**0.02**	**0.02**	**0.02**	0.02	**0.02**	0.01	0.00
	(.004)	(.003)	(.004)	(.005)	(.005)	(.008)	(.006)	(.008)	(.008)	(.008)	(.009)
Cross-pressures Scale, Moral					0.11	-0.23	**0.02**	**0.05**	**0.02**	**0.02**	**0.03**
					(.321)	(.474)	(.008)	(.011)	(.009)	(.01)	(.011)
N	541	433	515	394	262	184	256	374	323	172	199
LR Chi-square	49.17	52.08	74.93	20.25	38.82	20.61	30.06	50.62	20.94	12.98	37.57
Pseudo R-square	0.153	0.11	0.12	0.05	0.15	0.14	0.21	0.29	0.14	0.13	0.26

Note: Bolded coefficients are statistically significant at $p < .05$. Reported are logit results of model predicting defection. Sample restricted to white Democrats (including leaners). Political knowledge is the interviewer assessment of respondent knowledge. Data source is the American National Election Study cumulative file.

Bibliography

Abelson, Robert, Ithiel de Sola Pool, and Samuel Popkin. 1965. *Candidates, Issues, and Strategies: A Computer Simulation of the 1960 and 1964 Elections*. Cambridge: MIT Press.

Abramowitz, Alan I. 1994. "Issue Evolution Reconsidered: Racial Attitudes and Partisanship in the U.S. Electorate." *American Journal of Political Science* 39:1–24.

Abramowitz, Alan I., and Kyle L. Saunders. 1998. "Ideological Realignment in the U.S. Electorate." *Journal of Politics* 60:634–52.

———. 2005. "Why Can't We All Just Get Along? The Reality of a Polarized America." *Forum*. 3:1.

Achen, Christopher. 1975. "Mass Political Attitudes and the Survey Response." *American Political Science Review* 69: 1218–31.

Achen, Christopher, and Larry Bartels. 2006. "It Feels Like We're Thinking: The Rationalizing Voter and Electoral Democracy." Presented at the annual meeting of the American Political Science Association, Philadelphia.

Ai, Chunrong, and Edward Norton. 2003. "Interaction Terms in Logit and Probit Models." *Economic Letters* 80:123–29.

Aistrup, Joseph. 1996. *The Southern Strategy Revisited: Republican Top-Down Advancement in the South*. Lexington: University of Kentucky Press.

Aldrich, John H. 1983. "A Downsian Spatial Model with Party Activism." *American Political Science Review* 77:974–90.

———. 1995. *Why Parties? The Origin and Transformation of Political Parties in America*. Chicago: University of Chicago Press.

Alexander, Kim, and Keith Mills. 2004. "Voter Privacy in the Digital Age." California Voter Foundation.

Allport, Gordon. 1954. *The Nature of Prejudice*. Cambridge, MA: Addison-Wesley Publishing Company.

Alvarez, R. Michael. 1998. *Information and Election*. Ann Arbor: University of Michigan Press.

Alvarez, R. Michael, and John Brehm. 2002. *Hard Choices, Easy Answers: Values, Information, and American Public Opinion*. Princeton, NJ: Princeton University Press.

Ambrose, Stephen. 1989. *Nixon: The Triumph of a Politician, 1962–1972, v. 2*. New York: Simon and Schuster.

Armitage, Christopher J., and Mark Conner. 2000. "Attitudinal ambivalence: A Test of Three Key Hypotheses." *Personality and Social Psychology Bulletin* 26:1421–32.

Arnold, R. Douglas. 1990. *The Logic of Congressional Action*. New Haven:Yale University Press.

Barber, Benjamin. 1984. *Strong Democracy: Participatory Politics for a New Age*. Berkeley: University of California Press.

Bartels, Larry. 1988. *Presidential Primaries and the Dynamics of Public Choice.* Princeton, NJ: Princeton University Press.

―――. 2000. "Partisanship and Voting Behavior, 1952–1996." *American Journal of Political Science* 44:35–50.

Basinger, Scott, and Howard Lavine. 2005. "Ambivalence, Information and Electoral Choice." *American Political Science Review* 99:169–84.

Berelson, Bernard R., Paul F. Lazarsfeld, and William N. McPhee. 1954. *Voting: A Study of Opinion Formation in a Presidential Campaign.* Chicago: University of Chicago Press.

Bergan, Daniel E., Alan S. Gerber, Donald P. Green, and Costas Panagopoulos. 2005. "Grassroots Mobilization and Voter Turnout in 2004." *Public Opinion Quarterly* 69:760–77.

Berinsky, Adam. 2004. *Silent Voices.* Princeton, NJ: Princeton University Press.

Billig, Michael. 1996. *Arguing and Thinking.* 2nd ed. New York: Cambridge University Press.

Bimber, Bruce A., and Richard Davis. 2003. *Campaigning Online: The Internet and U.S. Elections.* New York: Oxford University Press.

Black, Duncan. 1948. "On the Rationale of Group Decision Making." *Journal of Political Economy* 56:23–34.

Black, Earl, and Merle Black. 2002. *The Rise of Southern Republicans.* Cambridge: Harvard University Press.

Boller, Jr. Paul, 2004. *Presidential Campaigns.* New York: Oxford University Press.

Brader, Ted. 2006. *Campaigning for Hearts and Minds.* Chicago: University of Chicago Press.

Bradshaw, Joel. 2004. "Who Will Vote for You and Why: Designing Campaign Strategy and Message." In *Campaigns and Elections American Style*, ed. James Thurber and Candice Nelson. Boulder, CO: Westview Press.

Brady, Henry, Richard Johnston, and John Sides. 2004. "The Study of Political Campaigns." In *Capturing Campaign Effects.* Henry Brady and Richard Johnston, eds. Ann Arbor: University of Michigan Press.

Brady, John. 1997. *Bad Boy: The Life and Politics of Lee Atwater.* Reading, MA: Addison Wesley Publishing Company.

Brody, Richard, and Benjamin Page. 1972. "Comment: The Assessment of Policy Voting." *American Political Science Review* 66:450–58.

Burden, Barry C. 2007. *Personal Roots of Representation.* Princeton, NJ: Princeton University Press.

Calvert, Randall L. 1985. "Robustness of the Multidimensional Voting Model: Platform Motivations, Uncertainty, and Convergence." *American Journal of Political Science* 29:69–95.

Campbell, Angus, Philip E. Converse, Warren E. Miller, and Donald E. Stokes. 1960. *The American Voter.* Chicago: University of Chicago Press.

Campbell, James E. 2000. *The American Campaign: U.S. Presidential Campaigns and Pre-National Vote.* College Station: Texas A&M Press.

―――. 2001. "Presidential Election Campaigns and Partisanship." In *American Political Parties: Decline or Resurgence*, ed. Jeffrey E. Cohen, Richard Fleisher, and Paul Kantor. Washington, DC: CQ Press.

Campbell, James, Lynne L. Cherry, and Kenneth A. Wink. 1992. "The Convention Bump." *American Politics Quarterly* 10:287–307.

Carmines, Edward, and Michael Ensley. 2004. "Strengthening and Weakening Mass Partisanship: Issue Preferences and Partisan Attitudes in an Increasingly Polarized Party System." Annual Meeting of the Midwest Political Science Association, Chicago.

Carmines, Edward, and James Stimson. 1989. *Issue Evolution: Race and the Transformation of American Politics.* Princeton, NJ: Princeton University Press.

Carmines, Edward, and Richard A. Zeller. 1979. *Reliability and Validity Assessment.* Beverly Hills: Sage Publications.

Carsey, Thomas M. 2000. *Campaign Dynamics: The Race for Governor.* Ann Arbor: University of Michigan Press.

Clark, Clifford, and Richard Holbrooke. 1991. *Counsel to the President.* New York: Random House.

Conley, Patricia H. 2001. *Presidential Mandates: How Elections Shape the National Agenda.* Chicago: University of Chicago Press.

Converse, Philip. 1964. "The Nature of Belief Systems in Mass Publics." In *Ideology and Discontent*, ed. David Apter. New York: Free Press.

Dahl, Robert. 1961. *Who Governs? Power and Democracy in an American City.* New Haven: Yale University Press.

———. 1989. *Democracy and Its Critics.* New Haven: Yale University Press.

Darman, Richard. 1996. *Who's in Control?: Polar Politics and the Sensible Center.* New York: Simon and Schuster.

Davis, Otto A., Melvin J. Hinich, and Peter C. Ordeshook. 1970. "An Expository Development of a Mathematical Model of the Electoral Process." *The American Political Science Review* 64:426–48.

Dawson, Michael C. 1994. *Behind the Mule: Race and Class in African American Politics.* Princeton, NJ: Princeton University Press.

Dent, Harry S. 1978. *The Prodigal South Returns to Power.* New York: Wiley and Sons.

Dillman, Don A. 2000. *Mail and Internet Surveys: The Tailored Design Method.* 2nd ed. New York: John Wiley and Sons.

DiMaggio, Paul, John Evans, and Bethany Bryson. 1996. "Have Americans' Social Attitudes Become More Polarized?" *American Journal of Sociology* 102:690–755.

Downs, Anthony. 1957. *An Economic Theory of Democracy.* New York: Harper and Row.

Druckman, James. 2004. "Priming the Vote: Campaign Effects in a U.S. Senate Election." *Political Psychology* 25: 577–94.

Druckman, James, Lawrence R. Jacobs, and Eric Ostermeier. 2004. "Candidate Strategies to Prime Issues and Image." *The Journal of Politics* 66:1205–27.

Dulio, David A. 2004. *For Better or Worse? How Political Consultants Are Changing Elections in the United States.* Albany: State University of New York.

Eagly, Alice H., and Shelly Chaiken. 1995. "Attitude Strength, Attitude Structure, and Resistance to Change." In *Attitude Strength: Antecedents and Consequences*, ed. R. E. Petty and J. A. Krosnick. Mahwah, NJ: Erlbaum.

Edsall, Thomas B. 2006. *Building Red America: The New Conservative Coalition and the Drive for Permanent Power*. New York: Basic Books.

Edsall, Thomas B., and Mary D. Edsall. 1992. *Chain Reaction: The Impact of Race, Rights, and Taxes on American Politics*. New York: W.W. Norton and Company.

Enelow, James M., and Melvin J. Hinich. 1984. *The Spatial Theory of Voting: An Introduction*. New York: Cambridge University Press.

Erikson, Robert S., and David Romero. 1990. "Candidate Equilibrium and the Behavioral Model of the Vote." *American Political Science Review* 84:1103–26.

Evans, Geoffrey, and Robert Andersen. 2006. "The Political Conditioning of Economic Perceptions." *Journal of Politics* 68:194.

Fair, Ray C. 2002. *Predicting Presidential Elections and Other Things*. Stanford, CA: Stanford University Press.

Feldman, Stanley, and John Zaller. 1992. "A Simple Theory of the Survey Response: Answering Questions versus Revealing Preferences." *American Journal of Political Science* 36: 579–616.

Fenno, Richard. 1978. *Home Style: House Members in Their Districts*. Boston and Toronto: Little Brown and Company.

Festinger, Leon, and James M. Carlsmith. 1959. "Cognitive Consequences of Forced Compliance." *Journal of Abnormal and Social Psychology* 58:203–11.

Finkel, Steven E. 1993. "Reexamining the 'Minimal Effects' Model in Recent Presidential Elections." *Journal of Politics* 55:1–21.

Fiorina, Morris P. 1981. *Retrospective Voting in American National Elections*. New Haven: Yale University Press.

———. 1990. "Information and Rationality in Elections." In *Information and Democratic Processes*, ed. John Ferejohn and James Kuklinski. Urbana: University of Illinois Press.

———. "Whatever Happened to the Median Voter." Presented at the MIT Conference on Parties and Congress.

———. 2005. *Culture War?: The Myth of a Polarized America*. New York: Pearson Education.

Fishel, Jeff. 1985. *Presidents and Promises: From Campaign Pledge to Presidential Performance*. Washington, DC: Congressional Quarterly Press.

Franklin, Charles H. 1991. "Eschewing Obfuscation? Campaigns and the Perceptions of U.S. Senate Incumbents." *American Political Science Review* 85:1193–1214.

Frymer, Paul. 1999. *Uneasy Alliances: Race and Parties in America*. Princeton, NJ: Princeton University Press.

Frymer, Paul, and John David Skrentny. 1998. "Coalition-building and the Politics of Electoral Capture during the Nixon Administration: African Americans, Labor, Latinos." *Studies in the American Political Development* 12:131–61.

Gaines, Bryan J., James Kuklinski, and Paul J. Quirk. 2007. "The Logic of the Survey Experiment Reexamined." *Political Analysis* 15:1–20.

Geer, John. 1988. "Assessing the Representativeness of Electorate in Presidential Primaries." *American Journal of Political Science* 32:929–45.

———. 1988. "What Do Open-ended Questions Measure?" *Public Opinion Quarterly* 52:365–71.

——. 1996. *From Tea Leaves to Opinion Polls: Politicians, Information and Leadership*. New York: Columbia University Press.

Gelman, Andrew, and Gary King. 1993. "Why Are American Presidential Election Campaign Polls So Variable When Votes Are So Predictable?" *British Journal of Political Science* 23:409–51.

Genovese, Michael. 1990. *The Nixon Presidency: Power and Politics in Turbulent Times*. New York: Greenwood Press.

Gerber, Alan S., and Donald P. Green. 2000. "The Effects of Canvassing, Telephone Calls, and Direct Mail on Voter Turnout: A Field Experiment." *American Political Science Review* 94:653–63.

Germond, Jack. 1993. *Mad as Hell: Revolt at the Ballot Box*. New York: Warner Books.

Gershkoff, Amy R. 2005. "The Importance of Properly Measuring Importance." Presented at the American Association of Public Opinion Research Annual Conference, Miami Beach.

——. 2006. "How Issue Interest Can Rescue the American Public." Presented at the American Association of Public Opinion Research, Montreal.

Glaeser, Edward, Giacomo Ponzetto, and Jesse Shapiro. 2005. "Strategic Extremism: Why Republicans and Democrats Divide on Religious Values." *Quarterly Journal of Economics* 120:1283–1330.

Glaser, James. 1996. *Race, Campaign Politics, and the Realignment in the South*. New Haven: Yale University Press.

Graber, Doris A. 1984. *Processing the News: How People Tame the Information Tide*. New York: Longman.

Green, Donald, Bradley Palmquist, and Eric Schickler. 2002. *Partisan Hearts and Minds: Political Parties and the Social Identities of Voters*. New Haven: Yale University Press.

Greenberg, Stanley B. 1995. *Middle-class Dreams: The Politics and Power of the New American Majority*. New York: Times Books.

——. 2004. The *Two Americas: Our Current Political Deadlock and How to Break It*. New York: St. Martin's Press.

Grossback, Lawrence J., David A. M. Peterson, and James A. Stimson. 2006. *Mandate Politics*. New York: Cambridge University Press.

Hacker, Jacob S., and Paul Pierson. 2005. *Off Center: The Republican Revolution and the Erosion of American Democracy*. New Haven: Yale University Press.

Hamburger, Tom, and Peter Wallsten. 2006. *One Party Country: The Republican Plan for Dominance in the Twenty-first Century*. Hoboken, NJ: John Wiley and Sons.

Hetherington, Marc J. 2001. "Resurgent Mass Partisanship: The Role of Elite Polarization" *American Political Science Review* 95:619–31.

Hillygus, D. Sunshine. 2007. "The Dynamics of Voter Decision Making among Minor-party Supporters: The 2000 U.S. Presidential Election." *British Journal of Political Science* 37:225–44.

Hillygus, D. Sunshine, and Simon Jackman. 2003. "Voter Decision Making in Election 2000: Campaign Effects, Partisan Activation, and the Clinton Legacy." *American Journal of Political Science* 47:583–96.

Hillygus, D. Sunshine, Norman H. Nie, and Kenneth Prewitt. 2006. *The Hard Count: The Political and Social Challenges of Census Mobilization*. New York: Russell Sage Foundation.

Hillygus, D. Sunshine, and Todd Shields. 2005. "Moral Issues and Voter Decision Making in the 2004 Presidential Election." *PS: Political Science and Politics* 38:201–10.

Hochschild, Jennifer. 1993. "Disjunction and Ambivalence in Citizens' Political Outlooks." In George Marcus and Russell Hanson, ed. *Reconsidering the Democratic Public*. University Park: Pennsylvania State University Press.

Hodson, G., G. R. Maio, and V. M. Esses. 2001. "The Role of Attitudinal Ambivalence in Susceptibility to Consensus Information." *Basic and Applied Social Psychology* 23: 197–205.

Holbrook, Thomas M. 1996. *Do Campaigns Matter?* Thousand Oaks, CA: Sage Publications.

Holbrook, Thomas M., and Scott McClurg. 2005. "Presidential Campaigns and the Mobilization of Core Supporters." *American Journal of Political Science* 49:689–703.

Horan, Patrick. 1971. "Social Positions and Political Cross Pressures: A Reexamination." *American Sociological Review* 36:650–60.

Hotelling, Harold. 1929. "Stability in Competition." *Economic Journal* 39:41–57.

Howard, Philip N. 2006. *New Media Campaigns and the Managed Citizen*. New York: Cambridge University Press.

Huckfeldt, Robert, and John Sprague. 2000. "Political Consequences of Inconsistency: The Accessibility and Stability of Abortion Attitudes." *Political Psychology* 21:57–79.

Hurley, Patricia. 1991. "Partisan Representation, Realignment, and the Senate in the 1980s." *Journal of Politics*. 53:3–33.

Hutchings, Vincent L. 2003. *Public Opinion and Democratic Accountability: How Citizens Learn about Politics*. Princeton, NJ: Princeton University Press.

Hutchings, Vincent L., and Nicolas A. Valentino. 2004. "The Centrality of Race in American Politics." *Annual Review of Political Science* 7:383–408.

Hutchings, Vincent L., Nicholas A. Valentino, Tasha S. Philpot, and Ismail K. White. 2004. "The Compassion Strategy Race and the Gender Gap in Campaign 2000." *Public Opinion Quarterly* 68:512–41.

Iyengar, Shanto, and Adam Simon. 2000. "New Perspectives and Evidence on Political Communication and Campaign Effects." *Annual Review of Psychology* 51:149–69.

Jackson, John E. 1975. "Issues, Party Choices and Presidential Votes." *American Journal of Political Science* 19:161–85.

Jacobs, Lawrence, and Robert Shapiro. 2000. *Politicians Don't Pander: Political Manipulation and the Loss of Democratic Responsiveness*. Chicago: University of Chicago Press.

———. 2005. "Polling Politics, Media and Election Campaigns." *Public Opinion Quarterly* 69:635–41.

Jacobson, Gary C. 2000. "Party Polarization in National Politics: The Electoral Connection." In *Polarized Politics: Congress and the President in a Partisan Era*, ed. Jon R. Bond and Richard Fleisher. Washington, DC: Congressional Quarterly Press.

Jacoby, William. 2004. "Ideology in the 2000 Election: A Study in Ambivalence." In *Models of Voting in Presidential Elections: The 2000 Election*, ed. Herbert F. Weisberg and Clyde Wilcox. Stanford: Stanford University Press.

Jamieson, Kathleen Hall. 2006. *Electing the President 2004: The Insiders' View.* Philadelphia: University of Pennsylvania Press.

Jamieson, Kathleen Hall, and Paul Waldman. 2004. *Electing the President, 2000: The Insiders' View.* Philadelphia: University of Pennsylvania Press.

Johnston, Richard, Andre Blais, Henry E. Brady, and Jean Crete. 1992. *Letting the People Decide: Dynamics of a Canadian Election.* Stanford: Stanford University Press.

Johnston, Richard, Michael Hagen, and Kathleen Hall Jamieson. 2004. *The 2000 Presidential Election and the Foundation of Party Politics.* New York: Cambridge University Press.

Just, Marion, Ann N. Crigler, Dean E. Alger, and Timothy E. Cook. 1996. *Crosstalk: Citizens, Candidates, and the Media in a Presidential Campaign.* Chicago: University of Chicago Press.

Kahn, Kim Fridkin, and Patrick J. Kenney. 1999. *The Spectacle of U.S. Senate Campaigns.* Princeton, NJ: Princeton University Press.

Kaplan, Kalman J. 1972. "On the Ambivalence-Indifference Problem in Attitude Theory and Measurement: A Suggestion Modification of the Semantic Differential Technique." *Psychological Bulletin* 77:361–72.

Kaplan, Noah, David Park, and Travis Ridout. 2006. "Dialogue in American Political Campaigns? An Examination of Issue Convergence in Candidate Television Advertising." *American Journal of Political Science* 50:724–36.

Keith, Bruce E., David B. Magleby, Candice J. Nelson, Elizabeth Orr, Mark C. Westlye, and Raymond E. Wolfinger. 1992. *The Myth of the Independent Voter.* Berkeley: University of California Press.

Key, V. O. 1959. "Secular Realignment and the Party System." *Journal of Politics* 21:198–210.

———. 1966. *The Responsible Electorate: Rationality in Presidential Voting 1936–1960.* Cambridge: Harvard University Press.

Kinder, Donald R. 1983. "Diversity and Complexity in American Public Opinion." In *Political Science: The State of the Discipline*, ed. Ada Finifter. Washington, DC: American Political Science Association Press.

Kinder, Donald R., and Lynn Sanders. 1996. *Divided by Color: Racial Politics and Democratic Ideals.* Chicago: University of Chicago Press.

King, David C. 10 March, 2003. "Congress, Polarization, and Fidelity to the Median Voter." Unpublished manuscript, Kennedy School of Government, Harvard University.

King, Gary, Christopher J. L. Murray, Joshua A. Salomon, and Ajay Tandon. 2003. "Enhancing the Validity and Cross-cultural Comparability of Measurement in Survey Research." *American Political Science Review* 97:567–84.

Klinker, Philip. 1994. *The Losing Parties: Out-party National Committees, 1956–1993.* New Haven: Yale University Press.

Kotlowski, Dean. 2002. *Nixon's Civil Rights: Politics, Principle, and Policy.* Cambridge, MA: Harvard University Press.

Kousser, Thad, and Mathew D. McCubbins. 2005. "Social Choice, Crypto-initiatives, and Policy Making by Direct Democracy." *Southern California Law Review* 78(4): 949–84.

Kramer, Gerald H. 1977. "A Dynamical Model of Political Equilibrium." *Journal of Economic Theory* 16:310–34.

Krosnick, Jon A. 1990. "Government Policy and Citizen Passion: A Study of Issue Publics in Contemporary America." *Political Behavior* 12:59–92.

Krosnick, Jon A., and LinChiat Chang. 2001. "A Comparison of the Random Digit Dialing Telephone Survey Methodology with Internet Survey Methodology as Implemented by Knowledge Networks and Harris Interactive." Unpublished report, Ohio State University.

Krosnick, Jon A., and Richard E. Petty, eds. 1995. *Attitude Strength: Antecedents and Consequences.* Mahwah, NJ: Lawrence Erlbaum Associates.

Kurland, Phillip, and Ralph Lerner, eds. 1987. *The Founders' Constitution*, vol. 5, amend. I, doc. 8. Chicago: University of Chicago Press.

Lamis, Alexander P., ed. 1999. *Southern Politics in the 1990s.* Baton Rouge: Louisiana State University Press.

Lau, Richard R. 2003. "Models of Decision Making." In *Oxford Handbook of Political Psychology*, ed. David O. Sears, Leonie Huddy, and Robert Jervis. New York: Oxford University Press.

Layman, Geoffrey C., and Thomas M. Carsey. 2002. "Party Polarizations and 'Conflict Extension' in the American Electorate." *American Journal of Political Science* 46:786–802.

———. 2006. "Changing Sides or Changing Minds? Party Identification and Policy Preferences in the American Electorate." *American Journal of Political Science* 50:464–77.

Layman, Geoffrey C., Thomas M. Carsey, and Juliana Menasce Horowitz. 2006. "Party Polarization in American Politics: Characteristics, Causes, and Consequences." *Annual Review of Political Science* 9:83–110.

Lazarsfeld, Paul, Bernard Berelson, and Hazel Gaudet. 1944. *The People's Choice: How the Voter Makes Up His Mind in a Presidential Campaign.* New York: Columbia University Press.

Lenz, Gabriel S. 2005. "Learning, Not Priming: Reconsidering the Evidence for the Priming Hypothesis." Unpublished manuscript, Princeton University.

Lillenker, Darren G. 2005. "The Impact of Political Marketing on Internal Party Democracy." *Parliamentary Affairs* 58:570–84.

Lord, C., M. Ross, and M. Lepper. 1979. "Biased Assimilation and Attitude Polarization: The Effects of Prior Theories on Subsequently Considered Evidence." *Journal of Personality and Social Psychology* 27:2098–109.

Luskin, Robert. 1987. "Measuring Political Sophistication." *American Journal of Political Science* 31:860.

Magleby, David B., J. Quin Monson, and Kelly Patterson. 2006. *Dancing without Partners: How Candidates, Parties and Interest Groups Interact in the New Campaign Finance Environment.* Lanham, MD: Rowman and Littlefield.

————. 2006. "Mail Communications in Political Campaigns: The 2004 Campaign Communications Survey." Presented at the Annual Meeting of the Midwest Political Science Association.

Maio, Gregory, David Bell, and Victoria Esses. 1996. "Ambivalence and Persuasion: The Processing of Messages about Immigrant Groups." *Journal of Experimental Psychology* 32:513–36.

Malchow, Hal. 2003. *The New Political Targeting.* Washington, D.C.: Campaigns and Elections.

Margolis, Michael, and David Resnick. 2000. *Politics as Usual: The "Cyberspace Revolution."* Thousand Oaks, CA: Sage Publications.

Markus, Gregory B., and Phillip E. Converse. 1979. "A Dynamic Simultaneous Equation Model of Electoral Choice." *American Political Science Review* 73:1055–70.

Mayer, Jeremy D. 2002. *Running on Race: Racial Politics in Presidential Campaigns 1960–2000.* New York: Random House.

Mayer, William G. 1996. *Divided Democrats: Ideological Unity, Party Reform and Presidential Elections.* Boulder, CO: Westview Press.

————. 2007. "The Swing Voter in American Presidential Elections." *American Politics Research* 35:1–31.

Mayhew, David. 2002. *Electoral Realignment: A Critique of an American Genre.* New Haven: Yale University Press.

McCarty, Nolan M., Keith T. Poole, and Howard Rosenthal. 2006. *Polarized America: The Dance of Ideology and Unequal Riches.* Cambridge: MIT Press.

McGraw, Kathleen M., Edward Hasecke, and Kimberly Conger. 2003. "Ambivalence, Uncertainty, and Processes of Candidate Evaluation." *Political Psychology* 24:421–48.

McKelvey, Richard. 1986. "Covering, Dominance, and Institution-free Properties of Social Choice." *American Journal of Political Science* 30:283–314.

Medvic, Stephen K. 2000. *Political Consultants in U.S. Congressional Elections.* Columbus: Ohio State University Press.

Mendelberg, Tali. 2001. *The Race Card: Campaign Strategy, Implicit Messages and the Norm of Equity.* Princeton, NJ: Princeton University Press.

Miller, Gary, and Norman Schofield. 2003. "Activists and Partisan Realignment in the United States." *American Political Science Review* 97:245–60.

Miller, Joanne M., and Jon A. Krosnick. 2000. "News Media Impact on the Ingredients of Presidential Evaluations: Politically Knowledgeable Citizens Are Guided by a Trusted Source." *American Journal of Political Science* 44:301–15.

Morrow, E. Frederic. 1963. *Black Man in the White House.* New York: Coward-McCann.

Mueller, John E. 1970. "Presidential Popularity from Truman to Johnson." *American Political Science Review* 64:18–34.

Murphy, Reg, and Hal Gulliver. 1971. *The Southern Strategy.* New York: Charles Scribner's Sons.

Mutz, Diana. 2006. *Hearing the Other Side: Deliberative versus Participatory Democracy.* New York: Cambridge University Press.

Nelson, Thomas E., Rosalee A. Clawson, and Zoe Oxley. 1997. "Media Framing of a Civil Liberties Controversy and Its Effect on Tolerance." *American Political Science Review* 91:567–84.

Nie, Norman H., Sidney Verba, and John R. Petrocik. 1976. *The Changing American Voter.* Cambridge: Harvard University Press.

Nisbett, Richard, and Timothy Wilson. 1977. "Telling More than We Can Know: Verbal Reports on Mental Processes." *Psychological Review,* 84:231–59.

Nixon, Richard. 1978. *RN: The Memoirs of Richard Nixon.* New York: Grossett and Dunlap.

Norrander, Barbara. 1989. "Ideological Representativeness of Presidential Primary Voters." *American Journal of Political Science* 33:570–87.

Novak, Robert D. 1965. *The Agony of the GOP, 1964.* New York: McMillan Company.

Okeefe, Daniel J. 2002. *Persuasion: Theory and Research.* Thousand Oaks, CA: Sage Publications.

Ornstein, Norman J., and Thomas E. Mann. 2000. *The Permanent Campaign and Its Future.* Washington, DC: The American Enterprise Institute and the Brookings Institution.

O'Shaughnessy, Nicholas. 1990. *The Phenomenon of Political Marketing.* New Hampshire: Macmillan.

Page, Benjamin. 1978. *Choices and Echoes in Presidential Elections: Rational Man and Electoral Democracy.* Chicago: University of Chicago Press.

Page, Benjamin, and Calvin C. Jones. 1979. "Reciprocal Effects of Policy Preferences, Party Loyalties and the Vote." *American Political Science Review* 73:1071–89.

Page, Benjamin, and Robert Y. Shapiro. 1992. *The Rational Public: Fifty Years of Trends in Americans' Policy Preferences.* Chicago: University of Chicago Press.

Petrocik, John R. 1996. "Issue Ownership in Presidential Elections, with a 1980 Case Study." *American Journal of Political Science* 40:825–50.

Phillips, Kevin. 1969. *The Emerging Republican Majority.* New York: Arlington House.

Philpot, Tasha. 2007. *Race, Republicans, and the Return of the Party of Lincoln.* Ann Arbor: University of Michigan Press.

Pomper, Gerald M. 1980. *Elections in America: Control and Influence in Democratic Politics,* 2nd ed. New York: Longman.

Popkin, Samuel L. 1991. *The Reasoning Voter: Communication and Persuasion in Presidential Campaigns.* Chicago: University of Chicago Press.

Popkin, Samuel L. 2007. "Public Opinion and Collective Obligations." Unpublished Manuscript, University of California San Diego.

Price, Vincent, and John Zaller. 1993. "Who Gets the News? Alternative Measures of News Reception and Their Implications for Research." *Public Opinion Quarterly* 57:133–64.

Prior, Markus. 2007. *Post–Broadcast Democracy.* New York: Cambridge University Press.

Prysby, Charles. 1982. "A Note on Regional Subsamples from National Sample Surveys." *Public Opinion Quarterly* 46:422–24.

Rahn, Wendy M. 1993. "The Role of Partisan Stereotypes in Information Processing about Political Candidates." *American Journal of Political Science* 37:472–96.

Rea, Nicol. 1989. *The Decline and Fall of the Liberal Republicans, from 1952 to the Present*. New York: Oxford University Press.

Remini, Robert. 1990. *The Life of Andrew Jackson*. New York: Penguin.

Ridout, Travis N., Dhavan V. Shah, Kenneth M. Goldstein, and Michael M. Franz. 2004. "Evaluating Measures of Campaign Advertising Exposure on Political Learning." *Political Behavior* 26:201–25.

Riechley, James. 1981. *Conservatives in an Age of Change*. Washington, DC: Brookings Institutien.

Riker, William H. 1996. *The Strategy of Rhetoric*. New Haven: Yale University Press.

Rivers, Douglas. 1988. "Heterogeneity in Models of Electoral Choice." *American Journal of Political Science* 32:737–57.

Rosenstone, Steven J., and John Mark Hansen. 2003. *Mobilization, Participation and Democracy in America*. New York: Longman.

Rossiter, Clinton. 1960. *Parties and Politics in America*. Ithaca: Cornell University Press.

Salmore, Barbara G., and Stephen A. Salmore. 1985. *Candidates, Parties and Campaigns: Electoral Politics in America*. Washington, DC: Congressional Quarterly.

Schattschneider, E. E. 1942. *Party Government*. New York: Farrar and Rinehart.

———. 1960. *Semisovereign People: A Realist's View of Democracy in America*. New York: Holt, Rinehart, and Winston.

Schier, Steven. 2000. *By Invitation Only: The Rise of Exclusive Politics in the United States*. Pittsburg: University of Pittsburgh Press.

Schlesinger, Arthur. 1960. *Kennedy or Nixon: Does It Make Any Difference?* New York: MacMillian Press.

Schuman, H., and J. Scott. 1987. "Problems in the Use of Survey Questions to Measure Public Opinion." *Science'* 236:957–59.

Sears, David O., James Sidanius, and Lawerence Bobo, eds. 2000. *Racialized Politics: The Debate about Racism in America*. Chicago: University of Chicago Press.

Sellers, Patrick. 1998. "Strategy and Background in Congressional Campaigns." *American Political Science Review* 92:159–71.

Shafer, Byron E., and Richard Johnston. 2006. *The End of Southern Exceptionalism: Class, Race and Partisan Change in the Postwar South*. Cambridge: Harvard University Press.

Shaw, Daron R. 1999. "A Study of Presidential Campaign Event Effects from 1952 to 1992." *Journal of Politics* 61:387–422.

———. 1999. "The Effect of TV Ads and Candidate Appearances on Statewide Presidential Votes, 1988–1996." *American Political Science Review* 93:345–61.

———. 2004. "Door-to-door with the GOP: When It Comes to Mobilizing Supporters on Election Day, Have the Republicans Finally Caught Up to the Democrats?" *Hoover Digest* 4.

——. 2006. *The Race to 270: The Electoral College and the Campaign Strategies of 2000 and 2004.* Chicago: University of Chicago Press.

Sides, John. 2006. "The Origins of Campaign Agendas." *British Journal of Political Science* 36:407–36.

Sigelman, Lee, and Emmett Buell. 2004. "Avoidance or Engagement? Issue Convergence in U.S. Presidential Campaigns, 1960–2000." *American Journal of Political Science* 48:650–61.

Simon, Adam F. 2002. *The Winning Message: Candidate Behavior, Campaign Discourse, and Democracy.* New York: Cambridge University Press.

Smith, Tom W. 1987. "That Which We Call Welfare by Any Other Name Would Smell Sweeter: An Analysis of the Impact of Question Wording on Response Patterns" *Public Opinion Quarterly* 51:75–83.

Sniderman, Paul M., and Thomas Piazza. 1993. *The Scar of Race.* Cambridge: Belknap/Harvard Univ. Press.

Sniderman, Paul M., and Sean M. Theriault. 2004. "The Dynamics of Political Argument and the Logic of Issue Framing." In *Studies in Public Opinion: Gauging Attitudes, Nonattitudes, Measurement Error and Change,* ed. Willem E. Saris and Paul M. Sniderman. Princeton, NJ: Princeton University Press.

Sosnik, Douglas B., Matthew J. Dowd, and Ron Fournier. 2006. *Applebee's America: How Successful Political, Business, and Religious Leaders Connect with the New American Community.* New York: Simon and Schuster.

Sperlich, Peter W. 1971. *Conflict and Harmony in Human Affairs: A Study of Cross-Pressures and Political Behavior.* Chicago: Rand McNally.

Stanley, Harold, and Richard Niemi, eds. 1990. *Vital Statistics on American Politics,* 2nd ed. Washington, DC: Congressional Quarterly Press.

Stimson, James A. 2004. *Tides of Consent: How Public Opinion Shapes American Politics.* New York: Cambridge University Press.

Stimson, James A., Michael B. MacKuen, and Robert S. Erikson. 1995. "Dynamic Representation." *American Political Science Review* 89:559.

Stokes, Donald. 1963. "Spatial Models of Party Competition." *American Political Science Review* 57:368–77.

Sundquist, James L. 1983. *Dynamics of the Party System: Alignment and Realignment of Political Parties in the United States.* Rev. ed. Washington, DC: Brookings Institution.

Swanson, David, and Paolo Mancini, eds. 1996. *Politics, Media and Modern Democracy.* Westport, CT: Praeger.

Taber, Charles S., and Milton Lodge. 2006. "Motivated Skepticism in the Evaluation of Political Beliefs." *American Journal of Political Science* 50:755–69.

Tate, Katherine. 1994. *From Protest to Politics: The New Black Voters in American Elections.* Cambridge: Harvard University Press.

Treier, Shawn, and Sunshine Hillygus. 2006. "The Contours of Policy Attitudes in the Mass Public." Presented at the annual meeting of the Midwest Political Science Association, Chicago.

Valentino, Nicholas A., and David O. Sears. 2005. "Old Times There Are Not Forgotten: Race and Partisan Realignment in the Contemporary South." *American Journal of Political Science* 49:672–88.

Van Onselen, Peter, and Wayne Errington. 2004. "Electoral Databases: Big Brother or Democracy Unbound." *Australian Journal of Political Science* 39:349–66.

Verba, Sidney, Kay Lehman Schlozman, and Henry E. Brady. 1995. *Voice and Equality: Civic Voluntarism in American Politics.* Cambridge: Harvard University Press.

White, Theodore H. 1961. *The Making of the President 1960.* New York: Atheneum Publishers.

Wielhouwer, Peter W. 2003. "In Search of Lincoln's Perfect List: Targeting in Grassroots Campaigns." *American Politics Research* 31:632–69.

Wilson, Shaun, and Nick Turnbull. 2001. "Wedge Politics and Welfare Reform in Australia." *Australian Journal of Politics and History* 47:384–404.

Wittman, Donald. 1983. "Candidate Motivation: A Synthesis of Alternative Theories Source." *American Political Science Review* 77: 142.

Wood, W., C. A. Kallgren, and R. M. Preisler. 1985. "Access to Attitude-relevant Information in Memory as a Determinant of Persuasion: The Role of Message Attributes." *Journal of Experimental Social Psychology* 21:73–85.

Wright, Gerald C. 1989. "Policy Voting in the U.S. Senate: Who Is Represented?" *Legislative Studies Quarterly,* 14:465–86.

Xenos, Michael, and Kristen Foot. 2005. "Political as Usual, or Politics Unusual: Position Taking and Dialogue on Campaign Web Sites in the 2002 U.S. Elections." *Journal of Communication* 55:165–89.

Zaller, John R. 1992. *The Nature and Origins of Mass Opinion.* New York: Cambridge University Press.

———. 1999. "Perversities in the Ideal of the Informed Citizenry." Paper presented at conference on "the Transformation of Civic Life," Middle Tennessee State University Murfreesboro and Nashville, Tennessee.

———. 2004. "Floating Voters in U.S. Presidential Election, 1948–2000." In *Studies in Public Opinion: Attitudes, Nonattitudes, Measurement Error, and Change,* ed. Willem E. Saris, and Paul M. Sniderman. Princeton, NJ: Princeton University Press.

Zaller, John R., and Stanley Feldman. 1992. "A Simple Theory of the Survey Response: Answering Questions versus Revealing Preferences." *American Journal of Political Science* 36:579–616.

Index

Note: Campaigns are listed by year prior to the main index.